NIGHT FLIGHT

By the same author

Attacker: The Hudson and its Fliers
Battleship Barham
Raider: The Halifax and its Fliers
The Month of the Lost U-Boats
Under Three Flags

NIGHT FLIGHT

Halifax Squadrons at War

Geoffrey P. Jones

WILLIAM KIMBER
LONDON

First published in 1981 by
WILLIAM KIMBER & CO. LIMITED
Godolphin House, 22a Queen Anne's Gate,
London, SW1H 9AE

ISBN 0-7183-0338-5

Typeset by Jubal Multiwrite Ltd, London SE13
and printed in Great Britain by
Redwood Burn Limited, Trowbridge

Contents

		Page
	Foreword	9
	Acknowledgements	11
1	Wuthering Heights	13
2	Breighton Bound	44
3	They also served	56
4	Berlin – Key of the Door	69
5	Lord Haw Haw welcomes Canadians	83
6	Shiny Ten	112
7	Active Australians	135
8	All return from the Happy Valley	148
9	Gardening in April	157
10	Coastal Halifaxes	169
	Glossary	216
	Additional Reading	217
	Index	218

List of Illustrations

Mess at Elvington	21
No 77 Squadron crews	21
Crashed French Squadron Halifax	41
No 76 Squadron Halifax	46
No 78 Squadron Halifax	46
Outside locker room at Breighton	49
Breighton send off	49
Pam Finch interrogates	65
WAAF MT drivers	65
The King and Queen at Tempsford	67
Squadron briefing	71
Berlin raiders	81
Pete Cadman and crew	81
No 405 Squadron Halifax	85
No 432 Squadron Halifax	85
No 427 Squadron Halifax	87
No 420 Squadron Halifax	87
The King inspects damage	90
U-Uncle being uncovered	90
The Queen chats to aircrew	91
The Padre chats to aircrew	91
Decorated crew of 429 Squadron	95
The King with Gordon Ritchie	95
Honours board at Leeming	96
Three miles high	100
No 425 Squadron Halifax	100
RCAF Halifaxes . . .	103
. . . at Tholthorpe	103
Crew of U-Uncle . . .	109
. . . and their No 419 Squadron Halifax	109
P/O R. A. Kalle and crew	110
No 10 Squadron Halifax . . .	114

... and crew in the Middle East 114
Early No 10 Squadron Halifaxes 1·19
Mark II Series 1a (Special) Halifax 121
Overhaul on 10 Squadron Halifax 121
Crashed 'Farouk' 125
Checking bomb bay 125
No 462 Squadron Halifax 137
No 462 Op' Record map 137
No 466 Squadron at Driffield 142
Y-Yoke running up 155
No 77 Squadron crews 167
F/Lt A. I. Sladen DFC 171
F/O Griffiths and crew 175
Veteran 58 Squadron crews 189
No 58 Squadron Halifaxes 199
Coastal crew at Stornaway 209
No 58 and 502 Squadron crews 209

Maps

Yorkshire Airfields used by Halifaxes 12
Denmark and North Germany 159

Photographic Acknowledgements

E. G. Hill 41, 121 (bottom). R. Hines 137 (bottom). R. Holsgrove 67. JMB/GSL Negatives 114 (top). Public Archives of Canada 85, 87, 100, 103, 125 (bottom). G. Zwanenburg 109. Copyright of other pictures from the authors collection is unknown. Len Greenham and Mick Wright also kindly provided photographs.

Foreword

It is said that much too much history is written by academics, with hindsight, and not nearly enough by participants who had to face the day to day difficulties of the times in which they were living. As an historian I agree that the combatants should have their stories recorded in their own words, but feel that such recollections should be set in the context of the battle as a whole in order to provide a memoir of the times both for those who recollect them and for those who were not there.

I do not think it is generally realized that, although many flyers physically survived the war, mentally many are still on edge. Waking up at night in a cold sweat to the lash of heavy rain beating down upon window panes, they relax again thankful it is not flak hitting the wings and bellies of their Halifax. Snuggling down, they think of their missing comrades, just as they were, alive and happy. The picture lingers on in the screen of memory.

It is only recently that the Halifax aircraft has received the spotlight it, and its crews, so richly deserve. To get the authentic atmosphere while researching for this book, I travelled to Yorkshire, base of the Halifax squadrons. Yorkshire, abounding as it does in abbeys, castles and cathedrals, is a cradle of history. The Halifax flyers added another page to the devotion and deeds of their White Rose predecessors. I met, or spoke to, most of the contributors to this book. I followed this up with visits to France, Denmark, Sweden and Germany (twice). These visits relieved the intensity of research, the concentration of writing and the drudge of correspondence. I think it is all worthwhile.

For the interest of collectors and model makers I have included serial numbers wherever possible.

Finally, I should explain that I wrote a much longer book than is reproduced here. To produce the book, with illustrations, at a marketable price I had to forsake a chapter on Meteorological Halifaxes, many good stories on training and, worst of all, many good Mess anecdotes.

Acknowledgements

The main contributors are named in the text and index. Many others helped and are not otherwise named. These include Roy Benwell, Anders Bjoernvad (Denmark),* Bill Chorley,* Arthur Evans, Len Greenham, Joyce and Roy Inkster (Canada), Ole Kraul (Denmark), G Stuart Leslie, Richard Roberts and Angus Sladen. To all, go my thanks.

I regret that lack of space did not allow the inclusion of the story of Eric Lightly and others of 158 and 76 Squadrons.* The same applies to the contributions made by Neville Beale and Guy Pearman on Meteorological Halifaxes.

The Department of Defence in Canberra was helpful with RAAF matters. My brother Ted in Perth, Australia was responsible for the cartographical work.

The Yorkshire Post, *Northern Echo* and The York Evening Press Group newspapers were instrumental in bringing forth contributions from their readers. *Air Mail* and *Turret* brought responses from Coastal Command crews. I extend my thanks to the editors of these publications.

The recording of the 640 Squadron briefing belonged to the late John Viney. Assistance with tape transcripts was given by Elaine Kingsmill and Bas Sheppard. Ted Manning helped check the manuscript.

The story by Sandy Johnstone was first published in *Where No Angels Dwell*, published by Jarrolds. Jules Roy's book, based on his diary, was published in France and the English translation was published by William Kimber as *Return From Hell* (1954). My thanks to the authors and publishers in each case for allowing me to quote from these works.

*See Additional Reading

Yorkshire Airfields used by Halifaxes

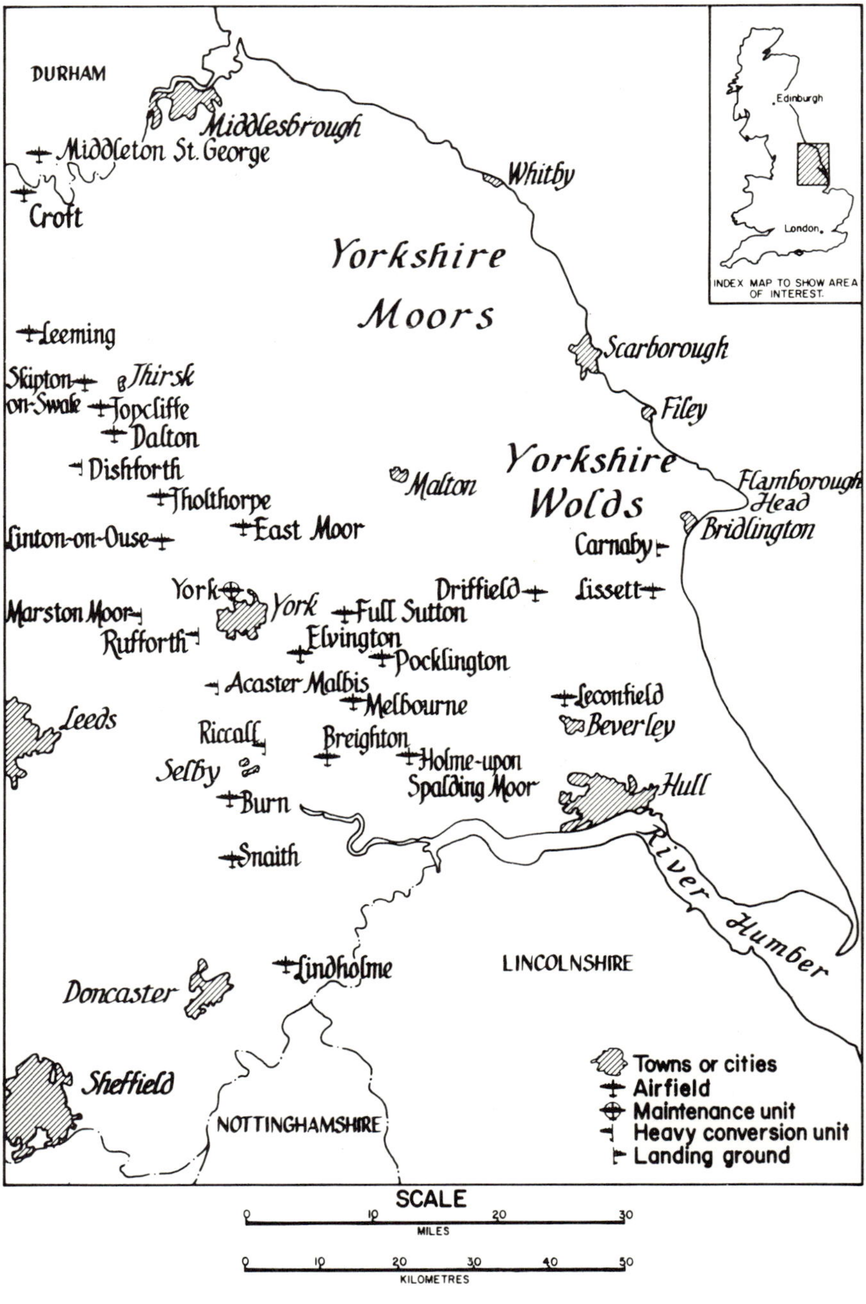

CHAPTER ONE

Wuthering Heights

Inside the porch of the eleventh-century parish church at Scawton, high on the North Yorkshire Moors, is a bronze plaque in memory of five French airmen who died when their Halifax, returning from a raid on Germany, crashed near the village just six weeks before the end of the war in Europe: George Ostre, Raymond Chevalier, Antoine Chemin, Henry Chabres and René Raymond.

I came to Scawton at the suggestion of Harry Mead, a journalist with *The Northern Echo* and an authority on the Moors. This area, abounding in memories of the Bronte sisters, was understandably referred to by the Halifax flyers as Wuthering Heights. At Scawton I met the vicar, the Reverend Albert Alderson, himself a wartime Coastal Command flyer, the church warden and local resident Mrs Alice Wood, who had vivid memories of that March night in 1945.

The Halifax, C-Charlie from 347 Squadron was returning to Elvington in the early hours when it crashed. 'It was dreadful,' recalled Mrs Wood. 'The aircraft circled round while it waited permission to land. We think the plane's instruments must have been faulty or broken and the crew did not know the altitude.'

I pointed out that it was clear from the memorial plaque that the survivors must have been the flight engineer and the rear gunner, who were probably both in the tail of the aircraft.

'That's right,' confirmed Mrs Wood. 'The tail was intact.' Originally, she told me, the plaque was fixed to the tree where the Halifax crashed, but it was moved when the tree died. 'We didn't pay for the plaque; it was probably provided by the French Air Force or Government.'

'But each Armistice Sunday we have prayers for the airmen mentioned by name,' added the church warden.

This moving story of the airmen who died so near to base on what was scheduled as their last operation, on 15 March 1945, made me decide to start this story of the Halifax's role at night with the Elvington base, and in particular to trace the last flight of these unfortunate French airmen.

Elvington airfield, to the south-east of York, became operational in the autumn of 1942. No 77 Squadron, flying Halifax II's, were the first to occupy the base, and in mid-1944 they were replaced by two Free French squadrons, Nos 346 and 347. The airfield was on the south side of the B1228 road, some eight miles from York. The living and sleeping quarters were spread either side of a tree-lined road. The quarters were typical war-time models, Nissen huts, wooden huts or concrete block huts. On the opposite side of the main road from the airfield, and dead in line with the main runway, lying a few yards back from the hedge, was a converted railway coach mounted on blocks. The elderly lady who lived in the coach served the airmen with mugs of tea and heavy bread pudding at reasonable prices in mid-morning in direct competition with the NAAFI. Maximum effort take-offs took the Halifaxes over the road and her hut at 30 feet, but she did not complain.

For the aircrew the station did not have much to offer: some wrote letters, played billiards or snooker, drank beer, made friends with the WAAF's and attended station dances; the majority went into York on stand-downs. Almost all missed the last 'Liberty Bus' back and had to walk, albeit a little unsteadily. The best method of getting round the camp was by bicycle, often a 'borrowed' one.

'It was in August 1943 that I was posted to No 77 Squadron at Elvington,' recalls Norman Barker, 'and on the next day found myself on battle orders as second pilot to Sergeant Brannigan. I well remember the sinking feeling as the wall map was uncovered at main briefing seeing the red ribbon zig-zagging right down into the heart of Germany. I never liked flying with anyone else and I think I was terrified, and terrified to show it!

'My very first op had to be Nuremberg! As a matter of fact, it turned out to be a piece of cake. A bit of desultory flak as we crossed the French coast, then an eerie and uneasy silence for the next two-and-a-half hours with only the occasional re-assuring bump of an aircraft's slipstream, with luck another Halifax, proving that we hadn't wandered from the main stream.

'The target had been well marked by the PFF and was well

alight, but as we turned onto the bombing run enemy fighters were dropping brilliant flares about 500 feet above us. We felt naked, almost like walking down Regent Street with no clothes on. I watched the tiny pin points of light as the eight-gun 88 mm batteries opened up, knowing it would take somewhere in the region of ten seconds or more to reach us and got my first smell of cordite as we flew through the flak. I marvelled at the apparently slow sweeping curve of the tracer bullets from other aircraft being attacked by fighters or, as very often happened, one Halifax firing on another. Our own gunners let off a few bursts but never reported an attack. I saw a 4,000 pounder cookie go right through the wing of a Stirling flying some 4,000 feet below us. We bombed on the Wanganui flares from 18,000 feet.

'On the way back I learned a valuable lesson about what happens if an aircraft gets separated from the main stream as I watched about a hundred searchlights, each operating with an eight-gun battery, concentrating on one aeroplane. I remember the feeling of relief: thank God it's him and they'll leave us alone. The more the pilot twisted and turned the longer he remained in the danger area. I resolved that should I ever get into this situation it would be the shortest distance between two points, nose down, taps open and hope the aeroplane held together until we were out of it.

'We arrived back without incident except for our anti-aircraft batteries opening up as we crossed our coast although we were carrying IFF. Running short of fuel, we landed at the "lame duck" base at Tangmere and flew home the next day. I did a few more operations from Elvington but didn't stay long as I had developed ear trouble, and, having previously been an instructor, I was sent back to Woodley to instruct instructors.'

Ex-rugby International Air Commodore S. A. 'Gus' Walker was AOC. He had earlier lost an arm.

The Station Commander was Group Captain E. Davy. Flight Sergeant Bill Trivett who was also flying with No 77 Squadron at this time says 'and the Commanding Officer was Wing Commander A. E. Lowe, affectionately known by the crews as Lapper or Lofty. He was by trade an armourer who rose through the ranks to be an officer air gunner.

'In his office he auditioned every new crew' recalls Bill. 'It was said that on the answers to his searching friendly questions he assessed whether the crew would get through those vital first five operations. He said that once over that hurdle one would have a reasonable chance and that only bad luck could then stop one finishing the tour. What he did not divulge to the crews was whether, in his opinion, they would complete the first few.'

Bill Trivett says Wingco Lowe was a very human person, and backs this up with the following personal story:

'During the summer of 1943 I hadn't written home for a few weeks and when I didn't receive a greetings card from home for my 21st birthday I was very moody. In the meantime my father had written to the adjutant asking if he could look into why there was no news from me. I was called in and told: "Don't upset them at home, get a pen to paper *now*".

'I was upset and wrote a letter containing details of what I had been doing. A few days later I was called into the office again, there on the table was my letter, returned by the Censor! The Wingco gave me a lecture, and that's being polite, about security. I had been standing to attention the whole time, and when he had finished he had reduced my 5 foot 6 inches to nothing. LMF or not, I felt like baling out and leaving the RAF to it, the floodgates were almost open. He dismissed me.

'As I was about to shut his office door, he called me back. I've never witnessed such a change in a man. He offered me a seat, and in a fatherly manner explained all about keeping families together, the worries of war for those not actively engaged in it but who had people at the front. I felt the biggest kit-bag of the lot. He also spoke about breaking people's hearts by failing to keep in touch – he'd broken mine in the first minute of his lecture. The great man then reached for the phone and dialled the Station Warrant Officer.

' "That you, SWO, I'm sending round Flight Sergeant Trivett. Put him on a 72 hour pass straight away. Oh, by the way, give him a free travel warrant."

'He dismissed me with a shake of his large hand.

' "I want you back here to celebrate your end of tour, and here's your letter, keep it for your memoirs, OK?" That man was a toff, one had to admire him.'

There were plenty of characters at Elvington in the summer of 1943 like ex-London policeman Flight Sergeant Daffey, Flight Lieutenant Pete Cadman and Flight Sergeant, as he was then, Brown. Bill Trivett continues:

'At mess socials the appointed Master of Ceremonies would be around the piano singing and when he pointed his finger in your direction you sang or told a joke. If not, the forfeit would be to buy a drink for someone. It was surprising how quickly one learned a song or joke.

'On one occasion it was Cadman's turn, not that he needed much prompting. He co-opted Daffey and the pair of them did their part. Pete had every respect for royalty and he would apologise previously for his mickey taking. He would begin by saying that he was the King visiting a station to decorate one of his brave fighter pilots. Daffey, of course, was the pilot in question. The Mess was full, respect for the artiste always.

Cadman, stuttering: 'I'm h-here to decorate one o-o-f my of-officer pilots.'

Daffey steps forward, salutes and stands at attention.

Cadman: 'I pre-present you with a med-medal f-f-for shooting down two Fok-Fokker Wulf 190's.'

Daffey, touching a pencil moustache. 'I do beg your pardon your Majesty, A-C-T-ually (blowing on his finger nails before brushing them on his tunic lapel) A-C-T-ually it was three Fokkers.' (A slight twist and a dropping of the shoulder.)

Cadman, looking at a piece of paper: 'Strange i-it says t-t-two F-Fokkers 190's here.'

Daffey: 'I beg to differ, Sir. A-C-T-ually, (more nail brushing on lapel) A-C-T-ually I can verify it was three Fokkers.'

Cadman (straight faced): 'Well Of-Of-Officer whether i-it was t-t-two Fok-Fok-Fokkers or thr-thr-three Fokkers, you're o-o-only going to get one bloody medal.'

Flight Lieutenant Mansan was one of the aircrew who played the piano quite well. When he wanted the ladies out of the room so that bawdy songs could be sung without giving offence, he would start off with, 'Goodnight Ladies'. The unattached males would all join in with gusto and the courting couples and early sleepers would make a dignified exit. There would then be a second chorus of the song. Slowly the WAAF's, or some of them, would drift into an ante-room. Finally it would be, 'For the third and last time of asking one and all, Goodnight Ladies'. It was meant to be a stag party, but for the few brazen, nay inquisitive WAAF's, who stayed behind, their ears would be wide open to the renderings of some wonderful Air Force ballads. Sometimes modesty would rise to the surface and they would leave. The three or four who stayed on were probably the daughters of the landladies who let the weekend digs.

According to Bill, the Halifax was believed, in some quarters, only to have been sent to the easy targets. 'Easy targets, where? Some were harder than others, that's all. Cologne, Essen, Hamburg, Mannheim, Nuremberg, Leipzig, Frankfurt, Berlin, the list is endless. The Halifax operated on these just as well as the Lancaster, although it took rather a back number in the Battle of Berlin. I saw Berlin four times in a Halifax. I also experienced the Halifax's tail wheel shimmy, which occurred on the earlier version. If on touch down the tail wheel wasn't straight with the runway the wheel tended to zig-zag. With the speed at about 110 mph on touch-down, just as one was relaxing in the rear turret, the last thing one wanted was to have the life knocked out of them. And, believe me, that's what one got in the turret, just as though someone was kicking your head from side to side. I thought we were silly enough without having to put up with that. They cured it on the later models, unless the wheel had dropped off and I hadn't noticed it. Another bind was the trailing aerial. This was some 100 feet in length with black beads three-quarters-of-an-inch in diameter at its flighted end, to hold it down. It would always be out during flight and was left to the wireless operator to wind it in on closing down his transmission. If he forgot it he would then rely on me to remind him. But sometimes I forgot and when the aircraft touched down there was a nice little trail of sparks as the metal beads made contact with the runway. The wireless operator would do his top and blame me for not reminding him to wind it back in. I spent much time polishing the perspex of the rear turret. There were no specks on my perspex! I was not the gunner who sent his pilot on evasive action before realising the aircraft he was tracking was a spot of dirt. The cut-away clearview panel on the turret was good thinking. I wonder how we rear gunners never froze to death? Sometimes I heard a request from up front, where they enjoyed engine heat piped down their necks, "Can we regulate this heat a bit?" How I wished someone could have devised a scheme to have extended this to the rear turret.

'I was once asked what the thickness of the armour plating was in the rear turret. My questioner would not believe me when

I told him it was non-existent, and when I followed up by explaining the centre was wide open to the atmosphere it was suggested that as a comedian I had missed my vocation.

'Microphones were a bother to me at the rear. When it was cold, as it always was, the hot air from inside the face mask would flow up to my eyebrows and would sometimes freeze there. I have really had ice on my eyebrows. In certain conditions my hot breath would turn to moisture and in due course settle as a pool of water on the mike which would cause difficulty in speaking. If I undid the face mask to wipe it dry, it would immediately freeze solid. I've known my wireless operator on occasions to run a shuttle service thawing out the spare microphone. I eventually cured the problem by unlatching the face piece every fifteen minutes or so just to wipe it clear. The first time it happened I was most put out. It was the skipper's usual practice to call each member of the crew in turn.

'Hello engineer, OK.'

'Engineer OK, skipper.'

And so on down the line until 'Hello rear gunner, OK?'

'I answered that I was all right, the next thing was: 'Hello, rear gunner' in a much sharper tone, 'Answer me'. I was answering. Then I heard the skipper say something that really hurt.

'Wireless operator, get down the back and see if he's dozed off.'

'In the turret I was raving mad, the skipper had really stung my pride. Me asleep in my turret, ME. When the poor wireless operator arrived I was ready to scalp him. However, it was my microphone that had frozen up and I could hear, but not transmit.

'After we got back I just had to have it out with the skipper. I was hurt to think that he didn't trust me to keep awake. He was man enough to give me a thousand apologies, but it rankled for a long time. Before the tour was over the crew had reason to know I never slept on the job.'

Pilot Ian Robertson joined 77 Squadron after conversion to Halifaxes at No 1652 HCU at Marston Moor, where the crew was completed with the addition of a mid-upper gunner and flight engineer. Pete Cadman was already at Elvington when he arrived. Both were to complete a full tour with the squadron. Ian Robertson, known to his colleagues as John, says:

'To get through a crew had to be lucky, without any obvious weak link and a bit positive in working at getting through, but mostly it had to be lucky. We never did relax until we were well over our own coast on the way back. We never did fly one mile on George. Occasionally we deviated a little from the flight plan when it was obviously causing avoidable risks. Above all, we were lucky enough, and perhaps efficient enough, to get away with encounters with German fighters.

'For this we have to thank Flight Lieutenant Palmer, who made fighter affiliation his speciality exercise as an instructor at No 20 OTU Lossiemouth. He should have flown with every OTU crew. Simply he threw the Wellington into the corkscrew manoeuvres in a manner never conceived by pupils or any other instructor.*

'Subsequently I used Palmer's technique on Halifaxes at Marston Moor, and on the squadron at base. In daylight, working with Spitfires at Elvington on a couple of occasions the fighter pilot's conservative comments were that "it was difficult to get a deflection shot at P-Peter aircraft". I adopted the same approach on operations. It resulted in chaos for the navigator with pencils, charts and anything loose flying about. We also lost considerable height and time, but we got away with the combats.

'On 29 September the target was Bochum. After all the usual aggravation and tension we had heard the words "Bombs gone" from Bill, the bomb-aimer, followed very quickly afterwards with a hesitant request to "go round again", as the bombs had *not* gone due to Bill making a cock-up about his bomb selection panel. After a pause there followed:

'Johnny the pilot: "OK, Bill, but don't hang about."

'Bill: "Thanks, Johnny. I'll be in trouble with the bombing leader otherwise."

'Alfie, the rear-gunner: "No skipper, drop them now, you know we must not go round again it's against orders." (Which was true, due to collision risk.)

'Johnny the pilot: "Shut up Alfie, it'll only take five minutes."

'Alfie the rear-gunner: "No! . . . no! . . . well I'm not coming!"

'Another incident at much the same time again involved Alfie.

*Squadron Leader R. A. M. Palmer DFC RAFVR was awarded a posthumous Victoria Cross. As a Path Finder he led a formation of Lancaster bombers to attack the Cologne marshalling yards in daylight on 23 December 1944. His citation says 'he disdained avoiding action, though heavily attacked, to mark the target. His aircraft was last seen ablaze'.

The Mess at Elvington. McClorry's name is chalked over the dart score

F/O Daffey (3rd left) with his crew. Pete Cadman (peaked cap) is next to his navigator E. G. McClorry, with his gunners Bill Trivett and Bill Batty on right of the picture

'Rear-gunner to Navigator: "We are just passing over a large town, I can still see some lights on."

'Navigator. "What . . . in the middle of the North Sea?" '

Matthew Holliday, who had already completed one tour, to be described later, now takes up the story:

'Tich Quine, who already held the DFM, and I arrived at Elvington at about 2230 hours on 1 November 1943 after imbibing a jar or two in York. We progressed through the camp, loudly singing the praises of Shiny 10 Squadron. Both being proud of having served on 10 Squadron we thought we would fly the flag a little. Fortunately we weren't lynched, and I went on to become very proud of being a member of No 77 Squadron. Tich was shot down before Christmas, he survived the crash. His commission came through later, and with typical aircrew humour we said he would be moving from a Stalag to an Offlag!

'I was to join Pete Cadman's crew as flight engineer, a wonderful crew with 18 trips to their credit. Mac, the navigator, Flying Officer E. G. McClorry, had been awarded the BEM for his work as a policeman in the Manchester blitz. We called bomb aimer Flight Sergeant Harry Clayton, "Clay" or "Straddle". The wireless operator was "Smokey", Sergeant A. Powell. "Scats", Sergeant Bill Batty, was the mid-upper gunner, and Bill Trivett the rear gunner.

'On 3 November 1943 the squadron was called on to make a maximum effort for a raid on Düsseldorf. The engineering leader was flying with Pete on that one, and as he was walking with me round the flight offices he complained of how difficult it was to make up crews when someone was ill. I made the appropriate noises of commiseration and he suddenly looked me in the eye and said, "Will you go?" Assuming what I hoped was a nonchalant air, I agreed. I hadn't flown in anger for many months and here I was about to be thrown in at the deep end and on my second day with the unit.

'I was to be flight engineer on C-Charlie, piloted by Squadron Leader Badcoe, one of the flight commanders. Take-off 1700.

'All went well until about a quarter-of-an-hour's flying time from the target when, as we were gently weaving along, the words "Fighter, fighter, starboard, go, go, go!" resounded through the intercom. With a sickening lurch we dived down and to the right – then up to port. I could see tracer bullets shooting between me, and my instrument panel. Within seconds down and starboard again, and up and then to port in correct fighter evasion drill, the fighter still sticking with us until suddenly I was jammed up in the astro-dome, unable to move. The aircraft had stalled and we were upside down and dropping rapidly. The bag in which I carried my equipment slowly rose and went leisurely down towards the rest position. This is it, I thought, my first trip with a new crew and I remembered an H. G. Wells film I had recently seen with the glass going across the room in *The Invisible Man*. As we were plunging to earth at a tremendous speed I was unable to move and expected the end at any second. Since then I have often reflected that my mundane thoughts were not in keeping with tales of one's past life rushing through the mind when death is imminent. Suddenly we were on an even keel; the pilot had managed to raise his feet up onto the instrument panel and with some superhuman strength had succeeded in gaining control. We had plunged from 24,000 to 9,000 feet and all loose equipment had made the inside of the Halifax a shambles. The navigator, in particular, had the difficult task of attempting to sort out maps, flight plan and his navigational equipment, not at all easy in a dark interior.

'Checking on all crew positions and finding everyone, and everything, in good order the pilot decided to press on towards the target although we were behind schedule, knew we would have to bomb when everyone else had departed for home and could not possibly make our bombing height. Checking on engines and fuel state, and deciding that, as the flight engineer's log was in a torn and crumpled condition, I would have to calculate on the fuel gauges, I began to cogitate on our reception over the target area. We would be bombing late, everyone else would have left for home, we would be sitting ducks for the enemy flak. With a bit of luck, we figured, the fighters would have landed at their bases. In the event we gained height and at 14,000 feet bombed a brightly lit Düsseldorf. Not a shot was fired at us. The defences had been swamped by the power of the Main Force attack. We bombed and turned for home.

'Shortly after leaving the target area I went aft to check visually that all the bombs had released, and then made my way in the dark to check the flare chute; in the hooded light of a torch I could see that it was empty. I returned to my position and we closed the bomb doors. Remembering the tracer bullets I had seen passing between myself and the instrument panel I checked for holes in the side of the aircraft, couldn't find any and realised that what I had seen was the reflection of the tracer bullets going past the aircraft showing in the glass of the gauges. So much for illusion and a vivid imagination!

'Returning over The Wash, one of the crew went back to use the Elsan: "Hello, Skipper, the photo flare is inside the kite!" When the aircraft had turned upside down the flare had fallen from the chute onto the floor. Not thinking of that, I had assumed that when the chute was empty the flare had dropped; the safety split-pin had indeed been pulled, but if a draught had removed the arming propeller . . . ! We opened the door and threw it out.

'Home and Elvington. On the final approach we had to overshoot and the port inner exhaust stubs exploded in a huge flash and bang, which added further to my grey hairs. Upon examination we found a hole made by a cannon shell in the starboard mainplane had removed most of the end of the wing, just missing No 6 petrol tank and the aileron. The back of Halifax JD385 was broken; she brought us home safely, but was herself consigned to oblivion. Squadron Leader Badcoe was awarded an immediate Bar to his DFC. This was announced at a crew conference and at the same time a general Group signal was read to the effect that when taking evasive action pilots should take precautions to avoid stalling the aircraft. If only the chairborne person who had drafted that signal had been in our Halifax on the night of 3 November!

'Pete Cadman: what a character, harum-scarum and full of fun on the ground – in the air calm and cool, a leader and a first-class pilot. He imbued one with a feeling of confidence in his own and your ability. My first operation with him was 18 November, take-off 1645, target Mannheim-Ludwigshafen. It was a successful trip, and as the coastal searchlights pointed our way on our return, I hoped the crews that manned the lights knew how much we appreciated them.

'Pilot to navigator: "Right, Mac, I know where we are." "Right Skipper" was the reply as Mac commenced to complete his chart and pack up. "That's not it, Mac, can you give me a bearing?" Mac does and tells the pilot to fly on it until he gets a fix. "Righto, Mac, I can see the drome."

'The intercom was busy for quite a while, while Mac gave Pete a heading, Pete flew it for a while, then said he could see base, found it was not Elvington and requested another bearing, but did not give the navigator time to get a fix before flying off in another direction. The result was that we became hopelessly lost. I was adding to my grey hairs by remembering the fuel state and calculating how much flying time we had remaining. Eventually we spotted a coded pundit beacon, but it was one on which we had no information! After several requests for a bearing the beacon was identified as flashing from Blackpool, Squire's Gate! Flying back to Elvington presented no difficulty, although a shortage of fuel was a constant source of worry until we arrived over base and landed JD462 safely. The other members of the crew were at pains to explain to me that the pilot was not always like that. Like most of my contemporaries I always assumed that if one landed back at base in one piece we were lucky. I suppose I said something to the effect that I was quite happy and would not wish to make any judgement on a pilot who had brought us safely through a raid over Germany. Mac was not so lucky however, despite the fact that the incident was not of his making I believe that he had his leg pulled shamelessly by other members of the Navigators Union and in due course a fellow navigator, a wag of a South African, substituted some words to a popular song of the day, one of the verses of which went:

'Oh, that looks like a pundit down there,
'We can sing as we fly through the air,
'And if it isn't too late
'We can call up Squire's Gate
'And come in on a wing and a prayer.'

'Only once as aircrew did I have premonition of disaster,' says Bill Trivett, who was rear gunner of the same crew. 'I experienced a bad dream. We as a crew would go missing. I didn't know how it was to be but we would not be coming back. I visualised also a crew, captained by young Brownie, now commissioned, half of them baling out and the captain bringing the aircraft back. The target in my dream was Frankfurt.

'Two nights later I was on Ops to Kassel. Although we were coned in a mass of searchlights and dropped from 18,000 to 12,000 feet we arrived back all right. At the time I wondered if I had got the target wrong! On the third night after my dream

I was on Ops again and the target this time *was* Frankfurt. I didn't say a word to anyone regarding my dream; it was bad enough for one to be uneasy, never mind the other six blokes. The battle order also included Flying Officer Brown.

'Came the take-off. Running up the engines, one of the port engines ran hot and there was also a slight loss of revs. A call to control. Out comes an engineer, then a debate, then "I think it will be OK, see how it goes with the cold air flowing". With the odds on chance of an engine cutting on take-off, and with this load of bombs, it could mean certain death. Knowing what I already thought I knew, I was already squeezing my buttocks. We hiccoughed, spat, gasped for breath and staggered off down the runway. In the rear turret I had already died a thousand deaths. I knew now it was going to happen! We made wheels up and tried a circuit of the airfield; the temperature was still rising and we were fighting hard to climb, to flight plan height. After about twenty minutes smoke came past me in the rear turret, from the port engine. The mid-upper and myself battled for honours to be first with the news: "Port engine on fire".

'The gallant old Halifax lurched to one side as the engine was cut, and then staggered manfully to support its full bomb load on three engines. There were houses below, our houses. That damned premonition, it was all happening. Was this where we were to go missing? It suddenly dawned on me, I couldn't move my turret so I informed the skipper of my predicament. Yes, of course, the rear turret was useless because it received its power from the crippled engine. God, now there was another alternative: we could blow up, pile in, or now bale out. The skipper spoke over the intercom.

' "OK, navigator, give me a course for the coast. We'll abort and discharge the bomb load in the sea." The navigator checked the statement.

' "You mean we are turning back?"

' "Yes", replied the skipper, "I would have risked going on three engines but not with the rear turret out of action as well. We could have need of it at Frankfurt."

'I couldn't believe my ears, or luck. We were a crew with 16 operations behind us; it could not have been an easy decision. After we'd touched down I went behind the rear turret and offered a silent prayer of thanks. We then went to Flying Control to see the other crews return some hours later. Amongst those who did return was, I'm pleased to say, young Brownie, with his crew intact. So much for the premonition. But that wasn't the end of the story. Some six operations later, on the night of 20/21 December 1943 the target was once more to be Frankfurt, which that night was defended by Flak Regiment 29(0) consisting of 84 x 10.5 cm guns and 416 x 8.8 cm guns.

'This time we completed our operation. Amongst the squadron missing was none other than young Brownie. Pilot E. A. Brown was flying LL127 H-How. Forty miles from the target the aircraft was attacked by a fighter and hit in the fuselage and starboard wing. Electrics, intercom, instruments, hydraulics and mid-upper turret became u/s. Brown gave the order to bale out and the second pilot, navigator and wireless operator left the aircraft. The pilot, however, then corrected the spiral dive and righted the Halifax. He continued on and bombed the target. Although the pilot, engineer and mid-upper gunner were injured, Brown, assisted by the bomb aimer, brought H-How back and landed at another airfield. He was awarded an immediate DFC.'

One of the aircraft that did not return to England from the raid was G-George LL121 flown by Flight Sergeant Leslie Howard. Take-off time was 1645 and the Halifax was attacked en route to the target by an unidentified night fighter which was shaken off by vigorous evading action. The crew found the approach to Frankfurt as formidable as on the previous two occasions they had attacked the same target in their 16 operations. There appeared to be a solid wall of searchlights in multiple groups with a controlling bluish radar-controlled beam. It was impossible to do other than go through the wall and the sight of other aircraft ahead caught in the cones and exploding after being blanketed by flak was unnerving. The bomb-aimer dropped the bombs on the visible markers and the aircraft turned on a north-west-north course.

The wireless operator remained in the second pilot's position for a short time after bombing and Flight Engineer Tich Quine remained in the astrodome, watching for fighters. Soon wireless operator Neville Short returned to his position to resume 'windowing' and monitoring night fighter controllers. About twenty minutes after bombing, a long double line of flares were dropped by the Luftwaffe along the bomber stream, against which the Halifax was silhouetted. Almost as soon as the Halifax went into a dive to gain speed it was attacked from astern and below. Cannon fire burst in the fuselage, the starboard outer and the wingtips. The Halifax immediately went into a spiral to starboard against which the pilot fought to regain control. The starboard outer had stopped and flames were being trailed well back. Burning petrol was jetting into the fuselage and the pilot issued instructions to abandon aircraft. The wireless operator placed the pilot's parachute on his chest clip before baling out of the forward hatch from between 17,000 and 18,000 feet. The aircraft crashed five miles south of Ahrweiler. The pilot's body was found near the aircraft. The bomb aimer was missing but the rest of the crew were made prisoners of war.

The Halifax was attacked by the *Schräge Musik* method of upward firing guns. It is almost certain that it was shot down by Hauptmann Martin Becker who commanded IV/NJG6 and personally shot down three bombers that night.

Matthew Holliday remembers that Tich Quine had just bought a Morgan three-wheeler and parked it outside the operations block. 'In the usual manner of aircrew I said: "Can I have that if you don't come back?" It felt very strange seeing the car stuck outside Ops until a corporal disposed of it. As I mentioned earlier, fortunately Tich was made a prisoner of war.'

Among Matthew Holliday's other recollections of his Elvington operations are:

'Leverkusen: when I felt the old line-shoot about getting out and walking on the flak was very appropriate.

'Berlin, the big city: After briefing one of the flight engineers pulled the legs of the rest who had not been there before. To say the least, he implied we would not like it over there and he was right, although we did not appreciate his telling us.

'Stuttgart, and being diverted to Tangmere when we returned. Saturday evening out in Chichester, all wearing our flying gear, feeling like little heroes for a change. On Sunday we returned to Yorkshire, and observed disasters all over the place. The Yorkshire-based Halifaxes had been told to land in the south because of mist in Lincolnshire, and the Lancaster squadrons were to land in Yorkshire. Unfortunately fog had obscured some of the Yorkshire airfields and many of the Lancasters crashed; two or three had pranged in the vicinity of Elvington.

'Disaster: we returned from an evening in York to discover that certain members of the squadron had decided that the mess piano had had its day – small wonder after all the beer slops that had been administered to its wires and other internal organs. They had proceeded to dismantle the piano and given it a decent Viking funeral by placing the pieces reverently upon the large open fire. Our skipper, Pete, was one of the ringleaders and seemed to have enjoyed the exercise – that is until the pay-off. The Groupy failed to see the joke and promptly ordered all concerned to pay for the damage. The price quoted for a replacement seemed exorbitant at the time and it would have cut down the beer intake of the culprits for many days to come, and so it was decided to ask all the members of the Mess who wished to do so to let a proportion of the cost be added to their mess bill. Disaster indeed! I can still feel the pain as I appended my name to the list of assenters.

'Christmas 1943: I hadn't expected to survive so long with all the losses being sustained by Bomber Command. There were celebrations in the mess, helped by words which had been written by the South African wag, to the tunes of popular carols. To the tune of "We Three Kings" there was a verse about each member of the crew, and then the chorus:

"Stirlings are a ropey kite,
"Lancasters they fly by night,
"Halifaxes, just like taxis,
"Owls and dimwits fly by night."

'March 1944. A sad moment for me: my crew had finished their first tour. (I had completed 13 trips of my second tour). They were screened and departed after a celebration in the local with those grand, conscientious, hard-working, loyal ground crew lads to whom we owed such a debt of gratitude. I had to soldier on as a spare bod until I had completed my quota.

'The ubiquitous 4 Group Battle School attacked us at 77 Squadron and the South African wag and scribe was up to his usual tricks. After the attack was over the participants repaired to the various Messes for refreshment, liquid and otherwise, and a great repast was laid out in the Officers Mess. Our intrepid navigator decided it would be good fun to drop a thunder flash down the ante-room chimney; unfortunately he dropped it down the dining room chimney by mistake, he says it was a mistake. An unlighted, rectangular stove was at the base of the chimney, the doors were closed, the result magnificent. The four sides of the stove neatly laid out, the chimney pipe in splendid isolation, with soot everywhere, on white tablecloths, sandwiches and all else was a layer which some thought enhanced the scene. The spread was for the guests only, otherwise our remarks might not have been so charitable.'

The South African incidentally was Wing Commander J. A. Roncoroni's navigator. Bill Trivett recalls one evening when the Wingco came into the Sergeants Mess:

'Wingco Roncoroni was a 6ft 6in rugby player. A mess social was in full flight when he entered; his intention was to introduce himself. Taking advantage of the piano player stopping to sup his beer, the Wingco stood on a table to make a short speech. He did just that, applause all round. The lads closed in tight around the table, and in the blink of an eyelid he'd lost his trousers. What did he do next? Minus his trousers and in a very high pitched voice he shrilled out the song to the tune of *La Donna e Mobile*.

Arse-holes are cheap today, cheaper than yesterday,
Smally boys are half-a-crown, standing up or lying down, etc.

'The Wingco took it all in his stride, he was quite a lad.'

The Wing Commander was a great man, in every sense. It was said he was the baby of the family of boys and he was the smallest of the lot, despite his being tall and broad with it. He once jumped from a high scaffolding being used in the Mess for painting the ceiling, into the mess carpet being held by the rest of the members 'A la firemen'. Matthew Holliday says 'The sound of his knees banging the floor as he landed in the carpet, which slipped from our hands, still rings in my ears, he didn't turn a hair.'

In the Sergeants Mess at Elvington a small piece of the ceiling was reserved for aircrew to write their names. But not any old crew, not any Tom, Dick or Harry. Special crews, only those who had completed their tour. It was an honour to write your name, and after a social mess do a crew would do just that. There would be a cheer for them, drinks would be plentiful. Woe betide any other beer-sodden crew without the required credentials who tried to write upon the ceiling! To their embarrassment the offending crew would be hailed down with united chorus of a song that finished with, 'Not entitled, not entitled, to write your bloody name'. Some even got incensed about it.

Matthew Holliday, who was completing his second tour as a

spare bod continues: 'During the spring of 1944 we lost about two-thirds of the squadron in a very short time and there were many strange faces on the flights. I sat in the mess one day quaffing a pint and reading a newspaper, I overheard the station engineer officer in full flow with his back to the fire in the manner of squires of old, expounding to a new crew the exploits of a certain crew whose aircraft turned upside down over Düsseldorf. The faces of the sprog crew were a joy to behold as they listened spellbound, a mixture of awe and wonder and a certain amount of apprehension about what the future held in store for them spread across their countenances. Suddenly the speaker stopped in midflow, looked across at me and exclaimed, "You were in that plane, Curly, weren't you?" "Yes, I was", I murmured, assuming what I imagined was an air of great aplomb and returning to my paper and the adventures of Jane and Just Jake. A great moment to remember.

'When I was awarded my DFC Wing Commander Roncoroni was one of the first to congratulate me, but when he won his gong he said it was an award to the squadron, not to him – the modesty of the man! His award was well earned and no one deserved it more.'

There were other decorations for the Squadron. Ian Robertson was awarded a DFC while Mike Walters and Alfred Presbury received the DFM. At the end of the tour DFM's were also awarded to Jack La Planche, George Paine, Bill Spears and John Symes. This fully decorated crew was said to be a precedent at the time. The crew were invited over to Group at Pocklington by the Air Officer Commanding.

On 17 May Squadron Leader Egan-Wyer took over command of the squadron from Wing Commander Roncoroni. The squadron remained at Elvington until the end of the month when they transferred to Full Sutton.

By June 1944, 346 and 347 Free French Squadrons were at Elvington. Most of the French flyers were older than their Royal Air Force counterparts. They were from the professions, craftsmen and men who had made a start in life. Lieutenant Colonel G. E. Venot was appointed Commanding Officer of 346 Squadron which had an establishment of 16 Halifaxes, plus four in reserve. The French Halifaxes were easily recognisable; their roundels had a blue centre piece and red on the outside, the reverse of the RAF's. In addition the fins of 346 Squadron aircraft were criss-crossed in red for easy identification.

In the RAF the pilot was always in charge of the aircraft, whatever his rank. With the French, it was different. Jules Roy, a bomb aimer, was a captain in the French Air Force, and as senior officer was in charge of his Halifax. He joined 346 Squadron early in July 1944 and fortunately kept a diary, from which we will follow French squadron life at that time. His first operation, to bomb a V1 launching platform, ended in disaster. Coming in to land in the early hours, his Halifax collided with another which went down in flames. His aircraft swayed, one engine caught fire and two of the crew baled out. The damaged engine was stopped and the remainder of the crew landed safely with the aircraft. An official enquiry exonerated the surviving crew; their seven comrades were recovered and buried.

Hundreds of bombers carried out attacks to relieve the invasion force which had landed in France a month earlier and was getting bogged down outside Caen; then there was a raid on a station just outside Paris; Frenchmen were killing Frenchmen.

On a raid to Stuttgart a Halifax was hit by gunfire and a shell pierced the navigating cabin and the bomb aimer jumped out over France. Jules Roy was listed for his first operation over Germany on 26 July. He remembers:

'The Tannoy relayed during the afternoon: "Dinner at 2230 for the crews flying tonight. Navigators to the navigating room at 1900 hours." I am always struck by the silence and the reserve which reigns at these meals for the *morituri*. The airmen split into groups by affinities, by age or length of service. One gets the impression that each one is wondering if perhaps this is not the last meal he will take among men. No popular or witty buffoon who provokes laughter and retorts. Nothing but smiles, winks and whispered conversations. The boys come and go, take their plates, eat quickly and disappear. There is that little paper pinned up in the corridor which sends shivers down your spine.

'At last, lurching heavily like stones released from the top of a slope, we arrive at the briefing room. The course hidden by an unrolled screen, but supplementary maps on tables. Titles of the maps: Essen, Frankfurt. Not possible. The screen is raised like a curtain of a theatre and the slender blue and red lines of the itinerary cross Holland to reach the heart of an enormous scarlet patch, the Ruhr. Target: Wanne-Eichel, a synthetic-oil plant near Essen. The name which the RAF has given to the Ruhr has begun to circulate, and from thirty tables a clamour arose: "The Happy Valley, the Happy Valley".'

One of the Halifaxes arrived six minutes late over the target and nearly paid the price, the compass was put out of action without the knowledge of the crew and the aircraft flew round in circles for 25 minutes while thinking it was on its way home. The Halifax survived the two pierced tanks and ninety holes it received. The bomb aimer was wounded and had to be replaced.

Early the next month one of the squadron pilots wound his wheels up too soon, with the result that the propellers touched the ground. The pilot fortunately retrieved the situation by pulling the stick back. The Halifax crash-landed at Carnaby.

At the beginning of September there was a huge explosion at Elvington when a Halifax returned from France with a 500 lb bomb still aboard. The bomb became unhooked as the aircraft landed and blew it to smitherines but miraculously the pilot was thrown clear – the only member of the crew to survive.

A few days later on a raid to Münster the pilot who had previously touched the ground with his propellers was amongst the Halifaxes that all returned damaged. His bomb aimer was killed just as he released the bombs and his aircraft was permeated with acrid smoke when the flare cartridges caught fire.

Bochum, in the Ruhr, was attacked on 9 October. Jules Roy was in Halifax III MZ709, one of the 400 aircraft taking part. It was a murky evening as the Halifax took off from its Yorkshire base at 1710.

By this stage of the war the Germans had been pushed out of most of France to their own borders, and as the Halifax crossed this area gun-flashes disclosed the firing line. The aircraft was loaded with five and a half tanks of fuel and five and a half tons of bombs. At the border the Halifax started its climb to bombing height. Although some of the fuel had been consumed the climb through the cloud was laborious. Eventually twenty thousand feet was reached. Through occasional gaps in the cloud decoy fires were observed. Bochum was bombed, and then the Halifax made a quick dive down to 9,000 feet where it levelled out between two layers of cloud. Then it climbed up to 16,000 feet to come out over Holland. Searchlights could be seen in the distance well before the English coast was reached, and then it was back over the Yorkshire airfields until the letters E V flashed up identifying Elvington. Home at 2247, another mission completed.

A crew goes missing. Jules Roy recorded his thoughts:

'Who is really sorry for them? Through our emotions we turn our glances towards ourselves. What happened to them can easily happen to us tomorrow. Their fate interests us in so far as it is the one we may suffer, and it is only the shadow of a thought – or rather as reflection – which stops us and becomes the true thought. A crew disappears and each one calculates in his own small way the happy results for himself . . . one more crew gone to destiny's bag, one more crew, and you are still safe. The missing are effaced from this world with prodigious ease.'

At the end of October 346 Squadron were briefed to attack Cologne. Jules Roy took off in reserve Halifax LL583. Soon after take-off the oil pressure on the starboard outer engine fell from ninety to sixty-five, then to sixty, then to fifty. The engine had to be cut at sixty according to regulations. The aircraft made height as it flew out over the North Sea but the faulty engine did not right itself and so the pilot flew the required eighty miles out from the coast before releasing his load. Despite the 7,000 feet altitude the aircraft was still shaken as the load exploded. For the crew, it meant an early return at 1500 in fine sunny weather.

Cologne again on 31 October. Jules Roy once more:

'Near the plane we embarked upon the agony of the day. We were loaded to the limit and were only just airborne at the end of the short runway, but the engines fired well. We flew straight on a northerly course and climbed to 8,000 feet. Through a gap in the clouds we could see the station. We scaled a fringe of light cumulus and came out into a sea of bulging clouds cut into ravines. The sun, which had already set, threw out an extraordinary afterglow, while to the east the full moon climbed in a dark and misty twilight. From all sides, like wasps, the aircraft plunged into the Saharan fragrance of gold or crimson through the whole range of purple, violet and mauve. The horizon looked like dunes of sand. I had no time to study it for long. I did not want to look, I was too busy watching the other aircraft.

'The first difficult change of course. The stream was as close together as in daylight, but a few aircraft passed us, all the same.

Why are they so crack-brained? I was badly placed in the nose because the glass distorts the images. Gradually the moonlight grew stronger. I was weary of my thoughts and tried to suppress them. In this flight of eight hundred wasps I was merely one insignificant insect.

'After Reading the stream thinned out. We skimmed over the upper layer of clouds, which gave us a great sense of speed. We met some Lancasters over the Channel. The whole of Bomber Command was out on the job. We were involved in something very big, but we had eyes only for ourselves and those around us. Little by little we climbed to avoid the clouds, in a prolonged silence.

' "She vibrates at times," said the rear gunner.

' "Yes, you know this plane always does."

'Poor "tail-end Charlie" perched there in his turret over the void between the two tail units.

'More cloud. We climbed to 19,000 and then to 20,000. At the last change of course we were a little ahead of time; then suddenly we came out into an enormous valley lit with the scarlet, green and white clusters of the marking flares above the terrible glare of the bombs. The gunners overwhelmed me with signals indicating the aircraft above and behind us.

' "I couldn't care less. I'm not bothered about *them*."

'The flak was in action but very far below. We were protected by 12,000 feet of cotton wool. It was not very serious, and there was no reason to get nervous, but all the same I was rough with the gunners. Bomb doors open. Pressed the tit, but it was stuck. Nothing fell. Quickly found the fault. I repaired it in a flash and at last saw the cluster of bombs whistling down towards the ground with the ugly 2,000 pounder staggering in the middle.

' "We're for it now if there are fighters about in this clear sky."

'But it was difficult to descend because of the icing, and the other aircraft making for the target blind would collide with us if we did not avoid them in their circus of death. To the south-east of Cologne we went down among the tracer bullets towards Coblenz and then after Bonn set a south-westerly course. I spent a long time looking back at the target. What a feast. What a feast for Death. He gives fine and magnificent feasts!

'I felt tired as though I lacked oxygen. Sat down for a moment feeling faint. We shaved the clouds. A light powder of ice had formed on the engine cowlings. To the north of Rheims we turned again and crossed the coast between Dunkirk, still held by the enemy, and Ostend.

'Relaxation over the North Sea. I switched on the navigation lights. We were flying high so as not to be bothered by the others. Counted the minutes of fuel that remained. It was nearly as clear as day. We were the first to arrive at base. We landed immediately while the others began to call out their names on the intercom. A slight bank of mist hindered us while we made our circuits. Twenty minutes later the mist thickened. The others had great difficulty in circling and the last of them were diverted elsewhere.

'To Bochum early in November with F-Freddie MZ709. Heavy losses, 346 Squadron lost five aircraft with their thirty-five crewmen.'

After more raids, in the middle of December Air Commodore Walker, still at Elvington, spoke to the crews, as Jules Roy remembers:

'He tried to tell us in French: "I have had great experience of the RAF and Bomber Command during the past four years. Well, you are worthy of the famous squadrons." To see this man, who had lost an arm over Germany and whose eyes flashed in a sunburnt face, struggling with his vocabulary moved us to the vitals. The esteem and affection of a type like him almost made me shed tears.'

On 22 December there was a call for crews at 0900 for a daylight raid on Cologne, but just as the aircraft were on the point of taking off at midday it was washed out. The fog probably prevented the fighter escort from flying. A new briefing was arranged at 1300 with take-off at 1600. Jules Roy was on the raid:

'Old F-Freddie struggled to pull her thirty-three tons into the air, but we were pleased to be on board and to be leaving by daylight. The stream was not very dense. Over the south of England a compact layer like swansdown. Darkness enveloped us over Charleroi. Anxiety about our return. What would happen if the fog closed in? The aircraft that glided at our side brought us the comfort of knowing we were on course. Markers fell in two unexpected places and before time; perhaps they forgot to tell us of other attacks. At zero hour our flares rained down ahead of us. The markers, quickly absorbed by the fog and the clouds, filtered through in a pink gleam. We attacked in the first wave and made our run at 1836, thirty seconds late. Heavy and accurate flak.

Flares to port and the bright glare of bombs well released. Hampered in our photographic run by another Halifax. Our red markers with green stars burst behind us followed by the sharp flash of the bombs. Lying on my belly in the forward cockpit to watch for fighters above the crescent of the new moon in the opalescent night. Over the coast the weather grew infinitely worse and the gunners were tired from their vigil. A sparkling rain crackled on the perspex, with the visibility almost nil but improving a little on the English side. In the distance I thought I could see the glare of fires, but as I drew nearer I recognised the flaming display of Fido at the reception station trying to absorb the fog. The sky was well lit up. Peacefully we glided down in order to be the first to arrive, and old F-Freddie responded well.

'Guessed at the airfield ground-lights and saw the circle about a mile away. We called on our intercom and landed almost immediately forgetting to put our nose light on.

'The refrain of all the crews: "One more, that makes one less."

'It was so dark that I returned on foot, completely exhausted and panting, my lungs on fire after five hours of oxygen.

'On 24 December we took off at midday with a visibility of 500 yards and a ceiling of 150 feet. We got through the cloud at once and into formation at 8,000 feet, with the usual fear of other aircraft.

'Over the sea the pilots jockeyed for position and had difficulty in doing so, like runners in a marathon. Just before Holland things grew calmer. I do not care much for these daylight raids, when the sun burns your eyes if you have forgotton your black glasses.

'Our fighter cover was invisible and the gunners grew restless. We could not see them, but they must have been there, for a few sparkling vapour trails spread out very high in the sky. Our formation was closing in more and more. We were carrying bombs with very sensitive fuses. If a burst were to touch them they would go off. The guns did not attack us until shortly before Essen. As our comrades were slightly in front and above us, we were liable to run into their bombs, so I gave the order to gain a few hundred feet to avoid them. The black clusters burst in front of us or to one side, but never near us. At Gelsenkirchen they were close enough for the aircraft to echo under a hail of steel. Disturbed by the other aircraft and by the gunner's orders, I brought F-Freddie back on an even keel and released my bombs slowly and well, counting them as they went down. The huge town of Essen, covered with the smoke of its factories, was still working in spite of all the preceding raids. A solitary aircraft flew over Düsseldorf, to be received by shattering flak. The Halifax burst into flames, dived and crashed on the outskirts of the town near the Rhine.

'Coming home we received a message from base: "Approach the airfield at 2,000 feet and wait for your instructions." Fog. After the Wash the fog was so low-lying that the tops of the trees and the steeples hardly emerged, and at Melbourne Fido was raging to try to disperse it. Received orders to make for Carnaby where Fido consumes petrol at the rate of 104,000 gallons an hour to dissipate the fog. After three attempts to get a reply, we landed at 1754 without waiting for instructions on the mile-and-a-half runway behind a hundred other aircraft. Much later a convoy of lorries returned us to Elvington.

'We took off at 1800 on 30 December, for another raid on Cologne railway station. At the moment we started up the engines it was noticed that we were too overloaded to take off: more than 66,000 pounds instead of 65,000. I telephoned for the loaders to take off two 250-pound bombs and we left on time.

'Suddenly, before starting to climb, traces of ice formed behind us in the exhaust of our engines. A hundred, more than four hundred vapour trails like bridal veils. Two minutes before zero hour red clusters burst slowly ten miles to the north of the target. It was a decoy. A minute-and-a-half late our real markers tumbled out of the sky and the blast of the shell burst flung us about. A bomb remained caught, which I had to jettison in the sea on the way back. The fighters were deceived once more and did not manage to intercept us, so back to base on the stroke of midnight.

'New Year's Eve was sacred for the RAF and a big party had been arranged for Elvington. Girls and WAAFs had been bussed in, the orchestra was rehearsing when suddenly the Tannoy summoned the duty crews to visit the 'Happy Valley' once again. By the time the mission returned the party was in full swing. There was no better way to unwind.

'Ludwigshafen the next day, and new dangers. The American ack-ack on the front-line was trigger happy and MZ984 of 347 Squadron was brought down near Verdun.'

Like Wing Commander Lowe earlier, Jules Roy appeared able to recognise those destined not to complete a tour, for he says:

'I seemed always to recognise on the faces of those who are going to die. The signs of their sentence, as though a kind of melancholy had cast a shadow over them. There were certain crews that were marked and I was sure they would not go far.'

Jules Roy had just six more operations to complete when his faithful F-Freddie was due to take off for the Ruhr at midnight on 6 January, 1945, but the Halifax behaved capriciously on its return from overhaul. Jules Roy continues:

'The port outer engine began to bang violently three minutes before take-off. We pulled out of line, tried it on full throttle and everything seemed normal, but we had no sooner got to the runway than it began to backfire so loudly that revs had to be reduced. We went to the end of the runway and returned to our dispersal pen. Another test. Perfect. I felt I had to try once more and I decided to leave. We took off at last without a hitch and easily made up our delay.

'Towards the Ruhr at nightfall there was a long row of false markers and decoys. Over the target badly protected by 2/10 cloud, a few aircraft passed us dangerously. We returned by a series of changing altitudes. If we hadn't returned they would have said, "He tried to leave three times that evening. He took off at the third attempt." '

January 1945 in Yorkshire was snowy and on the 19th there were also heavy storms that threatened to blow over the airmen's huts. Raids were laid on and then cancelled as the snow came down harder. One of the French airmen who taught geography in civilian life had, he said, deceived hundreds of children by teaching them that Britain has a 'mild and temperate climate'. In their huts the men huddled round their stoves and poked them furiously. A Halifax failed to return from a raid; one of the crew who baled out and survived said the accident took place very quickly. One engine was iced and another caught fire.

The Frenchmen discussed the length of operational tours according to the customs of the RAF. A total of 120 points was needed to complete a tour. Three points were awarded for a mission not further east than three degrees and four for the longer ones. This meant forty small trips or thirty long ones, or any combination. For those just starting, the total was awesome.

At the beginning of February terrible news arrived for those crews nearing the end of their tour: the total of operations was to be increased, each crew would have to complete thirty-six missions to finish a tour, instead of thirty. There was uproar on the squadron which the higher-ups were unable to smooth over.

A raid on Leipzig in support of the Russians took place in mid-February. Jules Roy:

'What shall I remember of Leipzig before the bombing and the colossal explosion which lit up the sky for a few seconds when we were directly over the town? A firework display, the sharp report of flak, the glow of bombs, our changing course, that aircraft crossing our bows which the pilot had to leap over, and the other one just above us. To the south-east an attack on Dresden was in progress. We were lit up as though in broad daylight. Desultory flak near Cologne then Manston with its searchlight as erect as a column. At 0250 we arrived over base, preceded by ten other aircraft.

'Had it not been for the new orders in force I should have finished my tour of operations. I was one of the first to be hit by the order of six supplementary missions and now I should have been out of danger.'

On 20 February every available crew was rounded up for a night operation on Reisholz. Jules Roy flew in MZ738.

On 3 March Jules Roy tested his F-Freddie on a cross country flight in the afternoon after three engines had been changed. That same night there came the final fling of the *Nachtjagd*. The Luftwaffe was launching its long-planned operation Operation Gisella, the first large-scale intruder operation against the bomber airfields since the late summer of 1941.

As Allied aircraft withdrew from bombing Kamen and Ladbergen and made for their bases in England, more than 100 German night fighters scrambled into the air and headed westwards in hot pursuit. Two waves of aircraft, comprising mainly Ju88's but with a few He219's, swept over the North Sea and made for targets in Norfolk, Suffolk, Lincolnshire and Yorkshire. At Elvington the Tannoy blared out an alert: 'Attention, Attention! Threatened raid of intruders! Check your blackouts!'

A burning Halifax NR235, from 347 Squadron, spiralled slowly in the sky above the base; then it went into a vertical dive and exploded like a star with a terrifying beauty. The moon was up

P-Peter of a French Squadron following a heavy landing

and the German fighters were searching for stragglers. The speakers gave a new warning, 'Attention, attention. Risk of a ground strafe. All personnel to the shelter!' A twin-engined marauder circled the airfield then attacked with cannon fire. A bomber, obviously low on fuel, attempted to land without a light, he overshot.

Elvington was only one of 27 airfields that were attacked and 22 bombers were shot down for the loss of six intruders. A Ju88 crashed on the outskirts of York after hitting a tree. Its crew of four were killed as were two women in the farmhouse it crashed on. There was a warning given of a further raid the following night but nothing developed.

On the morning of 14 March Jules Roy learned that his name was on battle orders for his thirty-seventh, and last operation. It was a short trip to the other side of the Moselle to smash concentrations of enemy troops at Homburg. When he landed, in MZ737, by the sodium flares on the runway the Wing Commander was waiting to congratulate the crew despite its being just thirty minutes before midnight. There was the usual banter and talk of veterans. The following night a note arrived from

4 Group ordering the station not to release crews in future until they completed a minimum of 144 points, which gave most of them another trip to do. It was not retrospective, Jules Roy was saved – if he had not taken off that night at the third attempt in early January his crew would have had another operation to perform to complete the tour.

George Ostre was not so fortunate. He should have completed his tour at the same time as Jules Roy, but he did not fly on that evening.

Ostre took off at 1830 on 15 March for Hagen. He was afraid of his last mission, as he admitted to the padre and to the rest of the world. He was never at ease on that last evening. He had difficulty keeping his 347 Squadron Halifax C-Charlie NR287 on course. When he arrived back over Elvington at 6,000 feet he heard an aircraft being given permission to land. 'We shan't be among the first', he said. 'We'll go down a little to the north and then come through the mush to the south.' He ordered the engineer to check if all the bombs had gone, and sent for the bomb aimer. In the bays the engineer had the shock of his life, for when he opened the hatch he saw the ground and the trees speeding past them in the dark. Then there was a crash. He fainted. He woke up to the sound of petrol flowing from the burst tanks and got out. He whistled and a second whistle replied. The two survivors found some people who looked after them. On the first impact the Halifax had hit a stone wall at the edge of a field on the slope of a hill. The wings and the four engines were ripped off and the body bounded on another two miles, which gives one the impression that it was flying at a terrific speed. The navigator was killed by the stone wall, and so was the wireless operator. Perhaps Ostre, too, and the rest of the crew.

'In friendly territory,' Jules Roy says 'the navigator never dared to correct a course which Ostre, whom he worshipped, had once given. He had therefore got into the habit of never making any comments. In this way he did not check his altimeter, for the one in the pilot's cockpit was faulty (otherwise one cannot conceive why the second pilot made no comment on the descent).'

A squadron leader at Elvington had another theory: he thought that Ostre had fainted in the air. Flying tired him a great deal. Once he even fainted on the ground. He was examined by doctors, who could find nothing to stop him carrying on, but his crew apparently were very anxious.

The news was received at Elvington at 2300; 'Ostre crashed forty miles north of here. Only two survivors.' Ostre and Chevalier dead . . . Chevalier had been a priest.

On 21 March the war in Europe had 48 days to run as Jules Roy attended the funeral of his colleagues:

'At the funeral parade I looked on the crosses of the tombs for the names of comrades I had known. I could have been lying under one of them. The grave-diggers have plenty of work. The holes are dug just wide enough to fit the shoulders, the walls are sheer beneath a first layer of black frozen earth, which the spade cuts and detaches in sods. So this was the Holgate Cemetery which I had never before dared to visit!

'Opposite there is the gentle slope of a valley, very flat below, and on the crest a long rambling farmhouse surrounded by meadows dotted with enormous solitary oaks. The hedges are springing to life and the sowing-machine is crossing the tilled fields, followed by the harrow. They are sowing the spring corn and covering in the soil, while here it was my comrades who were being laid in the ground.

'A bitter north wind was blowing which made us want to pull up our collars. At last the first two hearses arrived. The coffins were covered with tricolour flags of creased bunting and each set down beside its grave. On Chevalier's coffin they had unfurled a violet sacerdotal stole. The chaplain sang the *Libera Me*. How gentle was the prayer that followed and how moving that request for light for those who fell in the darkness. . . . Then arose the tolling for the dead, less pathetic than ours in France, less funereal also. A moment's silence, followed by a very short, almost happy echo like an unfinished note dying away.'

These gallant allies are remembered each time the parishioners enter their small church at Scawton and every Armistice Day, when they are mentioned by name. At this time also the thoughts of the congregation turn to all those other airmen who lost their lives while flying from Yorkshire bases.

CHAPTER TWO

Breighton Bound

Before the war Eric Pritchard worked for a London laundry chain, in charge of eighty-five depots. In 1939 he had undertaken St John's Ambulance, ARP and Fire Service courses. At the outbreak of hostilities he was considered to be in a 'reserved occupation'. As well as his fulltime job Eric was a despatch rider during the Blitz. Tiring of pulling wounded people out of shelters, Eric wished to retaliate. Six times he volunteered for the Air Force and was rejected each time, his age, thirty-three, and his reserved occupation were against him.

The RAF then started recruiting a new category of aircrew, the flight-engineer, for four-engined bombers. Eric volunteered once more and was successful.

After preliminary training, he was sent on to St Athan, a beautiful camp with every facility, but recruits suffered as they did in every Training Command camp. There were 32 airmen to each hut with a corporal in a room at the end. The course explored every part of the aircraft in the greatest detail and there were weekly tests, to check progress. There were cutaways and parts of aircraft, but no complete aircraft was seen in detail. A big drawback was that there was too much theory and one never had a spanner in the hand. Spare parts were passed round but the rest was all diagrams and theory. As the course progressed the trainees were allowed to run up a Tiger Moth's engine that was mounted on a handcart. Next, sitting in a cockpit of a Magister and run the engine up. Finally the trainees had to sit in a Stirling and run an engine.

During the course instruction had been on what turned out to be the wrong Mark of Halifax. Eric Pritchard and his friends qualified and were passed out as sergeants. As Eric says: 'There is no one better than the British services at taking people one step removed from an idiot and in a short space of time turning them out as an expert.'

From Wales the flight engineers moved to Wombleton and No 1666 Heavy Conversion Unit, for familiarisation and crewing up. For the new arrivals it was an eye opener. The Halifaxes were the early Merlin engined types, and in poor condition. They breathed fire all round, and glycol leaked out of the engines.

There was a certain amount of classroom work and during one of these sessions pilots arrived and were allowed to sit in and ask questions. They were then offered the chance to select their own engineer. Bill Rodney looked round the room, picked on Eric Pritchard and said, 'I'll try that one.' Eric was taken out to a Halifax, had a handkerchief tied round his eyes and asked by his new pilot to be shown through the aircraft. Eric Pritchard takes up the story:

'Fortunately we had been allowed to clamber over these Halifaxes thoroughly during the early part of the course and I must have coped all right because he accepted me. I didn't quite know what I was letting myself in for at the time for in some ways he was quite a martinet despite being only twenty-one at the time. Bill came from Canada with a complete crew, except for an engineer. In the evening we would go out and he would take a sextant or astro compass and we'd take star shots. Every morning before we started he would inspect the Met. Bill was extremely keen to learn all he could about engine handling and there was never a dull moment. I put in a total of 15 hours day and night flying at Wombleton. The first time I went up it was with a crew that I think was a bit flak-happy. It was a familiarisation flight and we were flying along straight and level at 10,000 feet when one of the blokes at the front put his arms round the feet of the pilot who promptly put the aircraft in a screaming dive, lashing out with his feet to free himself with the result that this bloke hurtled backwards and fell flat on his back in the perspex nose. One of the flight engineers who had spent nine months with me at St Athan seized hold of the nearest thing he could get hold of when he got into an aircraft for the first time, and wouldn't let go until he was back safely on the ground. This was the end of his flying career – he was washed out. They should have had flying familiarisation early in the course at St Athan.'

The new crew were posted to 78 Squadron at Breighton in March 1944. The station was a satellite of Holme-on-Spalding Moor, home of 76 Squadron. To the airmen this was a diabolical

(***Above***) P/O Len G. Smith flying a 76 Squadron Halifax I in July 1941; (***below***) F/Lt Long in 78 Squadron's P-Peter landing at Breighton from a daylight sortie on Essen 25 October 1944

place to be posted, for it was low-lying and misty.

On its first attack with Halifaxes, the squadron had attacked the docks at Ostend on 29 April 1942. In May it flew in the first 'Thousand Bomber Raid', to Cologne. In 1943 it participated in the Battle of the Ruhr. It moved to Breighton in the middle of June and two months later took part in the bombing of Peenemünde.

At Breighton Wing Commander A. Markland was squadron commander. He became the first wireless operator in Bomber Command to command a Bomber Squadron. He had a reputation for only having personnel on the squadron who would give one hundred percent; anybody who gave less he had posted. This made for a wonderful sense of unity right the way through the squadron.

'Much to my consternation' recalls Eric Pritchard, 'I found that the Breighton Halifaxes were of the Hercules variety whereas what little experience I had gained had been on Merlins. The Hercules engines demanded a high standard of handling, especially in the run down, coming back to base. If one did not go through the correct procedure the two bottom cylinder heads fell off the next time the engines were started up. Obviously there had to be some sort of further instruction. On the afternoon of arrival a conversion detail took off and immediately an oil coolant burst causing an enormous amount of black smoke and the feathering down of one engine. The experienced pilot of the Halifax burst one of the tyres on landing which finished the flying for the day.

'The following evening my skipper did his second dicky and the next day we were on battle order. I was so ignorant that I had to take my gen book with me because on this particular type of Halifax there were manually operated gills controlling the radiator temperatures; I had very little experience of these and had to keep looking at my notes to see what was going on. The most extraordinary thing was that up until this first operation I don't think the fact that it was dangerous had ever entered my head. We were cruising along and when we approached the target – one of the railyards just outside Paris – I got my head stuck into the astrodome and as I was looking round I was thoroughly enjoying the firework display that was going on all around. Suddenly tracer started shooting across the nose of the Halifax and I began to think, this is dangerous! I had gone through the whole of the London blitz convinced in my own mind that I would be immune to any sort of bomb attack and here we were being shot at while dropping bombs!

'As it was obvious on our arrival that none of us had any experience with this type of Halifax, our pilot set about rectifying this. If it was a quiet day he would march us all down to the flights and get hold of the chief and say, "Look here, Chiefy, my chaps want to know how 'George' works", and Chiefy would prime himself, get out all the charts and things and he would make sure we knew all there was to know about the thing. Bill would then say to Chiefy: "Right, get your boys together and we'll see how it operates in the air", and he took every possible opportunity to take the ground crew on training flights. So there was a tremendous bond between the air and ground crews.

'Bill seized on every opportunity to fly. If there was a damaged kite to be picked up from Manston or Woodbridge, then it was he and his crew that would ferry the crew that were going to fly it back. If there was any sort of local flying, bombing or H2S training he would be on it and he was also a sucker for fighter affiliation. He was particularly savage on some of these occasions; one day he corkscrewed so violently that the engine cowlings began to wrinkle and I had to order him to land before there was any serious damage. He was a superb pilot and took every opportunity of going on engineering and navigation courses, so that he was not only a good pilot but a first class Met man and quite a good navigator.

'I had a frightening experience on one occasion over France when a bird came bursting in through the astrodome splattering itself on the flight engineer's panel covering me with blood and feathers. I was knocked into the alley with the sudden decompression of air through the astrodome and was sucked up, but fortunately I was too fat to go out because of all the gear I was wearing. I fell flat on my back in the alley while returning to my position.

'We shared our hard-standing with another Halifax and the ground crew looked after both aircraft. They had a small hut where they kept their tools, and themselves when it was wet or cold. As No 78 Squadron was mainly Canadian, with a smattering of New Zealanders and some British, there were frequent food parcels from abroad. When these parcels arrived there was never

Outside the locker room at Breighton in August 1943

F/Sgt Schumann in A-Able being waved off at Breighton on 20 January 1944 for a raid on Berlin

any thought of their being opened privately and consumed. It was always "Party tonight in the flight hut". The party was always held on the hard-standing and the ground crew and both aircrews participated. There were some weird and wonderful concoctions, which all made for a good party.'

From March to June the squadron engaged in wrecking German communications in France, Belgium, Holland and Germany itself. This was part of the softening up prior to D-Day. This phase became known as the Battle of the Marshalling Yards, and included targets such as Le Mans, Trappes, Lille, Juvisy, to mention only a few.

'Dave, our navigator', continues Eric Pritchard, 'married a girl in York just the day before D-Day. Come D-Day itself, Wing Commander Markland completed his 50th trip with us. He was a man completely without fear; he had been shot down twice but managed to get back. I am certain that he had many other trips for which he had given the credit to other wireless operators, as he did on D-Day. He stood our operator down and said, "That's OK – I want to see what's going on". He was a more than adequate wireless operator, but on this particular occasion he kept leaping from his seat, peering out of the window, saying, "Wizard show, wizard show, I've never enjoyed myself so much in all my life." Our skipper got fed up with his bobbing about and said, "Sit down, shut up, and get on with your work." When he returned to base, the Wing Commander went round telling everybody how Bill Rodney had shut him up!

'We managed to get in two trips on D-Day. It was a wonderful experience. We flew out over the armada just as it was sailing out before dawn, bombing the gun emplacements and then we did a follow up during the day. It was marvellous flying in the dark over the ships, watching the blips on the H2S screen.

'We were out again the next night, attacking the rail yard at Juvisy. Over the target we were attacked by an Me110 and hit while corkscrewing both by the fighter and from flak. The bomb-aimer had his left knee-cap shattered from an AA shell and got a bullet through his left calf at the same time. Dave, the newly married navigator, was mortally wounded in the head.

'Our Halifax suffered complete loss of all hydraulics, which caused the bomb doors to remain open and the undercarriage to drop. The two starboard tank cocks were shot away, half the starboard elevator had gone and the starboard aileron was damaged, which meant that adequate control was only possible at low airspeed. To sustain the flow of fuel I had to crawl under the rest seat pulling the fuel cock wires with a pair of pliers.

'To escape a wide searchlight belt and the risk of further fighter attacks Bill descended to a mere 50 feet in the moonlight. He was so low that the mid-upper gunner could see the time on a church clock just above the tree tops. We just made West Malling and received a priority landing; the starboard wheel was punctured and the oil tanks were holed. Bill Rodney and bomb-aimer Hal Grimble were both awarded immediate DFC's.

'Our replacement navigator had us over the coast of France too early on one operation and gave the skipper a dog-leg course right over the heavy coastal batteries; this didn't please Bill one bit and he soon got rid of him. Fortunately, a navigator and bomb-aimer who were about to commence their second tour were posted to the squadron and Bill quickly snapped them up. The bomb-aimer had spent his rest period at Mamby on the bomb trainer with the result that he knew the German cities like the back of his hand. Both were so methodical and calm that a soothing attitude permeated the Halifax. The mid-upper gunner was a big wheat farmer from Manitoba and nearly always inflated his Mae West when climbing into his turret!

'The flight engineer, particularly in the Halifax, is one of the hardest worked members of the crew. It is one of the most demanding jobs in the business. In the first place there is nowhere to sit down. One is responsible for the transfer of all the "window" stored in the centre section; this means hopping over two main spars at some 20,000 feet, which means changing to the spare oxygen bottle and doing the same thing on getting back to the rest position where all the tank cocks are situated – there are 14 in a Halifax. On arrival at the target the flight engineer has to lie on the floor in the rest position, and take off the little round hatches over each bomb station and have a large spanner handy. A 160 mph wind comes up through the holes, bringing with it dirt and muck; then comes the 'bombs gone'. They are counted as they go, and if they don't go and it is thought there might still be one on a frozen hook it's belted with the spanner before the bomb doors close again. The skipper is told the bomb bay is clear. Next the flight engineer has to whip smartly down round the H2S blister to where the flare chute is situated and peer down the hole to make sure that the flare has gone and is not smouldering in the tube. Back again to act as an extra lookout, peering through the astrodome before going back down to secure all the hatches on the floor. At the end of an eight-hour trip the flight engineer has been extremely busy and entitled to feel a worthy member of the team.

'It was quite a bind making out the log every fifteen minutes while flying over a long period, but it was essential. If anything went wrong it gave the ground crew quite a number of clues as to what could have happened and in addition one knew exactly where they were and what one was doing. Some slap-happy engineers used to write up their logs while still on the ground. On one occasion a pilot called for an emergency landing because he was out of fuel and so was given priority. When he landed and his tanks were dipped it was found that there were 100 gallons of fuel left!

'The Wing Commander flew with us on a very memorable daylight trip on 25 June. At 20,000 feet over Montorgueil he saw a bomb smash through the wing of a Halifax flying slightly below us. The aircraft exploded in a blinding orange flash which hurled our S-Sugar upward, forcing Bill Rodney to dive and half roll to bring it on to a level keel.

'During the bombing of the Falaise Gap Lancasters went in first, we in the Halifaxes went in second and the Americans came in last. There were reckoned to be 2,000 four-engined bombers, in an unbroken screen. It was known as "Tedder's Carpet". Bombing from 4,000 feet pieces of tank and guns came up level with the aircraft. It was terrifying. As we flew over the coast of France it was just like a steel curtain in the sky, with black puffs of smoke. We wondered how we were going to get through it, but we did.

'When we secured our own S-Sugar it was considered to be the best kept and maintained Halifax on the squadron and so the Commanding Officer or any other top brass used to borrow it to go on operations. We lost two aircraft in this fashion; they failed to return. On one occasion, being badly battered, we had to land at Ford, in Sussex, and catch a train back to Yorkshire. We were only away a night and a day but it was extraordinary to find a brand new Halifax on the hard-standing with the painting of the squadron letters and our S-Sugar added.

'Another of our squadron Halifaxes crash-landed just behind us at Ford. The aircraft had been considerably shot up, there had been a fire on board and the whole of the H2S blister had disappeared leaving a gaping hole where it had been. The rear gunner had been mortally wounded and the pilot landed in very difficult circumstances in order to try to save his life rather than order the crew to bale out – he died an hour after touch down. It was obvious that the Halifax would be written off so the flight engineer carried out an experiment. He had always wanted to see whether the dinghy released, so he re-entered the wreck, pulled the tit and out came the dinghy from the wing, in perfect order. This was an extremely cool reaction from a crewman who had been under terrible tension for the past couple of hours.'

Eric Pritchard was commissioned as a pilot officer in September with the promotion backdated to August. He continues:

'During the latter part of 1944 when the offensive really got underway our squadron was doing two jobs a day, short daylight ones to the bombsights, which only counted as one operation for tour purposes. Quite a lot of crews came in and had a very short stay because flying in formation, as they were, at a fairly low altitude against radar predicted gunfire many of them were blown out of the sky. Actually we had some near misses ourselves. Once an aircraft was blown to pieces by a shell from below, we too were blown onto our back and it caused quite a bit of panic – just for half an operation!

'At no time while I was with 78 Squadron did the morale drop, despite considerable losses. There was quite a lot of mutilation of aircrew, crews returning with limbs blown off, but there were also some very lucky escapes. When I was on debriefing one night a chap came back, on the end of his oxygen mask he'd got about three inches of rubber piping and he said, "Look Sir, look Sir, look, a piece of shell came up through the floor right in front of my nose and cut the oxygen pipe in half, just like that."

'The ground crews were kept busy. Sometimes they would fuel the Halifax with a small load from the bowser, bomb up for an operation of the Pas-de-Calais and then perhaps that would have to be scrubbed; then they would have to take all the bombs back out, put more fuel in and increase the bomb load. Then, if this was also scrubbed, they would be back to square one again in the morning. They were working hard day and night.

'During the winter months the whole of the airfield was surrounded by water and had deep irrigation ditches dug on either side of the road. On a stand-down we attempted to go to York but the bus that passed the airfield started at Holme-on-Spalding-Moor and by the time it reached Breighton it was usually full. The only other way to get into York was to cadge a lift, sometimes even riding on top of a haycart. An alternative was to cycle out to the little village halt, for which in winter one had to take off both shoes and socks. Trousers were rolled up to the knee as often half the wheels were submerged in the water. On reaching the station one had to park the bike, take a towel from the saddle bag, dry feet and legs, replace socks and shoes then catch the train for Leeds. When one returned, usually somewhat the worse for wear, bike navigation was not all it should have been and often a luckless rider had to be hauled out from one of the irrigation ditches by his mates.'

One of the attractions of York for the seventeen squadrons based mainly south or south-east of the county town was Betty's Bar. Situated as it was right in the heart of Halifax country, it became the home of 4 Group's drinkers, a rendezvous for the many airmen and women stationed around York. The bar was downstairs, below Betty's Cafe, near the cathedral, in the centre of York. In mid-1943 it was suggested that the building should be requisitioned. This was successfully opposed on the grounds that it provided many meals for service personnel and the bar provided liquid refreshment and a meeting place for the armed services.

It was believed that the Intelligence Unit of the War Office regularly infiltrated the bar, to listen for any careless talk that could have cost lives; indeed it was rumoured that leave for some squadrons was cancelled because too much had been said in Betty's Bar. Wartime airmen who possessed diamond tipped pens, issued to VIP's, or diamond rings, were able to scratch their names on a mirror in the bar. A total of 582 names appear on the mirror, including the signatures of Canadians from 6 Group who made their way south to complement the British.

Betty's Bar became nationally known; there was a cartoon about it in the *Tatler*. Wartime photographs show a roadsign that says '2 miles to Betty's Bar'. The mirror and Betty's Bar held an honoured place in wartime history and happily remain as a memory of Halifax Squadrons.

Bill Rodney and Eric Pritchard finished their tour at Christmas

1944. Eric says: 'Never did I receive a scratch from the German bombs and didn't do too badly from their guns, apart from having a couple of teeth knocked out and a lucky escape when a nose cap of a shell lodged in the collar of my Mae West after coming through the windshield of the aircraft and bouncing off some other bits knocking me flat on my face.'

The beginning of 1945 opened for 78 Squadron with a successful attack on Ludwigshafen, but bad weather conditions during the month of January resulted in only nine operations being carried out during the month. From February the squadron carried on its good work attacking industrial targets, marshalling yards, rolling stock, synthetic oil plants, and concentrations of enemy troops and supplies. The Halifaxes flew into Germany in broad daylight escorted by Mustangs and Spitfires.

Wing Commander Young, formerly of 76 Squadron, had taken over at Breighton and took off for Wesel before midday on 17 February in T-Tommy NA278. A week later, in the same aircraft, he set off for Essen just after midday, an operation which would have been unthinkable weeks earlier. On 27 February and 3 March Mainz and Essen were his daytime targets, the latter with NA275.

With the capture of most of Germany's principal cities and towns, the Allied forces were witnessing for themselves the tremendous devastation caused by Bomber Command and the USAAF. In the last six weeks of the war Wing Commander Young attacked, in daylight raids, Sterkrade on 24 March in T-Tommy, next day Osnabruck, which received a 2,000 pounder from MZ460, and on 11 April NA220 attacked Bayreuth. The squadron's last raid was on 25 April.

From D-Day until the end of the war 78 Squadron dropped 7,000 tons of bombs. Their Halifaxes, which now included Mark VI's, had been operational for over three years and had given a very good account of themselves.

CHAPTER THREE

They Also Served

Pam Finch was the Intelligence Officer with 78 Squadron. Pam was one of only two WAAF Intelligence Officers to serve with the RAF. Norman Dimmock was her boss.

'It was the most interesting job in the whole war for women', says Pam. 'I left school with war threatening and I knew in my mind there was only one service which I wanted to join. My father had been in the Air Force and I wanted to join the Women's Air Force. We lived at Tiverton, in Devon, where I attended Greenaway, the girls' school. I went to drill at Plymouth even before war was declared and as soon as I could possibly get in I went, as an airwoman. Initially I was a general duties clerk and carried out secretarial duties. On being commissioned two years later, I thought I would get code and cypher, as did most of the girls. I had an interview with a darling of a man, he said to me, "Do you enjoy reading?"; after I affirmed this, he continued, "What are you reading at the moment?" I told him, and it must have been a book he too had read and enjoyed. I always reckon I passed because my taste was similar to his. I put down for Intelligence and later the Selection Board gave me my choice. I was delighted because code and cypher sounded rather boring. It was rather mundane, most of my friends worked on it. I had always wanted to travel and later I was to get the opportunity.

'I attended a photo interpretation course which I enjoyed and did a lot of work interpreting later. I had been with Bomber Command from the time of joining up and in July 1943 found myself with No 78 Squadron, then at Rufforth in Yorkshire. When I arrived it was Wings for Victory Week.

'The squadron was attacking main force targets with their Halifaxes and debriefing was clearly necessary. By 1943 most aircraft were equipped with cameras and there was a natural tendency for crews to think answers would be provided by their photographs. We had our stereotyped questions: what did you see, how much cloud was there over the target or whatever. When the men came back they knew they had to go through this routine when all they really wanted to do was to have a drink and go to bed. I think it helped if there was an understanding person about, and possibly it helped that I was not an old hard-boiled male. I thought at the time being female might have helped and I know now that it did. It was the most disciplined crews that provided the most useful information. I think sometimes a person might have had the knack, and I know it sounds rather conceited but I think I might have been able to get below the surface a little way with people in intelligence.

'Photographs would confirm information later on. There was always a great eagerness to see the bombing photographs which were developed very quickly and pinned up on a board in the library and all the aircrews came to view them.

'I was always there to meet the crews on return. Sometimes they returned at ungodly hours, like 0100 and 0200, I was told, "Don't bother coming down, Pam, you've been working all day." But I never wanted to miss any part of it at all; I always wanted to know who was coming back. I was absolutely broken up when one particular crew who were well known to me did not return from an operation. I think I eventually grew an extra shell. I had to.

'Some aircrew men would not be permitted to complete a tour. If it was thought that the skipper, or navigator or one of the key members of the team was getting edgy, for aircraft and aircrew safety they would be screened. It would be made to appear that they had completed the full thirty trips of a tour when in point of fact they had only performed three-quarters of them. It didn't happen very often.

'If it was suspected that there was any LMF it was hushed up. The chap would be sent off the squadron; sometimes we would wonder why he had gone somewhere else, and it would come out later. We never knew why he'd gone or where; it wasn't a thing that was discussed openly.

'We were very grateful for the ENSA shows. The performers travelled up to Yorkshire by coach. Sometimes we girls went by coach to other stations, such as Melbourne. There were some lovely pubs nearby and occasionally I had a dinner time drink in York's Station Hotel, and of course, I visited Betty's Bar.

'Because of the shortage of girls I had a lot of boyfriends and every boyfriend I had seemed to go missing. Word went round the chaps, don't go with Pam Finch because it was unlucky to do so. They didn't mean it, bless them, but at the time you also couldn't blame them. I think aircrew were very superstitious. There were a great number that didn't make it and it upset me terribly. As the war progressed the crews appeared to be younger and younger, like teenagers and babies coming in, but they were as good as the others, there was no deterioration of standards.

'I had a great love for the old Halifax. One of the skippers smuggled me aboard for a trip when the worst of the war in Europe was over. He took me on a Gardening mission. They all knew I wanted to do a trip and couln't wait to get aloft. If it had been known at the time, both I, and the crew that took me, would have been court martialled.'

Doreen Clarkson served as a WAAF from July 1940.

'As I was a store basher and worked on aircraft spares most of the time', she remembers, 'I got to know which aircraft were good and the ones that were not so good, and their faults. This led to my knowledge about "Halibags" as we always called them.

'I was posted to RAF Lindholme as a sprog and at that time we had Whitleys, the "flying coffin", with their huge wing span and long history of accidents; they were top heavy, I'm afraid. Then we had Hampdens, and later Halifaxes. These four-engined bombers were the talk of the station. Great stuff! Everyone thought the same, that they were the best we had ever had. I must admit I had less work ordering spares at that time and grew fond of the old dears. When large spares became u/s they had to be sent back to the MU's and that was also part of our work. I was often offered trips on test flights, for we could have been easily smuggled aboard. Many of the airmen used to go for a flip but I always refused. I left the Halifaxes in 1943 when I was offered a better post elsewhere, but I loved the aircraft although my favourite was the Lysander, the "flying bird".'

'Frankie' Allen was a girl when she joined the WAAF's in 1940; five years later she was demobbed as Corporal Mrs Booth.

'In my first year I was stationed with the Halifax Squadron at Middleton St George in Yorkshire. I was employed in the Administration Office, and it was here that I first encountered the horrors of war when a Halifax pilot came in to see us for a pass to take him to the plastic surgery unit of Sir Archibald McIndoe at East Grinstead. The poor fellow was horribly burned, with no ears, lips or nose; I never saw him again but I only hope that he was one of the guinea pigs who was given a new face. The atmosphere at the station was similar to that portrayed in the Gregory Peck film *One O'Clock High*. The squadron had suffered a large number of casualties and all the boys had the same look on their faces – fear. They eventually had to be sent on leave for morale purposes.

'The Waafery had been built at the end of one runway, and as the bombers took off with their full load, going over perilously low, we were all very unhappy and frightened. In the morning we used to be out early, counting them as they returned.

'Later I was posted to the headquarters of No 4 Group at Headington Hall, York. This building belonged to Squadron Leader Lord Deramore; he still worked there despite the fact that it had been commandeered. One of the jobs which I had to do involved going round all the squadrons in Yorkshire with the officer to whom I was secretary. We had to visit the squadron that had suffered the greatest number of casualties the previous night. This was a very harrowing job, dealing with the personal effects of aircrew, missing or killed in action. As we always went to the station where the most assistance was needed I had many letters to type. The airmen used to collect all the belongings from their lockers; all the wallets had to be gone through to make sure that nothing went back to relatives which would cause distress. We went to most of the airfields: Marston Moor, Dishforth, Pocklington, Snaith, Burn and Elvington, to name just a few. I received a Mention in Despatches for this work.

'After a while it became just a job until the day when I had to write a letter to one of my friends with whom I worked in Manchester prior to joining up. She was to be married shortly and her aircrew fiancée, whom I also knew, went missing. There was no hope; I was very deeply distressed.

'The worst thing that happened, however, was when one of my WAAF friends, a sergeant with a meteorological unit, took an unauthorised trip on a training flight in a Halifax. Of course, this was absolutely forbidden. Unfortunately the aircraft crashed in an electrical storm; the whole crew and the unauthorised passenger were killed. I was sitting at my desk ploughing through the routine work when a large brown envelope was put in front of me. I was totally unprepared for what was inside. It contained my friend's personal documents taken from her uniform, burned and covered with black. I felt violently sick, filled with terrible panic; I remember vaguely rushing up the stairs demanding to see the WAAF Squadron Officer. I was shaking like a leaf and absolutely distraught. I told her I could not go on. I had been doing the job so long and this seemed to be the end of the line. I was sent home on a week's sick leave and when I returned found I had been transferred to Air Operations. Here I worked with a wing commander, group captain and a commander on loan from the Navy. This was a very onerous job. Operations for the night were worked out at Bomber Command headquarters and then each Group Air Operations worked their routes, mustering numbers and all the thousand and one other details necessary to make the raids a success.

'I had one very embarrassing moment working there. An old family retainer of the Deramore family looked after the place, which is now the nucleus of York University. This old man perpetually "bumpered" the seemingly miles of corridors covered with brown lino until they shone and were permanently shiny and extremely slippery. When airmen up for commission, or new arrivals reported to be told to which squadrons they were to be posted, they had to be interviewed by the Air Vice Marshal. His office was the holy of holies but he always kept his door slightly ajar. This particular day there was a long line of aircrew waiting to be interviewed, all very nervous. I had been to take shorthand from my officers and was going back to my own office when I slipped helplessly, going forward on my stomach, headfirst and through the Air Vice Marshal's door. He gave me a withering look. No one dared help to pick me up.

'Whenever I was given any leave I went home to Manchester; it was only ninety miles but in those days it took about five hours by train. In wintertime, the last bus back from York left at 2000. There was never any money for a taxi so there was no alternative but to walk the three miles to Heslington. There was a snicket which ran around the back of the Hall from Heslington Road where the Waafery was; it took fifteen minutes off the walking time, but we had to contend with a flasher. He used to place himself strategically halfway down the snicket, with his bike, behind a tree, and we never knew whether he was going to be there or not, so we just had to take a chance. I experienced his presence twice, but the poor chap never used to touch anyone; he just did his turn and then rode off on his bicycle. He was eventually caught by the RAF police.

'Whenever we had any spare money, which was not often, we used to put two shillings each into a kitty and either go into York or to the King Charles Inn in Heslington. We spent some very happy times there, just drinking cider. The best times were at Elvington, with the Free French Squadrons. I used to be in charge of the bus which took us there. The RAF band played in the officers' dining room, the French band in the airmen's dining room playing marvellous quick French waltzes. Then there was a dark room, where everyone smooched to this marvellous music in the dark; now and again some spoilsport would put on the lights to the screams and anger of the couples in there. On occasions the famous Squadronaires played at Elvington. The girls I was in charge of were all general duty, which meant they did the more menial tasks, like washing floors, cleaning ablutions and helping in the cookhouse. Some of their escapades made my hair stand on end, particularly with the Corsicans and Algerians from the French Squadron. I couldn't be certain on every occasion that I had the right number of girls on the bus back!

'We quite often went to Betty's Bar in York where we used to have some marvellous, happy times, the aircrews just lived for the day, here today and gone tomorrow as they said. They used to scratch their names on the mirror, but eventually, I am afraid the place was put 'Out of Bounds'. York in those days was just a mass of men in uniform, both RAF and Army, in proportions of some twenty men to each girl. At the time there was the fabulous Glenn Miller type music. It really was fantastic to have a night out.

'When I received my three year chevron in 1943 it was an occasion for celebration, so we went into York with our usual kitty. It was a foul night, thick ice and snow lying on the ground and unfortunately I had a terrible fall, breaking my tibia and fibula. So I finished up in York Military hospital where all the wounded air crews were also taken. My mother was heartbroken; it was the week before Christmas, and my brother who had been wounded with the Desert Army in North Africa was in hospital at Liverpool.

'The hospital was showing the Christmas spirit as I was wheeled into the operating theatre: there were saws, hammers and horrible implements on display and above the door a sign said 'All ye who enter here, abandon hope'. I was wearing an ugly white gown, one woollen stocking on my good leg and some sort of white cap on my head, in which someone had stuck a paper rose. A figure in white came up to me, and, although his head and lower face was covered, those marvellous hazel eyes looked into mine and he explained what was going to happen, saying, "One little prick in your arm and when you wake up, you will be back in the Ward". A spark flashed between us. Complications had set in in my leg, and when I came round I was in terrible agony. The pain was so severe that I thought my leg had gone. Next to me this figure sat against my side, with a bunch of violets. It was my friend in white from the operating theatre. When I was feeling better he used to take me round the hospital in a wheelchair, with my plastered leg held straight out in front of me. He even danced with me in the wheel chair. The wards were full of soldiers and aircrew with the most awful injuries but they all attempted to join in the festive spirit. I became engaged to my soldier whilst I was still on crutches, and he it was who persevered and got me to walk, and even dance again, when I never thought I would.

'When, after many months, I was finally discharged from hospital, the atmosphere began to be electric and we knew things must be hotting up for D-Day. One night we were confined to camp and then the sky was absolutely filled with Halifaxes from all over Yorkshire, hundreds and hundreds of them. We all stood at the back of the huts watching this fantastic sight. Then we saw one coming low, its engines making a horrible noise, and it crashed behind the Waafery. All the bombs burst and machine-gun bullets were exploding. I was blown backwards down into the air raid shelter. When we came to our senses we all ran down the lane to a scene of utter devastation. There was just simply nothing left but pieces; shoes and clothing were hanging in the trees. It was the most awful sight of my life.

'I was married to my soldier whilst the war was still on. When the war in Europe finished a few of us were allowed to fly on "Cook's Tour" survey trips over Germany to see the damage. I should have met my husband that night but had to ring him at the hospital to say that I could not go. I was not allowed to explain why, and naturally he was very upset. I flew from Pocklington. The crew were marvellous. We were all issued with parachutes and the van was waiting for us to jump in to take us to dispersal. They all threw their parachutes in, as did I, but to my horror it opened and spread all over the van, so shamefacedly I had to fetch another one. What a job I had to get inside that Halifax, I was pulled and shoved and finally got in. I was allowed to sit in every position in the plane. The noise was absolutely terrible and we could only speak through the intercom. It was freezing cold and there was nowhere for me to go to the toilet! We came in low over all the terrible destruction and it made me realise the utter futility of war. It was a great privilege to be allowed to go on this trip and it is one I shall never forget.

'Soon after this I was appointed secretary to a new group captain, recently returned from Africa. He made my life a total misery. I had served in the WAAF's for five years through all the bad and good times. I had always felt I had been doing a worthwhile job but this person had been used to ordering people about like his playthings. I had to take verbatim notes at meetings attended by high ranking officers, and nothing I ever did pleased him. He would not let me have my leave at the same time as my husband, and although I went in great anxiety to my WAAF Squadron Officer she was powerless to help. However, soon after that my demobilisation came through just as the war in the Far East was ending.

'That night we had a dance on the camp. My husband was on theatre duty, so all we girls had our usual kitty and went to the pub. We came back well fortified. We sat reminiscing over the happy and sad times, when in walked the group captain and came over and sat right next to me. Full of Dutch courage I proceeded to tell him exactly what I thought of him. I cannot remember what I said but I really went to town, and all he could do was laugh, then he asked me to dance. I discovered that if only I had stood up to him in the first place I would never have had any trouble, but then it was too late. The next day I was demobbed. It was a privilege to serve with the WAAF's and with the airmen who looked after and flew the Halifaxes, I would not have missed it for the world.'

The consensus of Elvington's 77 Squadron WAAF's was: They had the rough end of the stick, poor pay, poor conditions, service discipline, service dress, restrictions. They probably envied civilian girls their dress and general freedom, as well as their money, but they did a great job, making tens of thousands of airmen available for other duties. WAAF batwomen had to be up very early, make their way to the officers' huts, heat the water, brew the tea, carry it round dispersed sites, and all by regulation wakey-wakey time. The officer aircrew mostly appreciated this – also being young they often found the batwoman's call, and a few words, a help and morale booster. Occasionally they ran the gauntlet, but rarely made official complaints, which had rather serious consequences at the discretion of the Wing Commander and head WAAF.

The WAAF's in the motor transport section tended to be the beauty chorus, smartly dressed, confident, much liked by the aircrew. They took the crews out and brought them back from the aircraft. The lads had quite a strong regard for them.

The girls in the parachute section, invariably spick and span and cheerful, tended to be hand-picked. The aircrew always had a cheerful word for them. There was a feeling of wishing to keep them happy and cheerful as an aid to perfect parachute packing. The crews wanted those chutes handled as they would dress their first new-born baby.

In the Control Tower the WAAF's handled communications for the officers in charge. It was their voice on the R/T that was heard when returning from operations after calling base for landing instructions. During that often hectic period in the early hours, they would receive requests for 'dates', and also regular threats of rape from voices known and unknown. Always they came back . . . 'Roger' . . .

In Wales in November 1943 Sandy Johnstone (now Air Vice-Marshal A. V. R. Johnstone CB DFC) was posted as commander of one of four sections in No 10 Group. This was a large area extending over the whole of South Wales, as well as out to sea as far as the south coast of Eire. The headquarters were situated at Fairwood Common, an airfield built on high ground about five miles west of Swansea. Sandy says:

'The distance between the accommodation sites and the various places of duty was a constant source of annoyance and discomfort to many of the personnel on the station. Owing to a lack of cars and lorries everyone had to walk or cycle, if they were fortunate

Intelligence Officer Pam Finch interviews a returning 78 Squadron crew

WAAF MT drivers preparing to drive out Berlin-bound crews of 77 Squadron

enough to get hold of a bicycle, between their place of work and sleeping quarters. In many cases these were several miles apart. As the airmen and airwomen were only issued with two pairs of footwear, one of these was always at the cobbler's shop being re-soled and heeled. On many occasions the second pair had completely worn out before the first pair had been repaired and were again ready for use.

'The WAAF were hardest hit of all as their living sites were furthest from the headquarters block. Presumably the architect who originally planned the lay-out had been endowed with puritanical morals and decided to banish the girls to a purdah-like existence as far as he possibly could. Unfortunately the only two sites which suffered any damage during the war were Nos 4 and 5 – the two occupied by the WAAF.

'During one air raid which took place nearly a year before my arrival the only bomb which dropped anywhere near the airfield made a direct hit on No 4 site, killing and injuring several of the girls as they slept.'

On 12 March 1944 a former 466 Squadron Halifax II, serial W7927, was sent to No 1658 HCU at Riccall Common. Four weeks later, on the night of 9 April, it was being taken on a night cross country flight. Sandy continues:

'Darkness had fallen when I was told that a Halifax bomber was in trouble near by. Two of its engines had packed in and flying control had prepared a full emergency to help the pilot get his aircraft down on the ground. Shortly after I arrived at the control tower the Halifax started to lose height quickly as it flew around the circuit. There was little the pilot could do and with a dull thump the bomber crashed straight into the middle of No 5 site. There was no explosion, just the tearing and crumbling of the masonry as the aircraft plunged headlong through everything in its path before coming to rest on its belly. Then an ominous silence.

'I got over to where the mutilated aircraft lay and met the crew coming towards me. They were quite surprised and also completely unaware that they had hit anything. But, clambering back into the site itself through a gap in the hedge made by the crashing aircraft, a scene of utter desolation met our gaze.

'Three low stone sleeping blocks full of WAAF personnel had been completely razed to the ground, while two others were

HM Queen Elizabeth and King George VI inspecting WAAF's at Tempsford – home of 138 and 161 Special Duties Squadrons. Halifaxes are in the background.

severely damaged and seemed in danger of imminent collapse. The sound of moaning and groaning came to us from beneath the piles of debris where many of the girls were trapped. The sounds of those in pain and fear seemed all the more terrible because of the darkness, broken only by a number of small fires starting up where coal stoves, which had been burning in all the destroyed huts, had been tipped over and smashed against the woodwork.

'Teams of medical orderlies were quickly on the scene, accompanied by rescue squads and soon everyone was busy heaving aside large sections of plaster and bricks in an effort to reach the victims. The Group Nursing Sister, Sister Stone, who had been visiting the station earlier in the day and was staying overnight, took charge of the first-aid side and seemed to be everywhere at once, tending injuries or administering morphia to those in distress. Despite the holocaust around them, made all the more terrifying by the darkness and the flickering of the fires, coupled with the frantic dancing lights of the hand torches, there was no sign of panic breaking out. Everyone, including the WAAF officers and NCO's, displayed a remarkable degree of calm and calculated efficiency.

'Rescue operations dragged on throughout the night, with the seriously injured being taken in whatever transport could be commandeered to one of the larger emergency hospitals in Swansea after receiving first-aid treatment in our own, but by now overcrowded, sick quarters. Many of the girls were in deep shock when pulled from the debris. It must have been a frightening experience for them; one minute they had been fast asleep in their barrack rooms; the next they were awakening in utter chaos, in the dust and rubble, many of them pinned in their beds by broken beams or large chunks of masonry.

'When dawn broke over the station and the weak light showed for the first time the complete scene of destruction I was only amazed that more people had not been killed outright. Shortly after daybreak the last of the girls was freed and the grim total of casualties was handed to me. One WAAF had been killed, eighteen were seriously injured and nearly forty were suffering from shock and other injuries.

'Anyone who had tended to take the presence of the WAAF's for granted before the crash soon changed his ideas when the station got down to work again later in the day. The domestic services were the most seriously affected as many of the girls were employed in the various messes or cookhouses. For several days officers and airmen alike had their meals in the vast airmen's dining hall, an arrangement which worked admirably and which also presented a first-class opportunity for all ranks to get to know each other better.'

Although the WAAF's were often exploited, they didn't resent it. Now, as they think back to their time on airfields, working with or for the crews, they remember that period as the happiest time of their life.

CHAPTER FOUR

Berlin – Key of the Door

On Wednesday 25 August 1943 the Air Ministry reported through the press:

'The Battle of Berlin has begun. For thirty-five minutes bombs rained down at the rate of fifty tons a minute in Monday night's biggest ever attack on the capital of the Reich. The load was over 1,750 tons – twice the weight dropped by the RAF in their previous record Berlin blitz, and four times the weight ever dropped by the Luftwaffe on London.

'Colossal damage has been done, according to first reports by pilots who went low enough to see through the smoke and fires. Within four square miles was a mass of flames, and the glow in the sky could be seen 250 miles from the target. It can be safely assumed that this great raid is but a preliminary in what is going to be sent to Berlin. While conditions may not be good for nightly attacks on the German capital, we may take it that Berlin is to receive a "Hamburging" in a series of devastating blows of this kind.'

'The Germans had long prepared their plans to meet the attack, which they knew would come as soon as the nights were long enough. Their plan appeared to be to engage our bombers all along the route – across Germany and back again across the North Sea – and to turn scores of fighters on to them right over the city in an effort to break up a concentrated attack.

'The sky above 12,000 feet – apparently the pre-arranged ceiling for flak that night – seemed to be swarming with enemy planes. One of our pilots saw fourteen of them in three minutes. Report of many combats are still being sifted at Bomber Command headquarters. But it is already known that at least twelve fighters were destroyed. Fifty-eight bombers failed to return. This represents over 400 airmen, but the crew of two bombers were saved when they were forced to land in Sweden. While the loss of so many bombers appears alarming at first sight, it must be remembered that they do not represent an unduly high percentage. Moreover, when you consider the enormous force of men you would require to carry out a land bombardment of Berlin, the loss of 400 airmen becomes very light, regrettable though their loss is.

'Our four-engined bombers were guided to Berlin by Pathfinders – and all the bomber crews praised the work of these "sheep-dogs".

'The "big boys" were shepherded in and dropped their "cookies" in accordance with a carefully worked-out timetable. The conditions were in favour of our bombers before midnight, but clear weather and a bright half-moon were all on the side of the enemy night fighters afterwards.

'As one of the Halifaxes was making its bombing run, an Me110 attacked it three times in six minutes. Cannon shells smashed the tail turret of the bomber wounding the rear gunner in the leg and arm. Despite his wounds the gunner kept on firing. A bullet hit the flight engineer in the ribs but he, too, remained where he was until the bombing run was over. His clothing caught fire. Sparks were coming from his flying suit, and the radio operator had to turn an extinguisher on to him before he could put out the flames.

'The crew of a Stirling watched one of the most dramatic incidents of the attack. They were about five miles from the target when they saw a bomber held in a cone of searchlights. Flak was being fired up the beams, and suddenly the bomber caught fire. The pilot, however, got out of the searchlights. He went across the target and levelled out and then the watchers saw the bombs go down. One of the crew said, "A huge explosion occurred as he was making his way out of a target area. It seemed right in the centre of the city, and must have been something really big."

'Berlin's chief industries are electrical equipment, general engineering, aircraft components and assembly, also aero-engines. Siemens, Osram, Daimler-Benz, Dornier, Heinkel and Focke Wulf all have factories in the area.'

Eight hours after the raid a reconnaissance aircraft took photographs of the target. The pilot reported that he had to fly over the capital for twenty minutes before he could find a gap in the smoke-blanket covering the city from the many fires started by the bombers. After the photographs had been developed Air Ministry interpretation experts, in their preliminary report, stated that when the reconnaissance flight took place nearly 100 fires were still burning in the centre of Berlin.

This was the heaviest raid carried out on Berlin up to that time: the cost was high, 58 bombers were lost.

Flight Sergeant R. J. Daffey of 77 Squadron, who has been mentioned earlier, flew Q-Queenie JB963 on the raid. When 270 miles short of the target oil pressure in the port outer engine started dropping, causing it to be feathered while still thirty miles from Berlin. After bombing the Halifax was nursed back to base on three engines. The following month the pilot was presented with the DFM. Pete Cadman, who entertained with Daffey in the Mess, was absent from the raid as his aircraft failed to take off. However, he was on the next trip to the Reich capital.

'On 31 August 1943, eight days after the attacks on Berlin had begun', recalls his rear gunner Bill Trivett whom we met earlier, 'Halifax JD462, squadron letters KN-N,.was at dispersal, and the aircrew were carrying out their usual daily inspection. The pilot and engineer were 'talking engines', the bomb aimer was checking his sights and equipment. The wireless operator was sending and receiving signal strength checks to headquarters whilst the mid-upper gunner and myself, in the rear turret harmonised our respective guns. The perimeter track showed signs of activity with the

Briefing at Elvington for the raid on Berlin on 23/24 August 1943

passing of a tractor towing a trolley load of bombs which indicated that a Bomber Command effort was to be made.

'Such was a normal operational day at 77 Squadron Elvington. After our morning duties were over we made our way to the mess and there surveyed the battle order on the squadron notice board. Eighteen aircraft were detailed for this evening's operation; I noticed my name was amongst the aircrew detailed.

'Dinner was served at the usual time and during this period, whilst in the mess, the announcement came over the Tannoy: "All crews report to briefing room 1500 hours". Lazing about in the mess during the afternoon many tried to speculate about the target. One clue was the full petrol tanks. If it did nothing else, the speculation helped to pass the time.

'Entering the briefing room, which was guarded by armed air force police, we awaited the arrival of the Station Commanding Officer. The noise of scraping chairs as the 130 or so aircrew came to attention heralded his arrival, and, with a wave of his hand in acknowledgement and a nod to the Winco to pull up the blind, the show was on. The board showed a large map of Europe, with a continuous red tape in an arc to Berlin, and back. The respective flight commanders gave us our briefings, what to look for as regards flares and target indicators and so on; this was followed by an overall summary by the CO. Then it was back to the mess for a meal. I enjoyed my egg-on-toast, we always had another on arrival back at base after Ops, and I was equally determined to be able to enjoy their second offering despite the usual chaff and banter from other crews, asking for our egg if we went for a Burton.

'We proceeded from the mess by wagon to the flights where various stages of changing were in progress by earlier arrivals and side-glancing these crews as I donned my electric flying suit, I had the impression of a cut-throat band of smugglers. The aircrews were decorated with gaudy scarves, balaclava helmets, an odd dagger strapped to a flying boot which the owner hoped would prove useful in the event of being one of the unfortunates.

'I plugged in my electric suit to the test rig in the changing-room to check that the heating was in working order as on a previous Op the suit I wore was faulty in as far as one foot became extraordinarily hot and one glove did not get warm. This proved very distracting and disturbed my concentration, to say the least, I took the precaution to see that it didn't happen again.

'Take-off time is drawing near; only another hour now. The wagons have arrived outside to take the aircrews to their various aircraft. Once at the dispersal the aircraft is entered for a quick last minute check over equipment. I check my turret sight, intercom and oxygen, the others in the crew check out their stations. Any defects are quickly attended to by the competent ground staff tradesmen. Satisfied with our check we stand outside having that last smoke; it will be eight hours before we can have another. We pass the time, which now seems endless, by telling the odd joke.

'The minutes tick slowly by, but the air of quietness is disturbed by the distant roar of one aircraft starting its engines, followed by another and another, and then above the cacophony of sound our skipper casually says, "OK, chaps, time to pile in."

'As I crawl down the fuselage to the rear turret I realise how cumbersome it is to wear the rear gunner's attire. It is a warm evening but the Met Officer warns it will be cold at 18,000 feet so here am I wearing long pants, short pants, trousers, vest, shirt, battle dress, scarf, balaclava, flying boots, electric suit, three pairs of gloves – silk, woollen and electric – and over all a Mae West; all this is held on by a parachute harness. Dumping my parachute outside of the turret I attempt to lift up my legs and hoist my sweating body into the tail. This sweat, caused by the exertion of crawling all the way to the rear turret, is a real curse, for one just sits there truly damp. On becoming airborne the ground heat is lost, the air is colder and a shudder runs down one's spine. For this moment alone I would gladly change places with any member up front who sits there in just their battle dress and Mae West, with the heat from the engines piped down their necks.

'Soon our engines are revving and we are taxiing from dispersal to the perimeter track. I notice the ground crew are now very energetically giving me, in the rear turret, the Victory sign, or at least I prefer to accept it as that! I elevate and depress my guns in acknowledgement.

'Arriving at the end of the runway we settle while the skipper aligns the aircraft for a straight run and take-off. I notice Flying Control is packed outside and on top with waving viewers. These personnel, flight commanders, aircrew, and WAAF's give each aircraft a good send off while they watch as the engines vibrate, and the tail becomes airborne. We sever our last link with terra firma;

roaring down the runway at 110 mph; the trees drop away, we unstick and are airborne. It is now 2015 and my guns are put to "fire".

'The pilot, bomb-aimer and engineer are going through their drill: "Wheels-up – flaps up – revs 2650". These instructions come over the intercom. Then the navigator calls: "Skipper, set course 065 degrees *now*."

'That is all on the intercom for about twenty minutes and then from the bomb-aimer: "We are crossing the coast *now*." The navigator acknowledges.

'The sky is still light, much too light for my liking. As I look around my thoughts almost run riot: what if Jerry had sent out intruder Ju88's? He'd have had a field day for I can see a hundred or more aircraft at various distances and heights.

'About ten miles out to sea the skipper gives permission for us gunners to test the guns, and in the ensuing chatter one is confident but conscious of the businesslike nature of our mission. We are now crossing the North Sea and as I look under the tailplane of the Halifax I view a wide expanse of this 300 mile crossing and I shudder to think how cold and unfriendly it seems down there. Glancing down some ships can be seen. I wonder – are they ours? How do they view us up here? Do they say "Good Luck" or "*Achtung*! *Achtung*!"?

'On this particular raid there are over 700 aircraft, carrying 4,900 aircrew, perhaps they are all too occupied in their respective jobs to ponder on the outcome, but the law of averages says some will not return. How strange it always seems that one never sees the cards stacked against oneself.

'Our height is now 12,000 feet climbing steadily and the sun has gone down. I am left alone with my thoughts but conscious of the growing darkness and the throb, throb, of the sturdy Rolls Royce Merlin engines. A call from the bomb aimer: "Searchlights ahead, navigator". This jolts my senses and I am immediately alert and vigilant.

'Various four-engined aircraft are seen dimly from time to time in the fast gathering dark, all flying in a steady stream all intent on crossing the enemy coast dead on track. This is one of the essentials if the losses are to be minimised.

'The bomb aimer reads a pinpoint from the enemy coast and informs the navigator we are dead on track but he is anxious about the absence of a route marker flare, as this would be our turning point. However, working on estimated time of arrival the skipper turns on a new course and as he does so a white marker flare goes down behind us. I inform the navigator and a "thank Christ for that" reply is all very reassuring.

'The bomb aimer informs us two gunners of a fighter station lit up to starboard; this is part of the reception for us, for they have been warned of our approach by radar. One can visualize them orbiting the route marker in the hope of picking up the odd straggler on the outside of the main stream, one object lesson for the need to stay on track. We are now climbing through thin cloud; the searchlights are gathering in concentration, however. We break cloud and level off at 18,000 feet but this thin broken cloud is proving quite a problem. The Germans are flooding the underneath of this cloud with their searchlights and one becomes conscious of an uneasy naked feeling of helplessness. Surely, to a fighter patrolling 1,000 feet above us in the inky blackness we must be easy prey silhouetted as we are above these illuminated clouds? My eyes are hanging out like organ stops as I scan above and to the sides, just waiting for a flicker of tracer that will reveal the position of an unseen fighter. There are so many contrasts in the degrees of light it seems incredible that one can be bathed in light yet above can be black, this really strains the eyes and it is folly to look into the light for too long.

'I ask the skipper to weave about a bit so as to make the night fighters' job a little more difficult. This, I am assured over the intercom, the skipper is only too willing to do.

'We are now past the searchlight area and I feel a little more secure, comparatively lost in the dark sky, but I know we are visible because I can see the glowing red-hot exhaust stubs of other aircraft as they pass to our starboard. I call up the navigator to inform him of these aircrafts' movements, he replies, "In another twenty seconds we will turn also". The order is given to turn after which the navigator calls me up on the intercom to thank me. Nice fellow – snag is if he got lost I got lost also. However, the art of being able to co-operate with one another is the recipe for making a competent crew.

'Way out on the starboard quarter an aircraft has jettisoned its bomb-load, a sure sign of fighter activity, and just to confirm my thoughts, a stream of coloured tracer cuts across the sky until the far end of the tracers grow into a red ball of fire, first blood to the fighters.

'The skipper calls up the mid-upper gunner and myself to tell us to keep a sharp look out, but my eyes are attracted to that unfortunate aircraft which is now going down like a shooting star. I cannot see any parachutes as it is too dark. It could have been worse, it could have been over the sea and I imagine that could be really hopeless for there are not many prisoners of war rescued from there.

'The flak is getting thicker as we penetrate deeper into Germany and as I change my search to port a vivid flash momentarily blinds me, but not before I am able to discern the disintegration of a four-engined aircraft. Obviously a direct hit by flak in the bomb bay, a chance in thousands.

'We fly on. Lucky are the wireless operator and navigator who seldom see outside the aircraft in flight. I console myself thinking these incidents could never happen to us, such is the reasoning one adopts.

'A blue searchlight is standing vertically on the distant port beam – this is an orbiting station for night fighters – so once again the skipper gets a request to get weaving. The navigator informs the skipper that ETA for target is ten minutes off and from now on the bomb aimer takes over. I can hear him describing the intense concentration of searchlights, but these are partially broken up by the clouds. The sky now seems full of red darting lights, some bursting yellow, some orange. These red tracer shells have a lazy way of climbing to the heights and then shooting past at incredible speed. It's all very uncanny.

'As I sit in my turret and scan all around, it seems like a bad dream. I couldn't run if I wanted to. Over the intercom the flight engineer comments, "Lanc coned over there, skipper". His dour reply: "– his luck" ends this informative conversation.

'I can hear the bomb aimer breathing very heavily and, come to think of it, I'm not doing too badly myself. The flak is pretty severe and the occasional *whoomp*! *whoomp*! becomes less occasional! The Path Finder Force have dropped the target indicators and these are raining red flares, dripping green flares. Then the skipper breaks in with "OK, bomb aimer, it's all yours now".

'A series of "left, left, right" and that agonising ten second "steady, s-t-e-a-d-y" seems like an eternity. Surely now is the time for the night fighters to pounce while we are trapped in that very steady run with us illuminated by the searchlights upon that very light broken cloud?

'How relieved we are when "bombs gone, Skip" is announced. The time is exactly 2325. The navigator has had his new course ready for just this moment and the skipper promptly turns on it to take us clear of the target area, and as we turn I am literally sitting on top of the world with a grandstand seat apparently sailing through space in a glass bottle.

'As I survey the scene during the course of my search I am left speechless with awe at the stage set before me. How did we get through those searchlights? Often I felt as though I could have put out my hand and cast rude shadows in those beams, but others are not so lucky as us. One chap is caught by a beam and instantly about thirty searchlights freeze on him. It was pathetic to watch that giant aircraft glittering and twisting like a silver moth around a lamp, until suddenly he could elude his captors no longer. It was only a matter of time as the tracer bullets from the night fighters ripped home and set him afire. Parachutes were seen to emerge and descend in the target area. During the aircraft's final dive to basement level tracers were still answering the challenge of the fighter from the gun turrets, but I don't suppose they could get out anyway. Not for them a decoration, or even survivors leave, but probably they were reconciled to their fate when they compared the reception that awaited the parachuted descent of their fellow comrades into that bombed and burning target area.

'Berlin had been littered with thousands of incendiary bombs and twinkled as a myriad of white sparklers. It gave me the impression of looking down on a reversed Milky Way. The incendiaries had obviously done the job expected of them for the broken clouds were now changing to a deep and rich crimson glow, reflecting the great fires that were raging below. This was a truly awe-inspiring sight of pure wanton destruction with its brilliantly illuminating white incendiaries starting the great red fires. The tall searchlight fingers all added to the effect. Red and yellow shell bursts mingled with the red and green target indicators, the dark rising smoke all helped to colour this moment and there in the middle of it all the Stirlings, Halifaxes and Lancasters, silhouetted black against the glowing red cloud flew serenely on. Such is the glory of war.

'As we pass out of the target area dense smoke can be seen billowing up to just below our own height of 18,000 feet. A click as a microphone is switched on, the roar of the engines amplified in the earpieces galvanise me instantly. A shrill garbled warning: "Fighter below, crossing to starboard gunner's"; it is the bomb aimer.

'Looking to starboard I pick the enemy out; he saw us as he passed below and came up level, slightly behind the starboard beam. He flies parallel for a few seconds giving at least sufficient time to warn the skipper "Prepare to turn to starboard, starboard, starboard". I see his wings flip to almost plan view. He is coming in and I conclude "Starboard *go*!"

'The next second my stomach is trying to get into my boots as the skipper flies the Halifax into a tight turn. With us travelling at 250mph towards the German Me109, and he towards us at probably 300mph, over a distance of 600 yards, there is little time for him to get a bead on us. We come back on course and never see him again. However, the time taken to read this far exceeds the time of action.

'We are now in and out of cloud, mighty thankful at times for a relief of constantly staring from darkness to light and back again to darkness, but how I dread being in cloud, especially at turning point when there is always a danger of collision. My eyes are beginning to feel like two balls of fire as I've now been searching for the past five hours, and base is still three hours distant. A hundred miles from the target a dull red glow can still be seen; it must have been sheer hell in Berlin. Seven hundred aircraft delivered a load of approximately 2,000 tons of high explosive in the space of forty minutes.

'In the distance searchlights have picked up an aircraft and it is surrounded by flak. Evidently the pilot had strayed over a big town. I tell the navigator and he confirms that Hanover is to starboard. During the course of my search I glance back at him every minute; he's still there twisting and turning – but suddenly he makes the break. There are no aircraft but plenty of searchlights and they seem to go mad, criss-crossing in all directions. When that kite gets home the ground crew must surely have some kind of mess to clear out! With the exception of the engine noise, all is quiet. The searchlights have now been extinguished and we are once more enveloped by darkness.

'In the loneliness of the rear turret I count my blessings and think how lucky our crew are to have a good navigator and skipper, a really good pair; together they keep us on track and away from most trouble. The journey back to the coast is uneventful, but all is not over yet. The searchlights and gunners on the coast are doing their best to hurry us home, but they need not worry, we're going home anyway.

'We cross the Dutch coast and maintain our height well out to sea, for the enemy has that nasty habit of placing flak ships off the coast just waiting to fire on low flying aircraft.

'I am conscious of the cold now, but I think it is due to the fact that nearing home one does not have so much activity to occupy the mind. The bomb aimer calls "English coast ahead" and as I swing my turret twenty degrees to port I can just see under the tailplane a thin white line, the sea pounding the cliffs. To me this has always seemed unfriendly but tonight the water must be doing a jig. Our height is down to 3,000 feet as I watch the coast pass under my turret. Flamborough Head is a familiar and welcome sight to us and the bomb aimer informs the navigator that we are visually dead on track. The skipper adds, "Well done".

'When we hit the coast I feel secure and always give my people in London a thought. I think of them now, asleep in their shelters; the time is 0345 but they can sleep soundly tonight – we've given the Germans a little bit of their own medicine. We see a few airfields illuminated and the mid-upper gunner sees our beacon flashing its predetermined letter and the skipper banks towards it. The wireless operator informs the skipper that the ground-to-air R/T is switched on and the skipper calls control asking permission to land. "N-Nan pancake" is the quickly-given response from Control.

'As we are on the downwind leg I can see two aircraft racing towards each other, each with its wing-tip lights on. It all happens so quickly, a blinding flash and they are locked together momentarily before plunging to burn on the ground. What an ironic turn of fate, having survived the German defences only to crash within view of their own base.

'I hear my skipper acknowledge Control "N-Nan Wilco out". The trailing aerial is wheeled in and suddenly the trees and huts are flashing past us with increasing speed as we drop lower and lower until, with a slight bump and a bounce, we are home. The time is 0415.

'We taxi to dispersal where we chat with the ground crew about the night's events while we await transport that will take us to de-briefing. Plenty of questions are asked by the Intelligence Officers such as fires, flares, flak, searchlights, fighters, explosions in target area, smoke, position of aircraft going down, parachutes seen and so on. As rear gunner I am not supposed to comment about fires as officially I am expected to look the other way to keep my eyes adapted for dark detection. However, the only one I knew who sat through a target area oblivious to his surroundings was a gunner riddled with bullets.

'We are given a tot of neat rum at de-briefing plus cups of coffee and I confide in the navigator that it was quite a good trip for my 21st birthday! He betrayed my trust in him by informing the CO Wing Commander Lowe. Somebody suggested a double rum issue and I drank a handy sized mugful and with the rather tired voices singing "Happy Birthday to you" I step outside and breathe deep the cold very fresh morning air.

'It really feels good to be alive.

'We wend our weary way back to the mess to enjoy that other egg that I was determined to see before we left for the Big City, and then – bed.

'I recorded this trip at great length for no other reason than that most people celebrate their 21st Birthday with a big party and happily recall it in later years as one of the happiest days of their lives. I came into the world at 2330 on 31 August 1922. I feel it would have been a short life if I had gone out of the world when that fighter attacked at exactly 2330 on 31 August 1943!

'I would like to remember in future years that my party was shared by nearly 4,900 aircrew, but the memory will be tragically marred by the loss of 57 aircraft and 400 comrades. Three of these aircraft were from our own squadron.'

Berlin was again the target three months later and Bill was on the trip with his usual skipper Pete Cadman. Pete was asked by the BBC to broadcast an account of the raid. This account went out to America, the South Pacific Islands and New Zealand on 24 November:

'There is always a more tense feeling in the briefing room when the Wing Commander announces that Berlin is the target for the night. Tonight it was just the same and all the crews were won-

Pete Cadman, Ian Robertson and Laurie Ellis with their crews. All had carried out a minimum of three raids on Berlin.

Pete Cadman with his air and ground crew at Elvington
(l to r) GC, GC, GC, E. G. McClorry. P. Cadman, W. Batty, M. Holliday, W. Trivett, GC, GC, A. Powell, H. Clayton.

dering how this trip was going to compare with previous Berlin visits. Actually we got along very nicely. Just before the enemy coast, cloud began to form beneath us until it became a solid mass which lasted to the target. We were well above this, however, but soon entered a higher sheet of cloud in which we flew for about an hour. Eventually this cloud began to break up and we could see all round us, except for the solid layer of cloud below.

'Eight minutes before reaching the target everything seemed so quiet ahead that I said to my navigator, "I say Mac, how are we doing?" He replied, "We're doing OK, skipper. You should be seeing things pretty soon. We're on the road all right." He was right. Very suddenly the sky ahead was lit up as the Pathfinding Force dropped their flares, and flak began to worry the boys in front.

'As we approached the target the Pathfinders dropped their special markers and I dived the aircraft towards these. All around us I could see hundreds of aircraft with their bomb doors open, all making their bombing runs. As I opened our bomb doors I could feel our aircraft lift as our load went down.

'Flak was thicker now but generally ineffective. There were no searchlights and we could see no night fighters. The clouds were lit up more and more as the glow of the fires caused by the incendiaries reflected through them. It looked as though Berlin was really getting a packet.

'As we turned for home the rear-gunner called out excitedly, "I say, Skip, there've been a couple of terrific explosions – wizard sight." He told me afterwards that a vivid white glow had penetrated the clouds. Thinking of the havoc we had left behind us we entered the cloud that we had encountered on our way out and the rest of the trip was quite normal except for the pleased and self satisfied look on the face of our bonzo dog we carry as mascot. It was quite evident that he too had enjoyed the trip.'

This was Flight Lieutenant Peter Cadman's 31st operation. He was later killed in a training aircraft when he had left the squadron.

CHAPTER FIVE

Lord Haw Haw welcomes Canadians

In April 1943 Jack Summers was one of twenty Radio Mechanics (Air) posted to HQBC to form the Squadron Centimeter Advisory Party whose purpose was to install H2S in all PFF and main force aircraft. 'We started at Wigton on 83 and 97 Squadron Lancasters and then split up and I went to 405 RCAF Squadron at Gransden Lodge where they were flying Halifax II Series 1A's. I spent a month there and airtested the H2S S-Sugar HX173.

'Between the quarters and the airfield there was about a mile of country road and halfway along it was a large house in which King Peter of Yugoslavia and his wife lived, in exile, with a handful of Yugoslav soldiers to guard them. For some reason the Canadians disliked the Yugoslavs and apart from shouting out "Hiya, Pete" if ever the King was in the garden they also used to rough up his guards in the pub at night. Soon an order was issued to the effect that all personnel are reminded that they must show the utmost respect to the Head of State of one of our allies. The Commanding Officer was Wing Commander Johnny Fauquier.'

Gerald South (now retired as Group Captain G. J. South DSO, DFC) remembers the CO as a founder member of 405 Squadron. He says he was an outstanding personality and most forceful and inspiring leader. He was formerly a bush pilot in Canada before the war.

'The squadrons were very mixed', he recalls. 'I am not a Canadian myself and we even had the odd Australian and New Zealander. I think 405 is worthy of especial mention as it was the first RCAF bomber squadron formed overseas, and the first and only RCAF Pathfinder Squadron. It converted from Wellingtons to the Halifax II in April 1942, was lent to Coastal Command and operated from Beaulieu from October 1942 until March 1943, and joined No 8 Path Finder Force Group at Gransden Lodge in April–May 1943.

'I joined them in July 1943 and started operations on Halifax II

Series 1A's, typical airframe numbers being HR810 and HR857. Johnny Fauquier always flew LQ-J (for Johnny) and if the original J was unserviceable for any reason, another aircraft had to be repainted with the appropriate letter. Johnny was accompanied everywhere, except in the air, by a pair of gigantic Irish Wolfhounds.

'Late in August we began to convert to the Lancaster and some of the Halifaxes went to No 35 Squadron at Graveley, the first RAF Halifax Squadron with the Pathfinders.'

On New Year's Day 1943 No 6 Group, an independent bomber group, all RCAF, was established and took over operational control of Nos 408, 419, 420, 424, 425, 426, 427 and 428 Squadrons.

Allerton Hall, near Knaresborough in Yorkshire, was requisitioned as the Group's headquarters. This immense country mansion soon became known as 'Castle Dismal' to the airmen. The Group, under the command of Air Vice-Marshal G. E. Brookes, 'Brookey' to all, took over control of some of the Yorkshire airfields for the Group's squadrons.

In May 1943, Nos 429 and 432 Squadrons joined the Group, as did No 434 in June, and 433 in September.

In October 1943 Jack Summers moved up to 6 Group and worked on every RCAF Bomber Squadron. He continues:

'As we always worked on new aircraft and flew on the initial air test when all the latest modifications had been incorporated, we used to have nice long trips while all the equipment was tested. At one time at Leeming on 427 and 429 Squadrons some of us returned on four engines for several weeks. The pilot would feather each prop in turn and then restore it to normal pitch, but there was some sort of fault on the Constant Speed Unit and at least one of the engines would roar away and it had to be shut down. The CSU on the port outer of 427 Squadron W-William LV883 went up in February 1944 and that of 429 Squadron V-Victor LV914 in March, both aircraft were Halifax III's.'

No 427 Squadron was first formed on 7 November 1942, the eighth of fifteen RCAF Bomber Squadrons, equipped with Wellingtons. On being transferred to Leeming in May 1943, it re-equipped with Halifaxes. Metro-Goldwyn-Mayer then adopted the squadron and allowed the names of their stars, including Joan Crawford, Greer Garson, Hedy Lamarr and Lana Turner, to be displayed on squadron aircraft. In addition MGM presented a bronze lion to the squadron, and from this came the name 'Lion Squadron'. The

Halifax II of 405 Squadron

Halifax VII of 432 Squadron

squadron also adopted one of Winston Churchill's lion cubs, Mareth.

One of the squadron flyers was Ron Burn, the flight engineer in a truly international crew. He was a Welshman and there were four Canadians, an American and a London Cockney.

'We liked to think we were the best crew in Bomber Command', Ron says. 'I was a twenty-year-old sergeant and on my 31st trip, flying easily above the Pas-de-Calais on the evening of 4 August 1944. The Halifax was U-Uncle 'See U in the morning'. Our target was a flying bomb launching site at Forêt-de-Neepe from which doodle bugs were being sent to blast London. This was one of our early daylight raids and as the aircraft droned along, we who were able, watched the other aircraft of our squadron and also those of our Group which formed the gaggle heading for the target.

'We were looking forward to the experience of watching the pathfinders at work on the target as we had bombed on their markings in the dark many times in the past. We were pleased to see them at ground level, placing the coloured smoke markers with precision.

'Bernie, our American mid-upper gunner commented, as we neared the target, that one of the Halifaxes was getting a little too close. However, as we were almost into our bombing run, under control of the bomb aimer, no serious notice was taken.

'At 16,000 feet we were flying above very accurate light anti-aircraft fire, which came from guns concentrated around the target. We night birds found the pock-marked sky very strange; the Womp! Womp! Womp! of near misses was however, an old experience.

'Looking through the astrodome I saw the Halifax above and to our port open its bomb doors and fly along with us on our run. I could see the rows of 1,000 lb. bombs hanging menacingly in its belly. It was not until the last moment, immediately prior to the release of our bombs, that it swung directly overhead, and dropped its load.

'Over our intercom came the usual "bombs gone", and the characteristic lift which followed the bomb release. As we rose three bombs, from the aircraft above, hit us. Fortunately the distance between the two aircraft was so short that the fusing mechanism had not had time to operate. The bombs therefore did not explode as they tore through. One hit dead centre of the fuselage behind the mid-upper turret. The other two took the

Halifax of 427 Squadron – Leeming September 1943

Halifax III of 420 Squadron being waved off from Tholthorpe 6 January 1945

trailing edge off the port wing. This wing immediately dropped, and although Murph, the pilot, aided by myself, struggled hard with the controls, it was impossible to move the aileron control surfaces owing to the fact that shreads of metal from the wing had jammed them.

'While this struggle went on we became suddenly aware that the aircraft had lost about 10,000 feet and was still going down. We noticed too, that our fighter escort were giving us a great deal of attention, "shooting up" our nose and waggling their wings. It took us some time to realise that we were still heading *east*! By using our engines, which were still running smoothly, we turned west. We trimmed the aircraft as far as possible, and I went back to take stock of things.

'One of the 1,000 lb bombs had punched a neat hole in the top of the fuselage about three to four feet astern of the upper turret. Directly below, a jagged hole the whole width of the floor appeared. Through this hole trailed oxygen tubes, wires and strips of metal. The hydraulic pipes, ammunition chute and control rods, which lie along the side of the fuselage were, however, fortunately intact. Standing there, in the strange light let in through the holes, I could detect the aircraft's tail vibrate and squeak above the sound of rushing air. Realising I could do nothing, I returned to the pilot and reported the extent of the damage.

'By running the port outer engine at full climbing power and starboard outer at a little more than tick over, it was possible to "crab" the Halifax along at a height sufficient for a parachute escape. Murph's voice came over the intercom telling all those in favour to jump. He explained that he had no idea how long he could maintain his present height or how the aircraft would behave when power was reduced for landing, if ever we reached British soil again. I do not think a landing in France entered my head. We listened carefully to the pilot and then all decided to stay with "Old Uncle", for maimed as she was she seemed to be doing all right.

'In view of the fact that the port outer engine was still running at full rated power, and would have to stay this way if we were to continue aloft, course was set for Woodbridge, the crash airfield in the south of England. After we changed course we noticed that the bomber that had bombed us was no longer in sight. It had flown with us, just a few hundred yards away, for the best part of thirty minutes, but not one of us could remember its squadron markings or number.

'While making for Woodbridge I kept an extremely careful check on the engines, which were behaving very well. We crossed the Channel safely, and as we began to circle our objective we again considered baling out. As the engines were still working satisfactorily we had another discussion on the intercom and decided to make a run for our Yorkshire base.

'By now the noise at the rear was becoming louder, and the wagging movement of the tail was being transmitted along the control rods to the stick. It was at this stage that we fastened on our parachutes. As we were safely over England the pilot ordered the gunners to leave their turrets, for he felt there was a better chance of escape from the main fuselage. Bernie came out of the mid-upper looking very pale. Little wonder, for when the bombs fell, even from my astrodome ten to twelve feet in front of the turret, they seemed to be heading straight for me. Bernie must have thought they were going to drop in his lap. Ken, the rear gunner, came out of his vibrating turret and stared at the hole for the first time. Stan, the navigator and myself were standing forward of the hole, holding on with one hand and reaching out offering help with the other.

'We could not speak to each other, but moved our arms encouragingly. Ken found that by having his parachute in position on his stomach, he was unable to hold on to the ammunition chutes and stride sideways across the hole. Each time he attempted to cross his parachute caught. We were afraid it might release itself, open, and pull him through the hole. After various unsuccessful attempts, and a lot of arm waving, we persuaded Ken to pass his parachute across the hole. Then very cruelly using it as bait, we eventually encouraged him to try crossing without it. He had no chance to change his mind for as soon as he could be reached we both grabbed him and pulled him across and to safety.

'In the meantime our faithful Halifax was crabbing along towards base, in the now failing light. Another check on the engines showed they were behaving magnificently. The port outer, now running well over its permitted time at this power, was doing fine. By the time we reached base Jimmy, our cockney wireless operator, had told them of our plight, and the runway was cleared for landing.

(*Right*) HM King George VI with pilot Murphy and the CO inspecting damage to U-Uncle

(*Below*) U-Uncle with covers being removed

(*Far right*) HM Queen speaking to Stan Niven while fellow Canadian Keith Young waits his turn

(*Bottom right*) The padre speaks to (l to r) 'Shadow' Bygraves, Stan Niven, Ron Burn, Bernie White and Johnny Cheese

CANADA

CANADA

Before letting down from our hard won height the pilot once again told us of his concern at what might happen when power was reduced. For the third time the offer to bale out was turned down. We entered the circuit and prepared to land.

'During the flight north the aileron controls had freed themselves a little, so Murph hoped that with a long, low approach, he would fly the beleaguered aircraft hedge high on to the runway. With the other aircraft keeping clear we commenced our approach. We six crew members were ordered to lie near the main spar, whilst only the pilot remained at the controls. Slowly, but surely, we sloped our way towards the runway, and, after what seemed an age, Murph called out, "Hold tight for the touch down".

'The touch down was a problem. While in the air our life-saver, the port outer engine, had held up the port wing, but now on the final approach any reduction in power on this engine meant a lowering of the wing. An added difficulty was the fact that the flaps on this wing were in ribbons.

'The port wheel hit the runway hard; a burst of throttle on the engines that side, not only lifted the wing, but gave the aircraft an extra pull along the runway. The wheel hit again and we bounced, then again and again, then suddenly we were running out of runway.

' "Hold tight, I'm going to brake," yelled Murph, and did so as soon as the main wheels touched the ground together. By braking and releasing quickly, the Halifax began to slow down. Just when we began to breathe easily the pilot shouted, "Brake pressure's gone".

'Once again, luck was on our side. In my position, forward, the mechanics had fitted experimentally an extra air cylinder for the brakes. Ours was the only aircraft on the squadron to have one.

'I jumped up from my position at the main spar, ran to the cylinder and opened the valve, tapped the pilot's shoulder and indicated the return of pressure. We had travelled so far along the runway by this time that the only thing left to do was to lock the wheels and hope for the best. With a scream of tyres, clouds of blue smoke, the Halifax shuddered, skidded and stopped. We cut the engines and suddenly it was all quiet.

'Murph caught my arm and pointed to the aileron control. It was jammed solid in the vertical, or full bank, position. Perspiration ran down his face.

'It was now dusk, and by the time our Halifax had been towed to dispersal our friends were there waiting for us. It was good to be home.

'The incident was followed by leave, and when we returned we learned that Murph had been awarded a well deserved Distinguished Flying Cross. It had certainly been distinguished flying.

'This was not quite the end, for King George VI, Queen Elizabeth, Princess Elizabeth and Princess Margaret visited the squadron a few weeks later and we were very proud to be lined up in front of our Halifax and introduced to them individually, and asked to give details of our experience.'

The other squadron Jack Summers mentioned, No 429, was formed at East Moor on 7 November 1942. After the squadron entered the Canadian Group in August the following year, they moved to Leeming and the personnel from then on were predominantly Canadian. The squadron also converted to Halifax Mark II's at this time and to Mark V's in November. In March 1944 the squadron converted to the Hercules engine Mark III's which were to be the mainstay of the squadron until the end of the war.

On the evening of D-Day, 6 June 1944, Gordon Ritchie was flying as rear gunner in V-Victor LW128. He takes up the story:

'We were detailed to attack Achères, a marshalling yard. We were all feeling elated as our pilot, Squadron Leader W. B. Anderson, who had taken us through some dicey do's at the Ruhr, Leipzig and Berlin, had just been appointed flight commander and given word, shortly before take off, that he had been awarded the DFC for a rather hairy do when we attacked Karlsruhe some days earlier.

'As we crossed the French coast at Dieppe, all hell broke loose as the ack-ack guns pummelled us. The pilot caught a rather large chunk of flak through his side and immediately gave us all the order to bale out. We were at approximately 18,000 feet. The aircraft went into a vertical dive as the pilot slumped over the control column. I had the turret swung out on the beam looking for fighter attacks from below; I immediately tried to centralise the turret, but in my rush I overcorrected and got it to a position where I could tear myself out. I left one of my flying boots wedged in it, as I extricated myself and picked up my parachute. I squeezed through the narrow opening between the fuselage and the tail wheel oleo jack. This is usually a difficult manoeuvre but when the aircraft is in a dive and heading for eternity it was a miracle.

'As I crawled forward to the escape hatch my face was being forced into the floor. It was then that I realised that the aircraft was being pulled out of its dive. I plugged in my intercom and learned that Flight Sergeant Gilbert Steere, the flight engineer, had dragged the wounded pilot from the cockpit and was straightening the Halifax. The mid upper gunner, John Mangione, and I learned that the navigator, bomb aimer and wireless operator had baled out over France.

'The pilot was in a terrible bloodied condition but still alive, and we administered morphine to ease his pain. We switched on some lights in the aircraft to see what we were doing, not realising we had inadvertently switched on our navigation lights. We jettisoned our bomb load near Dieppe and headed for England. At that time there was such a concentration of shipping in the Channel that they had orders to shoot at anything overhead. However, we had more to concern ourselves with than that, not the least of which was what we were going to do when we arrived over England.

'During this time the flight engineer was flying the aircraft, sitting in a bucket seat wearing a chest pack parachute and consequently could not see out of the aircraft, relying solely on the artificial horizon to keep us somewhat straight and level, so it was anything but a smooth flight back.

'The skipper rallied a little from time to time and we had hopes that he might pull through; it was only his great constitution that kept him alive as long as he did. He was a big man who had played professional football in Canada. We dragged him over the two main spars back to the escape hatch. This took a great deal of effort and we were pleased when we completed that task. We attached the buckeye snap on the static line to the D ring on his parachute and prepared to release him out of the hatch.

'We were in touch with several airfields after calling "Mayday" but we had no idea what part of England we were over. We advised them we were about to release the skipper, I was the last to speak to him and I told him what we were about to do, he asked for a little time and then said, "Good luck, OK let me go", and so we slipped him out.

'Then it was time for the rest of us to leave. The flight engineer

(***Above***) F/Sgt John Mangione, F/Sgt Gilbert Steere, F/Sgt Gordon Ritchie. All were later commissioned (below) HM King George VI decorating Gordon Ritchie with his DFM while the rest of 429 Squadron look on.

Centre section of the Honours Board at Leeming

was quite anxious for us to go as he was concerned about the petrol, so the other gunner and I went forward to the front hatch which did not look too appealing, and then back to the rear hatch. After another trip forward and back, neither looked too inviting, and I decided it was time to go, slid my feet out and the slipstream took my one remaining boot away. I slid my feet out again and away went my heated slippers; finally I summoned enough courage and out I went. It was such a relief when the chute opened; it was so heavenly to be out of that Halifax with all the noise, blood and clatter. My next concern was where I was going to land. We estimated we were flying at 12,000 feet at bale-out.

'I landed in my stockinged feet on a wire fence and blew into a field. I immediately reached for a cigarette, I had one of those Victory lighters and with my hand shaking I flicked the wheel right off the lighter, so there I was sitting in a field with a cigarette in my mouth and nothing to light it with.

'I looked behind me where there was a small white sign with red lettering which I could read by the limited light from the moon. It read "Beware of Mines". I decided I had to move, I made a straight line to the edge of the field and started towards our burning Halifax, across freshly ploughed fields, with mud oozing up between my stockinged toes. Then the ammunition started to explode, with tracers going in several directions, so I decided an about-turn was in order. I tried several houses, without success. I couldn't convince some of the Oxfordshire people that I was a Canadian airman who had just baled out. Finally, at a farmer's house, I was able to get my cigarette lit and found I was near Wallingford and that a little girl had lost her life running in the minefield some days earlier. The farmer drove me to RAF Benson where they were expecting me; the flight engineer had already arrived! Our pilot was found and brought to the mortuary at Benson where the station medics assured us that we had done all that was humanly possible for him.

'Within a week Gilbert Steere was awarded the CGM, John Mangione, the mid upper gunner from Ottawa, and myself were awarded the DFM. The bomb aimer and wireless operator were taken prisoner after a few days and the navigator returned to England after six weeks, courtesy of the French Underground.'

Jack Summers who visited all the RCAF bomber stations takes up the story again:

'The only time I was under fire was on air test from Skipton-on-Swale. As we flew over Huntingdon in a Halifax III from 433 Squadron the pilot saw a formation of eighteen Flying Fortresses setting out on a daylight raid so he said, "Let's go and waggle our wings at them". Next minute the mid upper gunner shouted out that the Yanks had got the wrong colour of the day – it shouldn't be red. "Hell," said the pilot, "that's tracer," and he put the nose up in a beautiful fast climb. Probably the Halifax III was so different to the Mark 1 that it seemed to the Americans to be a different type of aircraft.'

Jack Summers mentions 433 Squadron at Skipton-on-Swale. We will continue to follow its progress until the end of the war in Europe with Gordon Gross, an air gunner from Ottawa. By now there had been a change in command at the top. 'Black Mike', Air Vice-Marshal C.M. McEwan, took over command of No 6 Group from 'Brookey', his former First World War fighter pilot colleague.

Gordon Gross finished gunnery training in his native Canada in the autumn of 1943 and was posted to England, arriving at Liverpool in the *Mauretania*. From there he was sent on to Bournemouth, with a number of other Canadians. Their first introduction to war-time Britain was at a public house there, where they heard Lord Haw-Haw on the radio. He remarked about the *Mauretania* docking at Liverpool and gave a fairly good report on who was present and mentioned that Swordfish aircraft welcomed the ship during its final stages. He continued:

'For the sake of any of you young Canadians listening we could have gone over and sunk the ship before you entered Liverpool but we well know that most of you will either drink yourselves to death in the pubs or crash in training at an operational training unit. Of course, if any of you think I don't know what I'm talking about you will find that the clock in the Royal Bath is two minutes slow.' Much to the Canadians' chagrin, they found that the clock in the hostelry was two minutes slow, but they were assured that the clock had always been operated that way. Nevertheless it was quite an introduction to an operational theatre of war.

After ten days at the south coast resort, followed by leave, most of the gunners were posted to Pershore in Worcestershire and spent the winter flying Wellington III's on operational training. Next the gunners were sent on to Dalton for toughening up and battle school escape training in preparation for operations. From Dalton, they went on to nearby Topcliffe for a few weeks' conversion on to four-engined bombers before being posted to a No 6 Group squadron.

Gordon Gross and the rest of his crew started their tour at one of the most eventful periods of the war for a bomber crew. For their debut, a month before D-Day, there was a short trip to a gun position in France. Next, a bombing attack on the railyards at Aachen which turned out to be the roughest of the whole tour, a difficult night raid with fighter attacks and flak. Three days later a routine night flight successfully removed another gun position in France. A few days later Gardening operations dropped 2,000 lb sea mines on parachutes; there was a fighter attack by a FW190, which surprised and shook up the crew. Then came the eve of the invasion.

'We had another gun position to remove near the beach-head. It was very evident the beginning of the big invasion had come when we saw the briefing map. We were routed well east of the immediate Channel area and west of it for coming away. The story given to us in briefing was that the Americans were practising a night flying operation and since we all knew their ability in these lines, we were staying well east and keeping well west to be safe. Once airborne we could pick up parts of the Channel area on H2S. The bomb aimer was coming out with remarks to the effect that there were whole new islands in the Channel, which represented the clusters of shipping that were emerging on to the French coast at that time. We were told that we were quite successful in putting the gun out of commission in advance of the invasion.

'We were given a number of day operations on buzz bomb sites. These were comparatively easy, except over the immediate target area, where the direct flak was pretty hot.

'Some three weeks following the invasion we were sent to a large ammunition dump some distance south of Paris, Sautre Courte, which was difficult to locate. This was also a marshalling point for moving equipment to the front.

'On 4 July we were sent to the Paris area again, this time to the marshalling yards at Villeneuve St Georges. We received a shaking up on this trip. It was a fairly light sky and we had reason to believe a captured Flying Fortress had been sent up by the Germans to monitor our position and give details. As we went in on the

A Halifax of 431 Squadron photographed from another flying three miles above the flying bomb site target in France

425 Squadron Halifax III revs up at Tholthorpe

target area it was illuminated to daylight brilliance. We bombed from over 20,000 feet.

As mid upper gunner I was trying to preserve some semblance of night vision in one eye as the target area was very bright. We had moved on and arrived on our bombing run. Later, we were to receive a certificate for being very close to the aiming point. As we emerged out of the illuminated area the fighters moved in, no doubt locating us while over the target. A number of aircraft started to go down around us. We tried to record the position of these encounters as we saw them and where the aircraft were going down. There were so many that the skipper said we should forget about it and just watch out for our own aircraft. He then decided to change our briefing tactics and let down from 20,000 feet. We thus escaped from the many fighter attacks.

'We continued to let down as we flew across France with the idea that we would stay low until we crossed our own lines on the ground and then pull up to go out over the Channel. The navigator was doing his stuff on altitude to be sure we were not too low for safety. As a result we received a lot of flak from the ground, 20 mm calibre. We continued to keep veering west all the time and came hopelessly off track. We were not sure of our position but knew we were miles west of the corridor track laid out. We were still being intercepted by gunfire and it seemed to be the thing to do. As we crossed the coast we were fired on by naval flak and realised one of our own fighters had been tailing us at that time. We received most damage from the naval flak and some special accounting had to be done by the pilot and navigator because of this incident and our departure from briefing tactics. We believed we had done the best thing for our own safety.

'The Halifax III bomber certainly gave a great feeling of pride to those who flew in them, a sense of confidence in the aircraft, it was built like a tank, was rugged and gave a tremendous performance. The Halifax was quick in response on the controls and it was more than capable of very violent evasive action in a fighter attack. I knew, as a gunner, flying in the rear position, one could feel very intensive G when doing a corkscrew, often quite a bit of G felt in the mid-upper turret.

'At the end of the month, exactly a year after the fire raids on Hamburg we were again sent to Germany's second city. On 28 July 307 aircraft were despatched. It was a bad one for us. The situation was that it had been a very bright sky with light cloud below and it was evident the Germans had put up some aircraft in our stream as we emerged on the target. There was heavy white billowy cloud cover at 10,000 feet so the enemy turned the searchlights up and put all the illumination they could over the target area and we were like a bunch of flies crawling over white paper. We were very easily silhouetted and spotted from above. What surprised me more than anything else was the number of bombers in close proximity as we flew in the stream. We had never appreciated this previously, not having seen ourselves in the light up to this stage in any large force, whereas in daylight, on buzz bomb attacks the force was small compared to any big city raid. There was a lot of tenseness added with the proximity of all these aircraft especially looking up seeing aircraft above with their bomb doors open. We had a couple of bad scares with aircraft crossing through the stream and we were almost caught by a collision. I had to call for quick evasive action a couple of times to miss some of our own Halifaxes who seemed to be so intent on their own course that one wondered if anyone at all was keeping a look-out in them. A total of 23 aircraft were lost on the raid.

'All told, there were 234 Canadian heavies in the bombing force. The report of the raid said: "Good visibility, bombing dispersed among markers, several heavy explosions seen, enemy fighters active."

'The highest we ever flew in a Halifax III was something over 30,000 feet, but a number of raids were carried out at 27,000 and 28,000 feet. There was a bit of conceit on the part of us Halifax flyers, for although we did not have the range of the Lancaster we felt we were competitive in many ways. We certainly had more acceleration which we frequently liked to prove on returning from daylight raids. We'd be following along in streams at the prescribed speed when quite often a Lancaster would hedge along and catch up with us. We would fly abreast for a time and then take great pride in giving a booster power with the Halifax leaving the Lancaster behind. This was a sort of game we played on occasions.

'Sometimes we were diverted to American bases because of bad weather over our own field in Yorkshire. We looked forward to visiting these bases because of the difference in food, and the fruit juices. The actual landing was almost as bad as doing a late target across the Channel. We'd call up the base as we came into the

RCAF Halifaxes of No 425 (Alouette) Squadron at Tholthorpe

area; they would call back, after identifying us, and give permission to land. Unfortunately, they had done the same thing with everybody else, so at times there were twenty or thirty bombers milling around the base all attempting to land at the same time, and without lights! It was always a tense situation. On one occasion my pilot had to pull up to avoid an aircraft that was sliding in underneath him to land. Nobody could clearly see what was going on and the upshot of it was we were usually pretty taut and panicky by the time we landed. There certainly did not appear to be much pattern in the night control on the American bases.

'Once, while at Skipton, we were lining up opposite the main runway, about a third of the way up the line when one of the Halifaxes took off and seemed to lift prematurely, before it had adequate speed. It rose, went soaring straight up, hung on its propellers and then turned and came down, actually crashing just behind us. The port wing struck first and it went up in a pillar of smoke. It was thought that the second pilot's seat, which was a folding arrangement, may have given way, and in falling the flight engineer, or whoever was with the pilot, had grabbed the stick instinctively and caused the Halifax to climb involuntarily and then crash. I was completely hypnotised by this unusual event, it was a devastating thing to have to experience. In the course of squadron life one became used to unusual episodes, with aircraft taking off at something less than two minute intervals. We formed up over base before setting out for the target. On return to base we had a well-defined drill for getting in, being stacked and brought in. We had a great deal of confidence in our own airfield control in bringing us down.'

Contrary to the experience of other squadrons, 433 found that the greatest number of losses was to crews that were somewhere between their tenth to twentieth operation. This was believed to be due to an apathetic attitude, a sort of sense of confidence after the first initial trips and then later from twenty onward, when it was realised that there was a hope of completing the tour there was a sort of sense of determination and tenseness in seeing it through.

As a result of heavy losses an intensive training programme was ordered for the squadrons in No 6 Group. Naturally many of the aircrew were not at all impressed by this but it was the appropriate thing to do. Gordon Gross, as assistant gunnery leader, found himself being given the task of working up a training programme for all air gunners on the squadron. He went back to basics that had been learned before the crews joined an operational station. He incorporated gunnery practice, fighter affiliation exercises and intensified work on aircraft recognition. A great number of the aircrew were reluctant to give any time to this type of programme but a number of skills and techniques were refreshed. Gordon Gross thought it a very worthwhile effort as it was too easy to lose technical skills that had been brought to a high level before going on to operations. Some crews completed a full tour without ever encountering an enemy fighter at night.

At Skipton with gunnery and bombing training on the programme Gordon Gross remembers one incident when practice bombs were being carried:

'When we were warming up at dispersal one of the small bombs dropped off and there was a cloud of smoke. The pilot and flight engineer couldn't make out what had happened and believed from the smoke that an engine had caught on fire and gave us the panic word to get out. Those of us at the rear quickly jumped out of the back door while the flight engineer and pilot went out of the cockpit hatch and ran down the wing before jumping off at the end. The pilot received a badly sprained ankle. We all fled the aircraft like a bunch of rats and to our chagrin it was nothing but this practice bomb which had dropped off that caused the commotion.

'On 28 August there was a daylight raid on Brest. A ship was the target and the tactics were for a small force to detach from the main stream attacking another target and fly to the Atlantic port. We were briefed to fly over Brest harbour, identify the ship at the dockside and bomb it. We had to try to prevent the Germans bringing the ship out and sinking it at the entrance of the harbour. The garrison at Brest were holding out and putting up quite a bit of opposition.

'We went in following a main force over the continent and then set course for Brest. One or two of the earlier aircraft bombed an island area in the harbour but the latter part correctly identified the ship and were successful in laying their bombs over the dock area and damaging the ship. Our own crew was on target and we took a picture to prove that we had achieved direct damage on the ship. There was heavy flak in the Brest area but otherwise the trip was uneventful.

'Nights became longer in October, and we were assigned to night bombing in the Ruhr Valley: Dortmund on the 6th/7th, five lost out of a force of 523 aircraft; Bochum on the 9th/10th, six lost out of 435 and Duisberg blast furnaces on 14 October when all fifty aircraft returned safely. These were all heavily defended targets and in each case had a full complement of defensive measures which they threw against us including night fighters and predicted flak working with radar controlled searchlights. Several night fighters made passes at us before and after the target area but we were not damaged.

'It was about this time that we had our first non-starter. We had a full load of HE and incendiaries and were taking off in line when, about halfway down the runway, it was seen that the aircraft in front was in trouble and we had to swing. As a result we didn't make the trip. My first awareness from the mid-upper turret was the swing at the edge of the runway and then I realised that I was in the midst of four great columns of flame from each motor passing out beside me. Immediately I knew the thing to do was to jump out, and grabbed the release catch in the seat of the turret. I forgot that all the wires, my oxygen tube and seat belt were all connected. As a result when I slipped down the catch on my Mae West caught the dash panel of the turret and inflated and so I was hung up there and I had to recover myself, struggle back out, disconnect some wire and then come back down. In the meantime, those of the crew in the rest position saw a tremendous display of footwork as I went through and when I did get out of the turret all I could say, or rather mouth with my lips, was "Fire, fire, get out". I made for the rear door but I was passed by all of them; their reactions were faster than mine for I was still pretty well out of breath at this time. We all jumped out of the back door of the Halifax. At this time we weren't travelling too fast and when we came to our senses we were all running along the runway behind the aircraft which at this time was coasting to a stop. It actually stopped at the field at the end of the runway with its nose over the stone fence.

'What had happened was that we had swung but the pilot still thought he could bring the aircraft under control and so pulled back all the throttles; the raw gas in the manifold had ignited and this was the fire I had seen. We had done the safe thing but had many a good laugh later about chasing a burning Halifax.

'There was a big nuisance factor in having bombs that hung up; it was a matter of special concern and happened on all bombers. If they were discovered in time, before landing, it meant flying out over the North Sea, some eighty miles from Scarborough, and dropping them in the designated drop area.

'One of our crews on 433 Squadron came back to base and just as they touched down a fully primed 500 lb bomb dropped off and went sliding out ahead of them and moved off down the runway, fortunately without exploding.'

Gordon Gross made the last trip of his tour on a target near Dortmund at the end of November 1944. In the early spring of 1945 Gordon was back at Dalton when the Germans mounted their intruder raids. They crossed the coast and flew from the Midlands and caught the Halifaxes just as they were about to land at their Yorkshire bases. At Topcliffe they strafed some parked aircraft and a WAAF was killed when the barracks were hit. One intruder flew over the Dalton base where there was a party in full swing at the mess. There must have been a light showing for the mess was shot up. A few holes were put in the roof and the commanding officer's hut was machine-gunned. One burst went straight through his much prized copper tea kettle. Later a farmer handed the Canadian a machine-gun belt and some blank cartridges which he had found on his land at the back of the RAF quarters. This was probably where the intruder had cleared his guns after firing at the mess and living area.

Gordon was on his way back to Canada for a spot of leave, before being posted to the Far East, when news of the atom bomb raids was received, making his next posting unnecessary.

To return to Jack Summers, our guide through the Canadian Squadrons:

'When I was at Middleton St. George with 419 and 428 Squadrons the last train from Darlington to Stockton left about 2230 and it stopped at all stations. The first station was Dinsdale and the next, seven minutes later, was Eaglescliffe. The trouble was that the camp entrance was between the two, so that when the 'Dinsdale Belle' gathered speed on leaving Dinsdale there was always someone who pulled the cord as it neared the camp, and hordes of airmen would pour down the embankment.

'Things were no better at Ripon station. All the airmen from

Topcliffe and Skipton-on-Swale would travel from Baldersby to Ripon or Harrogate for the evening and on the return trip tickets were collected from those alighting at Baldersby. Talk about Fred Karno! There would be about 100 Canadians crowded into the Gents until the railway staff grew wise to this so the next thing was to watch the collectors moving from the back of the train and as they approached your compartment you opened the offside door and walked along the running board to the rear coach where tickets had already been collected. It sometimes took staff half-an-hour to collect tickets.'

On 31 August 1943 Wing Commander M. M. Flemming DFC, commanding officer of 419 Squadron, approved a design for the squadron crest submitted by the *Chester Herald*. The design consisted of a Moose in natural colours, depicted in a charging position. The motto on the crest was in crew language '*Moosa Aswayita*' which means 'Beware of the Moose'.

Two months earlier one of his all sergeant crews had been busy. On the night of 21/22 June U-Uncle JD214 piloted by Sergeant G.V. Neale bombed Krefeld. The following night the Halifax took off for a mining operation off the Frisian Islands but as Gee failed the pilot returned to base with his lethal cargo.

The crew were active for the third consecutive night when they took off at 2301 on 24 June 1943 to attack Wuppertal. At 0137 an SOS was heard from the aircraft which was then over the target. Seven minutes later a first class bearing of 118 degrees was given from Hull and another fix was requested. At 0149 a third class fix put the aircraft over Holland. The wireless operator then signalled he was unable to transmit any further messages; the position was unknown and nothing further was heard from the aircraft, which crashed in Holland.

Concluding the section on Canadian Squadrons the story of George Burton, from Halifax in Yorkshire, must be told. He joined No 420 Squadron at Tholthorpe from No 1664 Conversion Unit at the end of February 1944.

On 28 May he was flight engineer to Pilot Officer R.A. Kalle, and took off at one minute past midnight in G-George LW423. The Halifax was one of seventeen detailed to attack the Bourg-Leopold military camp as a prelude to the Invasion. G-George, loaded with sixteen 500 lb bombs, just had the pathfinder target indicators in its bomb sights at 0211 when it was attacked by a

Some of the all NCO crew of Sgt. G. V. Neale and their 419 Squadron U-Uncle which crashed in Holland

FW190 at 8,500 feet. The fighter had been observed earlier but the pilot thought he had shaken it off; obviously it had played possum until the aircraft was on its bombing run. The Halifax was set on fire in the attack. The pilot says:

'I did a steep dive, jettisoned the bombs and the fire went out'; he also told the crew to prepare to bale out. The mid upper gunner, who had been forced to leave his position due to the heat, abandoned the Halifax when flames spread to the wings during the dive – he must have thought the aircraft was out of control. He was obviously wounded for blood was found on his helmet and mask.

Rear gunner Laurence Metcalfe, from Vancouver, had the satisfaction of hitting the enemy fighter, see it slowly turn over, burst into flames and crash. But that was the end of the good news.

Kalle nursed the badly damaged Halifax back to England, with George Burton keeping an anxious eye on the fuel tanks. Navigator Lloyd Magson, also from Vancouver, was plotting a course for home when a signal was received telling all aircraft to land away from base as a heavy ground fog was covering Tholthorpe. G-George crash landed and was scrapped. Pilot Officer Kalle was awarded the DFC and Sergeant George Burton the DFM. Unfortunately the raid was considered to have been unsuccessful but all the Halifaxes returned, despite the fog.

P/O R. A. Kalle, who won the DFC and his crew, including George Burton who was awarded the DFM for 'gallant service and devotion to duty'

Two months later, when the Allies had secured a firm foothold in France, Kalle and his crew, now nearing the end of their tour, were detailed for an early morning raid.

On 30 July, a new G-George, Halifax III NA528, took off at 0529 carrying sixteen 500 lb bombs to attack Amye-sur-Seulles. The target was successfully attacked but one bomb hung up.

Back over England the pilot was forced to make a crash landing at the Air Transport Auxiliary airfield at White Waltham. At 0920 Kalle came in, overshot the short landing run and ran into a railway cutting on the north-west corner of the airfield and the 500 lb bomb exploded. All the crew were injured except, ironically, the mid upper gunner who had replaced the one who had earlier baled out. Some of the crew were badly burned and the rear gunner later died.

The crash made the national newspapers. One report read:

> A bomber which crashed on the main Great Western railway line near Maidenhead yesterday delayed arrivals of some trains at Paddington by 75 minutes. The bomber pilot tried to make an emergency landing on an airfield near, but because the runway was too short could not pull up in time.
>
> Fire followed the crash and the crew were trapped. Men of the NFS were soon there and dragged the airmen clear. The aircraft had buried its nose in an embankment and for two hours blocked both the fast and slow lines.
>
> Trains from Paddington to Wales and the west of England were diverted to the northern line, which normally carries the Birmingham, Wolverhampton and Birkenhead traffic. The station was still thronged by holiday-makers but since Saturday when its approaches had to be closed because of the congestion, the organisation had improved.
>
> 'I think we have got on top of it now, and can handle the traffic comfortably', an official said.

George Burton injured an arm and became one of Sir Archibald McIndoe's patients at East Grinstead.

Whether it was George Burton, an Englishman from Halifax Yorkshire, with a Canadian Halifax Squadron or Canadians from Halifax Nova Scotia with RAF Squadrons mattered not. What did matter was that Canadians and Canadian Halifax Squadrons were able to play a full part in Bomber Command's contribution to the defeat of Germany.

CHAPTER SIX

Shiny Ten

Fly high, fly low, wherever you go,
Shiny 10 Squadron will give a good show.

Following Nos 35 and 76, No 10 was the third squadron to be equipped with Halifaxes in October 1941. The squadron attacked the *Scharnhorst* and *Gneisenau* at Brest in December.

The four-engined aircraft were making demands on RAF manpower, requiring seven or eight crew for each bomber, including a new crew category, the flight engineer. One of the early ones was Matthew Holliday, who was a flight engineer/air gunner. A ground engineer, Matthew had little initial training either as an air gunner or later as a flight engineer, as he describes:

'Some of us were given a shortened gunnery course on Defiants, and posted to a squadron as a spare bod to await crewing up. We were expected to complete an eight weeks' course in three weeks – "You know all about hydraulics, so you won't need so much time."

'I had little training as a flight engineer either – an interview and a few questions by the Station Engineer Officer and that was it, a flight engineer! A lot of questions to other flight engineers, and flying with 10 Conversion Flight, and a little light began to dawn. We had an engine fire on my second operation and the engine could not be feathered although the fire eventually died out. Good flying by the skipper, Flight Sergeant Ernie Allen, got us home, as he was to do on many an occasion, and I think I was learning a little about what the job entailed. When I think of how the lads in that crew had to put up with an amateur like me at that time my blood runs cold at the thought of those days and I can only admire their courage.'

Wing Commander D. C. T. Bennett took over No 10 Squadron in April 1942. At the end of the month he crashed in a squadron Halifax on a bombing raid on the German battleship *Tirpitz*, holed up in Foetten Fiord, near Trondheim, in Norway. He escaped to Sweden, thence back to England and 10 Squadron again.

In July the squadron were taken off bombing German targets and ordered to the Middle East to assist in the bombing of the Italian Navy. The Royal Navy had suffered badly in the Mediterranean, in the previous year, following the evacuation from Greece and Crete. The battleship *Barham* was sunk in November and her sister ships *Queen Elizabeth* and *Valiant* were attacked and damaged by frogmen in Alexandria the following month.

The Wing Commander was none too happy with the new assignment for the squadron, even although it was intended to be a short term measure, as Matthew Holliday explains:

'The commander told us: "Special mission to bomb the Italian Fleet in Taranto Harbour, sixteen days only, take your best blue and leave everything else behind." The squadron flew down to Hurn and refuelled prior to leaving for the Mediterranean. It was here that the Wing Commander said, "I am not able to go with you, I have been ordered to stay behind." One of the flight commanders took over.'

The next day D. C. T. Bennett reported to the Headquarters of the Commander-in-Chief of Bomber Command and was appointed as Commander of a Path Finder Force. Matthew Holliday continues:

'That sixteen days stretched to eight months. At Fayid Air Marshal Tedder asked us if we had any questions and one flight engineer asked, "When are we going home?" This summed up the feelings of most of the crews. It might seem petty when one remembers what others out there had to put up with, but the point is that all the lads thought it was a shabby way to build up the Desert Air Force, and also, of course, quite a number of the aircrew were almost at the end of a first tour, and one or two of the ground staff NCO's had only just returned from overseas. The aircrew were lucky; at least we returned but some of the ground lads had to stay behind.

'Our aircraft, J-Jig W7717, force-landed by the side of a runway being built in the desert; it was short of petrol, and two of the fuel pressure lights came on as we made the final approach. The *Felaheen* charged round the aircraft and we thought of *The Four Feathers* and *The King of the Khyber Rifles*, stiffened

W1174 of 10 Squadron in the Middle East

(L to r) Bill Dill, Taffy Perkins, Mart Levine, Ernie Allen, Wally Everett and Matt Holliday with their 10 Squadron Halifax in the Western Desert 1942

our lips and manned the turrets, swearing to sell our lives dearly. The Royal Engineers in charge of the workings restored order, using fly-swats, and we breathed freely once again. Filling a heavy bomber in four gallon tins from 50 gallon drums which were sent for, and hauling them up to a mainplane which was too hot to stand on without engine covers under our feet, took a long time; and we still had the thought of a take-off from the sand in our minds, which was successful as it happened.

'Heat during the day causing a lack of sleep was the main difficulty during the early days. We'd be flying along after hitting the target area and suddenly the aircraft would give a lurch; Ernie had dozed off. I awoke from a deep dream one night to see two of the fuel pressure lights glowing; I broke records getting to the petrol cocks in the rest position. When I plugged back into the intercom Ernie said, "I think there's something wrong with the engines, Curly, we lost power a moment ago." I replied, "That's all right, skipper, I've just fixed it."

'One aircraft crashed on take-off. The flight engineer was a Jonah who had experienced many crashes and as soon as the kite stopped he was out of the upper escape hatch rapidly, onto the wing and jumped to the ground and, expecting the bombs to go off, shot off away from the crashed Halifax. In the dark he could not see where he was going and suddenly he fell over something; it was one of the bombs which had fallen off the aircraft on the first impact. Next day he came into the mess at Fayid with a leg swathed in bandages. He said his speed away from the bomb, with his damaged leg, was much greater than his impact speed.

'We were visited by Marshal of the Royal Air Force Lord Trenchard, and that great man gave us a speech.

'Our trip to Tobruk in H-How W1151 ended in a landing without brakes; we seemed to run on for ever until crossing a road wiped off our tailwheel assembly and slowed us down, helped by yards of telephone wires which wrapped around the two engines we kept running.'

Raids on Tobruk, christened 'Mail-Runs', were frequent. An Australian war correspondent flew on one of the raids. He had been on the wrong end of many raids on the town but this time he was dishing it out instead of taking it. His account appeared in an official Forces news-sheet:

After battling for hours through a violent electric storm, an RAF armada of Halifaxes and Wellingtons met over Tobruk one night recently.

It was the hundredth raid on Tobruk since the Axis troops occupied it, and the bombers dropped many tons of high explosives on jetties, storehouses and shipping. The attack was probably the most concentrated the little harbour has received. It was a spectacular performance seen from the co-pilot's seat in the squadron leader's Halifax.

For the men who went on the raid it was only a routine affair. For Squadron Leader Peter Warner and his crew it was their eighteenth consecutive raid on Tobruk. They had been in fourteen raids over Germany including three 1,000 bomber raids.

It was my first raid and not a routine matter. Our aircraft, 'Minnie the Moocher', had a winged arrow with the motto 'Straight to the point' on it. It had helped smash the Renault works near Paris, bombed the *Tirpitz* and helped to destroy Rostock.

I looked at the fearsome cargo of heavy bombs and thought of the little wharf at Tobruk where, one night just a year ago, I had sat round with men from the 2/13 Battalion of the AIF waiting for the warships to take us from Tobruk. We were to have been the last Australians to be evacuated but although we waited until 0300 the warships never came. They had been attacked by German bombers, and the one we were to have boarded had been sunk. The Battalion stayed until, with the British troops, it fought its way through the Tobruk corridor, and it made a glorious bayonet charge which drove the Germans from El Duda ridge.

But that night we were feeling bitter, and when the German bombers came over and dropped their bombs nearby some hard things were said about them. It was our target for tonight, and two of our bombs hit it fair and square. It was a long journey. Ahead vivid lightning flashes, rippled down from stars sheer to earth. Then lightning split the sky directly ahead of us. I thought of those tons of bombs just beneath. When the storm was behind us we were heading straight for flak and searchlights were sweeping the sky. Brilliant flares were cascading down from the Wellingtons and I could see every detail of that once familiar harbour. There was the derelict *San Giorgio*, used as a landing stage, there was the wreck of the gallant little *Ladybird*.

We turned over the point where the hospital is. Light ack-ack was being pumped up at us in blazing spurts of colour, and heavy guns were blazing from every point. A Wellington was caught in the cone of searchlights, and lurid flame was pouring into that cone. By the light of those steadily dropping flares, magnificently placed, the beach, roads, wharves, ships and marsh shone whitely.

We went into the thick of it. 'Bomb doors open' called the navigator. I could hear the bump, bump, bump of exploding shells. They must be close because, I can hear them above the engines. 'Left, left, right,' called the navigator. The pilot was manoeuvring for the target and watching the direction of the flak at the same time. Twenty-two and in charge of all this I thought, and my next thought was that I wished he'd let those bombs go. 'Bombs gone,' said the navigator. A searchlight caught us and I could see black puffs of bursting shells in the beam. Two parachutes billowed down. They had hit a Wellington.

The navigator was shouting, 'Oh what a beauty, two of them right on the shed at the shore end of the wharf'. I saw three great mushrooms of earth leaping up from the quay and shore. Somebody else's bombs were bursting.

The searchlight still held us but we were tearing for the open sea. We passed into the comforting dark. For twenty minutes we circled the area, watching the bombing until it was over, and then we turned for home. Another routine job was finished.

The crew I flew with came from the British Isles but Australians and New Zealanders were included in the others. Two of them Sergeant Ben Gibbons, of Sydney, and Albert Declerk, of Newcastle, have piloted Halifax bombers on nearly forty long operational flights, both have been over Germany over twenty times.

The long expected attack by the Eighth Army began in bright moonlight on the night of 23 October, at El Alamein. The squadron Halifaxes attacked the retreating Afrika Korps at the Sollum-Halfaya pass area in low level raids.

All the crews were declared tour-expired at the same time and the Halifaxes were taken from Derna, on the Cyranaica Plateau, to an airstrip known as Kilo 40. What happened to the aircraft will shortly be told in another chapter, but Matthew Holliday returned home by sea and air to join No 77 Squadron. His second tour has already been described.

Before moving back to rejoin No 10 Squadron at Melbourne, in Yorkshire, here is a poem written by Sergeant Steer, a gunner in a crew which did not return.

The Reaper

The aircraft droning up above,
The aircrew dozing in it.
Can all become a tangled wreck
In less than half a minute?

'But how?' you ask, and well you may,
You who stay on the ground,
The answer to the question is
The Reaper is around.

He plods the lonely skies at night,
His black beard dangling low,
His beetled eyebrows, long, thin nose,
His eyes a fiery glow.

Then suddenly he stops – he laughs
An ugly sinful laugh,
And swings his scythe along the skies
As though 'twere cutting chaff.

He hurries where his victim drones,
'A Halifax!' he cries,
'I'd sooner prang a Halifax
Than anything that flies.'

He creeps behind, his scythe aloft,
His evil lips drawn tight,
And with a cry of, 'Die, you dogs!'
He'll swish with all his might.

So aircrew take this warning,
Look out – and search the skies.
Remember – perhaps it's your turn next
To hear the Reaper's cries.

Wing Commander Carter was the squadron commanding officer at Melbourne when the airmen arrived back from the Middle East. In February Wing Commander D. W. Edmunds took over the squadron, which came under 42 Base, of which Air Commodore G. A. Walker, whom we met earlier, was in command.

Berlin and Essen were among the squadron's early targets in 1943 and many Ruhr targets, Hamburg and Stuttgart were bombed in the first half of the year. The squadron took part in the great fire raids on Hamburg in July and August. Les Fuller was a gunner with the squadron at this time, flying in O-Orange:

'In the early hours of the morning on 3 August as we approached Hamburg, the pilot, Flying Officer J. G. Jenkins, directed me to vacate the mid-upper turret and drop Window from the flare chute on the starboard side. Several large parcels were stacked here, the brown paper wrapping opened in readiness for the dropping. While back at Melbourne, during the long wait on the dispersal area, I had carefully positioned the packages within easy reach to avoid perspiring; working with the excessive amount of clothing worn by necessity against the intense cold of high altitude flying caused perspiration which froze easily in our clothing with very discomforting consequences.

'On leaving the Boulton Paul turret and after several hours of flying in total darkness, I was completely night vision adapted

Early Marks of 10 Squadron Halifaxes

and could see very well in the darkness of the rear half of our Halifax, "Farouk" (the name given to this aircraft by its former crew, because of Middle East associations). Sitting down on the floor over the rear end of the bomb bay, where a step was formed by a drop in the floor level, near the flare chute, I connected up to the oxygen supply and prepared the bundles of Window for dropping.

'Each bundle comprised hundreds of metallic strips about 15 inches long and ½ inch wide and about as thick as average paper. The strips were pressed together to form blocks about four inches wide and 3 inches deep, held together compactly by a piece of string, tied around each bundle, one third of the way up. Before dropping, the string had to be rolled down the bundle to within ¾ inch from the end; the bundle was held at the tied end in one hand, and the opposite end was fanned across the extremity by the free hand to separate the strips along the length of the bundle, so that when dropped throught the chute, there would be a maximum separation of the pieces to swamp the enemy's radar screens below and so hide the bomber force.

'Window had been dropped initially on the first of the four great Hamburg raids on 24/25 July and was an instant success. The chaos Window had obviously created, was evident from the cessation of the searchlights, flak and lack of activity by night fighters.

'Instructions at briefing were that the dropping procedure was to be rigidly adhered to, to make Window successful as a protection for the bomber force flying together, and I naturally stuck strictly to orders. It was difficult to appreciate the magic of these metal strips at the time, because they were so very simple and yet so very effective.

'I had many misgivings about being out of the mid-upper turret during this critical period over the target area, when the sky was illuminated by searchlights, with the conflagration below and fighter flares descending from above and when night fighter activity was probably at its maximum. However, the squadron order was for mid-upper gunners to drop the Window and no one queried it, although some aircrews thought that perhaps the wireless operator could do this duty.

'We were now flying over the North Sea and approaching the enemy coast. I was not aware of the weather conditions outside;

(*Top*) Take off in a Mark II Series 1a (Special). (*Below*) Overhaul of a 10 Squadron Halifax (note damage below rear turret)

my view was restricted to what was visible through the opening of the flare chute: about eight inches square. Bundles of window were going down and separating into thousands of metallic strips. The rear gunner was scanning the darkness of the sky for night fighters and I could see the movement of the turret in the darkness. This was our tenth operation and fourth visit to Hamburg. Only a quarter of the city now remained, we were told at the briefing: tonight would finish it!

'Suddenly the situation changed dramatically, "Monica" began to pip and the intervals between the pips were noticeably decreasing, indicating that an aircraft was approaching with a speed greater than ours. The rear gunner had not spotted the night fighter on our tail.

'The pilot quickly instructed the gunner to locate the enemy, realising that the mid upper turret was unmanned. The Canadian rear gunner reported a Ju88 about 400 yards off the port quarter, slightly above us, obviously preparing to attack. The next instant I heard the rear gunner confirm that the fighter was coming in fast on a curve of pursuit, and instructed the pilot to dive to port immediately, to increase the fighter's deflection as he sighted on us. The response was instantaneous, for in a moment "Farouk" had plunged into a steep dive to port and the bundles of Window around me left the floor and clung to the roof of the aircraft, as they were left behind in the dive. I was rolled over and my legs floated upwards. While I was rolling on the floor and feeling for anything to hang onto, a noise like a cascade of large hailstones hit the metallic fuselage. The fighter had fired a good burst and the experience was more terrifying than anything I had encountered previously. We had been hit from comparatively close range, from a position approaching our stern and had been raked by this fire as the bomber dived. As the rounds struck the metal on the port side of the Halifax, many ricocheted off, and in the pitch darkness I saw scores of circular areas of glowing metal, red hot for an instant, from the glancing impact, before they went out; it was a shock to see this from the receiving end.

'Still pressed to the floor by the force of G from our downward dive, I felt certain that the damage sustained by the fusillade was bringing us down and expected we would catch on fire any second. The rear gunner was firing and waves of cordite fumes from his guns swept through the fuselage, and the smell as it passed revived me with hope, despite the firing difficulties in such a steep dive.

'The rear gunner reported that the fighter had broken away on the starboard side, and the pilot called us on the intercom to see if there were any injuries. Amazingly no one had. I had just regained my feet when the rear gunner reported the fighter was some 400 yards off, some 60 degrees off our longitudinal axis. Hearing this, the pilot somewhat reluctantly ordered the bomb bays to be opened and the bombs jettisoned. "Farouk" rose upwards and we all felt relieved to be rid of our lethal load.

'The fighter came in again; we dived starboard and commenced firing. I was pitched sideways as projectiles from the Ju88 hit the tailplane area and starboard side of the fuselage, in the region of the rear turret, with shattering force. The noise sounded like a death rattle to me. The clouds of cordite fumes from the rear turret drifted past me as I searched for the oxygen tube bayonet to disconnect the supply, in order to return to my turret. The impact of rounds bursting into glowing red hot circles, like enormous sparks, gave a frightening effect. I was nauseated by the sight, sound and feel of the force of the rounds and shells as "Farouk" absorbed them all. I was astonished to realise that the rear gunner was still alive. I picked myself up from the floor again and managed to crawl along the floor and eventually reached my turret. I pulled up the hinged seat, locked the catch, sat down, plugged into the intercom and operating the control column, swung the turret round to starboard to try and locate the fighter. In my frantic effort to pick up the threads of the combat, so that I could now join in, I heard a lot of conversation between the gunner, pilot and flight engineer and was amazed and delighted to learn that the fighter had just blown up in mid-air. He had been hit by the gunner and the flight engineer confirmed that it had burst into flames and spiralled slowly downwards out of control.

'After heaping praise on the rear gunner, the pilot asked the navigator for the course home. We had dropped our load, and though we were disappointed it had not been on Hamburg, we were thankful to be alive.

'Soon after I had entered the turret I noticed the sky had grown rather brightly coloured and as we flew along the colouring increased in vividness, with red and purple predominating. I associated this with the burning and destruction of the night fighter, but shortly afterwards became suspicious that something was wrong. A chronic headache developed so I reported the facts to the pilot who promptly told me to check my oxygen supply – I found it was not connected. I plugged in and all was well again.

'The rear gunner reported extensive damage to the elevators on both sides of the turret. The pilot had expected to hear this as he was finding the controls heavy. Taff Jenkins told us about a 20 mm cannon shell hole alongside him through which the wind was whistling continuously. The journey back was dangerous, we had a damaged aircraft, we did not have the protection of Window or the main stream, we were a straggler, ideal prey to a lurking night fighter. We kept our eyes skinned in our turrets.

'Once back over England we lowered the undercarriage to check that it was functioning properly and were relieved when it went down. We notified Flying Control of our condition, confirmed we had dropped our bombload and after waiting a while we were given instructions to land, along with a warning of a capricious crosswind. We were the first Halifax back, and therefore had to be careful not to block the runway to prevent the others from landing.

'The pilot ordered most of us to the rest position, in accordance with crash drill. We touched down safely and "Farouk" raced along the runway. Then the treacherous crosswind caught us, and lacking the proper controls to correct our deviation, we were swung off the runway and raced along the grassy surface bumping and rocking perilously, wondering apprehensively what was going to happen next.

'The lights were on in the rest position, but there were no windows to see through for a glimpse outside of the aircraft, where in any case it was still pitch dark. We braced ourselves even harder and waited anxiously, the pilot remained silent because he had enough to concentrate on as it was.

'The bumpy ride soon ended when "Farouk" rose gently, lop-sidedly and then fell downwards, before coming to a halt, with a final lurch to port. The pilot told us to get out as quickly as possible, as he cut the engines. We needed no second bidding and as we jumped the crash tender and ambulance arrived alongside, as did a crowd of ground crew.

'The sudden quietness, after hours of roaring Merlin engine

Crashed 'Farouk' at Melbourne with (l to r)
J. Ollerton, J. Whatley, E. Saddington, A. L. Fuller, J. G. Jenkins, R. Hurst, J. Ryan. Sitting, ground crew.

A Canadian crew check the bomb bay. This picture shows how impossible it was to hack away the floor.

noise on our ears, gave one a floating feeling and an unreal atmosphere in which to terminate this operation of the Battle of Hamburg.

'The ground crews soon informed us of what had happened. "Farouk" had been brought to a premature halt by running up onto a shallow mound with the port wheel and then down into a ditch, which caused the Halifax's undercarriage to partially collapse in the hollow, damaging the portside propellers and engines. It was a stroke of luck that the ditch was there in our path because the aircraft was heading straight for a nissen hut housing ground crews awaiting the return of the other aircraft. It was certain the hut would have been written off by the bomber had we not stopped. The airmen, forewarned, had evacuated the hut in a great hurry and it was they that arrived at the same time as the crash wagon. A van collected us and we were driven to the briefing room where cigarettes and coffee were liberally handed round before debriefing.

'An officer of Air rank, who was present in the room, joined in the interrogation and listened intently to the details of the combat. Several times he made comments like "good show" and "well done" and in the end congratulated Flight Sergeant Hurst on his destruction of the night fighter and our pilot on his fine effort in piloting the crippled Halifax back to base.

'We complained about the folly of a mid upper gunner dropping Window instead of his proper function during the critical time. He said he would make a report to Group Headquarters.

'Later, when the crews were debriefed, we found that our combat with the Ju88 had been witnessed and logged by other crews and squadrons, and our claim was confirmed. The pilot and rear gunner were put up for immediate awards: a DFC for Flying Officer J. G. Jenkins and a DFM for Flight Sergeant R. Hurst were accompanied by a personal telegram from "Bomber" Harris, congratulating them both on their skill and bravery.

'After a meal and a sleep we examined "Farouk" by daylight. The cannon shell damage near the cockpit was a close call for the pilot, whilst in the mainplane there were two large holes, about six inches in diameter, on each side, made by shells, presumably when we went into steep dives at the beginning of our combat manoeuvres. Each hole was in a similar position on the port wing, as on the starboard, between the inner engine and the fuselage. It is hard to conceive how the shells went through the wings without causing major damage to the fuel tanks. The port engines and wing were damaged in the crash and "Farouk" DT792 was a write-off.

'Later on a modification was carried out on the operational aircraft: a chute was installed alongside the wireless operator and through the floor, for the dropping of Window. This allowed the wireless operator to listen out and discharge the bundles through the chute without any problems. This came about as a direct result of our report to Gus Walker, for it was he who was the Air rank officer who was at the debriefing. It subsequently transpired that No 10 Squadron had been the only squadron in which the mid upper gunner had dropped Window.

'On our next operation, to Mannheim, we had a new aircraft and it was named "Farouk II" by general agreement.'

A week after the last Hamburg raid, on 10 August, the squadron attacked Nuremberg and lost veteran Halifax II N-Nan JD198, which crashed into the Channel on the way home. A week later still the squadron participated in the well-known Peenemünde raid and thus delayed the launch of Germany's secret rocket weapons on Britain.

Les Fuller flew again with 'Taff' Jenkins again on 22 September, on their 14th operation. He takes up the story:

'In the afternoon, at briefing, Wing Commander Edmunds announced that a special honour had been paid to 10 Squadron in that one of our Halifaxes was to be fitted with a cine-camera which would operate automatically when the bombing run commenced and film, in colour, the inferno below, during the passage over the target area. It would be the first instance of a raid being filmed in this manner. The Commanding Officer revealed that the cine-camera had been fitted in the flare chute of the new N-Nan HR924, and that we were to fly it.

'I believe we were selected because of our recent completion of an H2S course, and were the only crew on the squadron at this time trained to operate this equipment. The new N-Nan had been allocated to the flight commander, Squadron Leader J. Sutton, but he was away doing the new H2S course. At this time H2S was so secret it was screened off with a black curtain and all members of the crew not directly associated with it were on their honour not to even look at the equipment, either working or switched off.

'The night operation was to Hanover and we took off at 1850 and the flight out was uneventful. As we approached the target we could see an ever increasing light in the distance as the pathfinders were releasing their coloured clusters. Cones of searchlights probed for the bombers. The atmosphere in the bomber grew tense as we waited the commencement of the bomb-aimer's patter. We had completely forgotten about the cine-camera. However, it was not the bomb-aimer's voice we heard, but the rear gunner's. The latter's Canadian voice came unexpectedly over the intercom, reporting a fighter below, a Me110, which appeared tc be manoeuvring in preparation for an attack. I could not see the fighter from the mid-upper turret. The rear gunner told us an attack was imminent, but he could not get his guns to bear, he had extended the hydraulic jacks to the full but the fighter was too far forward for him. We dived, but just an instant too late. A devastating burst of fire streamed upwards and raked the fuselage, seemingly from tail to nose. The burst of fire struck on the downward dive of our combat manoeuvre.

'After firing the attacker disappeared in the darkness. The attack had not been the usual curve of pursuit attack, but one with upward firing cannon known as *Schräge Musik'*.

'Once it had been ascertained that there were no injuries the pilot continued on course for the target which we were now approaching. On the run-in the bomb doors would not open; obviously the attack had caused some damage and this was confirmed when it was found that the H2S also was not functioning. On investigation it was discovered that the perspex cover had been shot completely away, leaving a large oval gaping hole some five feet by three through which we could see the searchlights below. There was hydraulic fluid which had leaked from a fractured pipe.

'Sergeant Monty Banks, the flight engineer, found a projectile from the attack embedded in the bullet proof plate glass protective panel positioned directly behind the pilot's head and when he withdrew it the round was still hot enough to burn his finger and thumb, causing him to drop it.

'Unable to drop our load our main consideration was to get away from the target area but we agreed to carry on over the target and return with the main bomber force, thereby retaining the protection of Window, which was still being dropped through a chute at regular intervals by the wireless operator.

'The night fighters began laying a lane of powerful flares, to silhouette the bombers as they left illuminated Hanover and re-entered the cover of darkness. Each flare lit up an extensive area of the sky and two separate lines, placed a considerable distance apart, laterally, so that each bomber had to fly between them, presented a frightening challenge. The fighters orbited above, to spot a bomber outlined against the descending flares. The lane extended in length as the mainstream of bombers flew out of the target area and more flares drifted down on their parachutes from the fighters.

'We ran the gauntlet successfully and now had the problem of what to do about our 4,000 lb bomb and incendiaries. We tried the doors again without any luck so it was suggested that the bomb be dropped on to the two long hinged panels, joining at the centre hoping that the great weight would force them apart. The pilot and engineer thought the risk too great; there was no guarantee it would work and we would be left with a loose bomb. We tried the undercarriage and found that did not work either; this meant a belly landing with a lethal load aboard. The pilot now decided that we would have to jump for it but the engineer raised our spirits by suggesting that we cut a pipe which would cause the bomb doors to open. He set about finding the correct pipe. A small hacksaw blade was produced and in a few minutes the pipe was cut. Nothing happened, the bomb doors stayed firmly shut. Someone then suggested hacking a hole in the plywood floor and, through the opening made, possibly forcing the long doors open, so that the bomb could be dropped safely, even if we had to try and shake it off, assuming this was feasible.

'In desperation it was agreed to try this and I was selected to do the cutting with the turret axe. The flight engineer took up a position in the astrodome to search for fighters while I was away from the turret.

'Unfortunately the floor area necessary for the opening was remote from the oxygen supply connection, so it meant working without the gas. The axe was more like a hatchet, with a 15 inch long handle, was very sharp but the blade made little impression on the tough laminated timber. Before long the lack of oxygen took its toll and this combined with the physical exertion compelled me to return to the oxygen connection and plug in for a time, to rejuvenate myself and relieve the chronic headache that had developed, along with the impaired vision.

'The ¾ inch thick plywood, with successive layers of grains running at right angles to each other, resisted the axe blows so the original idea had to be scaled down, and only a small hole was cut, just sufficient to put one foot through. I took a long whiff of oxygen and told the crew that I was about to try and tread the bomb free. I put as much weight as I could on it but it still held fast on its mountings. The pilot told me to abandon the idea.

'During the operation my intercom plug had probably dangled into an oil pool for when I plugged in a long squeaking noise became audible. The pilot told me to disconnect and stay off the system, so I could not keep in touch with what was happening.

'Eventually we reached Melbourne and got in touch with Flying Control. The Commanding Officer ordered us to abandon the aircraft. There was enough fuel for 25 minutes' flying so the pilot headed out to sea, telling us the order in which we were to bale out. The front escape hatch was to be used so that the pilot could see that the rest of the crew had abandoned before he switched over to "George" and left himself. The flight engineer helped the pilot on with his parachute as N-Nan was making for the North Sea, beyond Hull.

'The vision of plunging headlong out into the inky darkness at 0200 was a frightening thought and the only consolation and spur to going through with it was the knowledge that it offered the best prospects for survival.

'Ground defence had been alerted and we began circling Patrington, near Hull, at 8,000 feet with navigation lights on. Searchlights picked us up as we prepared to jump. We shared our cigarettes so that we all had one to smoke once we landed. The rear gunner jumped first and while I was waiting my turn I thought of the lecture we had received some four months earlier at the HCU Riccall. I decided to fall forward into the opening and dive out headlong.

'Just as I was about to leave the Halifax I was shocked to see that we were being fired on from below; somebody was firing at us with a machine-gun. At this juncture I knelt on the floor and rolled forward through the aperture and out into space.

'As I dropped through the cool fresh air, with the roar of

engines still in my ears, I started counting away the recommended ten seconds before pulling the rip-cord. I had reached five when I tugged the handle on the pack and flung it away, rather than wait unnecessarily longer, to get the first part of the ordeal over. The bundle of silk opened with a shocking jolt and the two heavy webbing straps snapped taut and smacked forcibly against both of my ears and made them sting.

'The searchlights appeared to have gone out as I descended in the darkness, although there was no feeling or impression of moving downwards at all, only that I was spinning backwards and forwards as the lines above were twisting and untwisting. I felt helpless, suspended in the air. At intervals loud cracking noises were evident aloft, when air was being expelled from pockets in the swelling silk canopy.

'Naturally I wondered where I would land, and felt comforted that I was still wearing my Mae West. I could barely discern some tree-tops racing up at me with surprising speed. I just had time to reach up, grasp the harness straps connecting to the cord lines above and draw my legs upwards with knees bent, before hitting the ground with a much greater force than expected. As soon as I landed I realised I had missed the trees and landed in a rough ploughed field. Luckily my legs were drawn up but the back of my head hit a clod of earth and I think I was momentarily knocked out. When I came to, and had recovered my breath I released my harness and took stock of my bearings as best as I could. I put the webbing round the base of the nearest tree and locked it.

'It was with difficulty that I traversed the ploughed field wearing fur-lined flying boots, but I reached grassed land and had not proceeded far before being challenged, out of the shadows, by a soldier.

'A fixed bayonet, placed perilously close to my throat, caused me to shout out "RAF" to the challenge. He inspected me with his torch and then told me his post had been alerted to look for us. He took me to a hut where another soldier made some tea; they were amazed to have an operational aircrew member among them on their gunnery site.

'When more ground defence men came in off duty, they admitted firing at us: they thought our Halifax was a Dornier 217 and in the searchlight beams had seen black objects falling out of the underside of the fuselage; assuming these were bombs, they commenced shooting at us with machine guns. Fortunately a radio message from their headquarters informed all posts that the circling aircraft was an RAF bomber from which the crew were baling out. They had successfully shot down an intruder some nights earlier and were after another.

'While I was drinking tea a message was radioed to their headquarters announcing my arrival, a message was sent back for my benefit saying that others from the crew had also been picked up and I would be collected later. Seeking to reward my rescuers I told them where my parachute was, thinking it would make some nice underclothes for their girl friends. I thought the RAF would have no further use for it. However, I was wrong, because personnel from the parachute section came later to collect all the parachutes, which were returned to use after inspection for damage and repacking. When we arrived at headquarters we were each given a bed for the night before being returned to the squadron. It was good to be reunited again after our enforced separation and we related our adventures after abandoning N-Nan on its first and last operation.

'The luckiest member of the crew was probably our rear gunner, Dick Hurst. He landed close to the edge of a cliff from where he could hear the sound of the waves beating on the shore below him. He moved inland for safety. After walking for some minutes he came to a barbed wire fence, laid in the military manner, and managed, with great difficulty, to wriggle through it. Continuing on he again ran into a similar barrier and again succeeded in extricating himself from the entanglement. He then encountered a third fence and again crawled through the twisting circles of the jagged wire. Beyond this he arrived at a roadside, boarded by hedging. As he climbed over to the highway he saw a large notice which read 'DANGER, MINED LAND – KEEP OUT'. It was a nasty shock which had an amusing sequel, for when the RAF wanted their parachute retrieved a team of Army specialists travelled up from London to rescue it!

'Monty Banks landed on the tiled roof of a large outhouse and bumped and rolled down the sloping surface; the billowing chute retarded his fall. Coming to the edge of the roofing he dropped down on to the village policeman. The two men were covered by the white canopy and floundered in the folds. The constable was bewildered, having no idea of what was happening, but after a struggle, and many harsh words, a hurried explanation by the shaken flight engineer retrieved the situation. They went to the policeman's home and over half a bottle of whisky a detailed narrative of the night's events was given.

'The skipper was the only one who retained his grip on the rip cord handle, when he pulled it to open the chute, and he proudly showed his trophy when we met up. I remember flinging my rip cord away, probably in jubilation when the chute opened. They were supposed to be returned to the parachute section; the penalty for not doing so was the purchase of drinks to those working in the department.

'It was a curious fact that those of us who baled out head first found an L shaped tear on our battle dress trousers at the front, about halfway up on the thigh on the right leg and those who went out feet first had a similar rip in the seat of their pants, also on the right hand side. We discussed this numerous times but failed to find a satisfactory solution to the mystery.

'I was the only one to sustain cuts to my ears, resulting from the straps clouting me when the chute opened.

'The next morning Wing Commander Edmunds, the Commanding Officer, entered our room, asked us how we were and where was the film? "What film?" we asked collectively. "The coloured film, of course." And then it registered. The film was at the bottom of the North Sea with the Halifax.

'It was a bitter blow to the Wing Commander, who had visited us specifically to enquire of the film of which he had such high hopes. Some strong words were spoken for a few seconds but then the CO, who was very human, cut short his reproof and admitted that in similar circumstances, he would probably have forgotten all about the cine-camera. In any case, it was doubtful whether the equipment had commenced to operate at the time the attack took place; but if it had, then the *Schräge Musik* attack would have been faithfully recorded.

'We journeyed back to Melbourne somewhat depressed over the film affair and on arrival were debriefed in the usual way. After lunch in the mess we retired to bed for some well earned sleep. Next day we had to report to the medical officer and on being found fit were given four days survivors' leave.

'Flight Lieutenant "Paddy" Keene, the squadron adjutant and a great friend of all aircrew, made an application for each of us for membership of the Caterpillar Club and in due course we received our membership card, plus a small gold caterpillar, with ruby eyes, in the form of a brooch, with name and rank engraved on the reverse side.

'One of the consequences of this operation on Hanover was the growing suspicion that the night fighters were homing on the new H2S equipment, which was being more frequently used. On several occasions we had been intercepted, whereas other crews, without H2S, had not been troubled by fighters. We discussed this ourselves and the possibility emerged and soon became a firm belief.

'The skipper reported the matter one morning at the crew conference and the Intelligence Officer agreed to submit the theory to Group Headquarters for their consideration. Later, when we were all assembled in the Briefing Room, we were told that an investigation had been carried out and it was considered extremely unlikely that the Germans had equipment capable of homing on to H2S. However, some months later, at the completion of our tour, it was revealed officially one morning that night fighters were now known to be homing on to the H2S equipment, and at this time nearly all the squadron aircraft were equipped with the navigational aid.

'Before proceeding on leave the crew examined the bomb bay of a parked Halifax with the ground crew, to study the operating mechanism. As soon as we saw the arrangement of the robust mechanism for opening and closing the doors and the fixings for the bombs, it was realised how hopeless had been the task I had tried to accomplish on the way back from the target.

'On our return from leave we carried on flying by night slowly notching up what seemed an excessive number of operations necessary for us to complete our tour. We learned that an appellation had been bestowed upon our pilot by the other crews, and often heard stories told about "Bring em back alive Jenkins" – a well earned and suitable sobriquet.'

CHAPTER SEVEN

Active Australians

In the last chapter we left the ground crew and 10 Squadron Halifaxes in the Middle East. The squadron amalgamated with some of 76 Squadron and became No 462 RAAF, at Fayid, on 23 September 1942. With very few exceptions personnel in the new squadron were drawn from the RAF, but the intention was that the original personnel should be replaced by Australians.

One of the interesting features of this squadron was the training of flight engineers. Matthew Holliday mentioned his 'do it yourself' makeshift course, but No 462 Squadron had the first flight engineers to be trained outside Britain. The training of these specialist personnel in the Middle East proved a success; only a dozen were wanted, but hundreds of applications were received from fitters. Among the twelve selected were five Australians, of which four came from Kalgoorlie, and these five were trained and transferred from ground to air crew.

The first operation of the squadron took place on 29 January 1943 when six aircraft attacked the rail ferry at Messina, Sicily, and during the succeeding months the main task of the squadron was the blasting of harbours and shipping in the island preparatory to the invasion that summer. In March it attacked troop concentrations, motor transport and airfields.

In May an outstanding story of courage and endurance was provided by one of the crews when they were forced to ditch in the sea seventy miles west of Tripoli and drifted in their dinghy for ten and a half days before reaching the shore. Detailed to attack enemy troop concentrations and motor transport in Tunisia, the Halifax was forced to make a ditching in very rough sea. The dinghy was released and all the crew climbed safely into it with their emergency pack. The crew, captained by Warrant Officer N. Vertican, were all very seasick at first and water was rationed at one-seventh of a pint per day and food on a similarly drastic scale.

After ten and a half days the dinghy drifted ashore between Tripoli and Homs, with the crew in a state of exhaustion after their ordeal. On landing they were looked after by Arabs who gave them food and water, took them to their village and sheltered them until the arrival of a Sudanese Desert Patrol. The captain, who already held the DFC, received the CGM and an immediate commission. Three other members of the crew were also decorated.

In September, S-Sugar W1169 made its 50th operational flight, the trip coinciding with its completion of its second tour of operations. This veteran aircraft had been flown to the Middle East by 76 Squadron.

During October, 886 operational hours were flown, in attacks on airfields and ports in Greece and Crete as well as in Rhodes and other islands of the Dodecanese. The Martisa airfield on Rhodes was rendered completely unserviceable by the persistent attention of 462's Halifaxes. Until December the squadron continued its operations over the Aegean Sea, but early in that month it began diversionary bombing raids on harbours to draw the fire while other aircraft went in low to mine waters. Salonica, Piraeus and Suda Bay were among many of the places visited. A new task in 1944 was leaflet dropping on Crete, Rhodes, Leros and Samos.

In March 1944 No 462 Squadron was disbanded and replaced by the newly formed No 614 RAF Squadron. By that time the squadron personnel included 200 RAAF ground staff personnel and a fair sprinkling of RAAF aircrew. Five months later, on 14 August, No 462 RAAF Squadron was reformed at Driffield where they were equipped with Halifax Mark III's. The first commanding officer was an Australian, Acting Squadron Leader D. Shannon, appointed to the acting rank of wing commander and posted from the sister 466 Squadron. The first operation, to Watten, was carried out on 25 August. While attacking Sterkrade, a Halifax was hit twice while over the target and set on fire. The navigator and bomb aimer were wounded but the crew brought it back to England in the face of what seemed at that time impossible odds.

Pilot Officer E. McCindle, the skipper from Melbourne, in describing the incident said that they were making their bombing run when they received a direct hit from heavy flak. The engineer's compartment was badly damaged and the bulkhead was set on

No 462 Squadron Halifax II in the Middle East

No 462 Squadron's Operations Record map at Driffield showing the heaviest concentration of raids on the Ruhr.

fire. At almost the same time, the Halifax was hit in the nose and great holes were blown in it. Then the engineer reported that the aircraft was on fire.

'I ordered the crew to bale out,' said the pilot, 'but as I did so, the wounded navigator called out in great pain and his voice drowned my orders which were not heard by the rest of the crew.'

The bomb aimer had not reported his injury until afterwards, but together with the wireless operator he went to the aid of the wounded navigator who could not be moved from the nose. Meanwhile the engineer had gone aft to fight the flames and had succeeded in putting them out with extinguishers and his bare hands. He then went to the rear of the aircraft, without oxygen although they were flying at a great height, and collected some dressings for the injured navigator. However, there were not enough of these dressings and the wireless operator tore up his own parachute although he knew he might need it and in this way improvised additional dressings for the wounded man. As soon as the navigator was as comfortable as his comrades could make him, the bomb aimer took over the wounded man's duties and gave the pilot the course home.

During the attack the port engine had been hit and was working at reduced efficiency, but the pilot did not feather it because he was anxious to get his wounded crew back as soon as possible. When they arrived within ten miles of the Channel however, the port outer finally packed up and he had to feather it. Air Speed Indicators had been put out of action and the other instruments were also useless, but the pilot battled on and made a safe landing at an emergency landing field.

Another outstanding operation, in October, resulted in Pilot Officer A. J. Cockerill, an Australian, being awarded the squadron's only DSO. He was the captain of a Halifax detailed to attack Duisberg. Nearing the target the aircraft was illuminated in the searchlights and subjected to much anti-aircraft fire. A fragment of shrapnel which tore through the windscreen struck the pilot in the eye and the wound was so severe that he momentarily lost consciousness. Although the aircraft went into a dive, the pilot regained consciousness just in time to level out and persisted in completing the bombing run, although the aircraft was still illuminated by searchlights. Although weak from loss of blood and suffering from shock, the pilot remained at the controls but was unable to see his instruments and the bomb aimer stood by to give the necessary instructions. It was with this assistance that the skipper flew the Halifax to England and, calling upon his last remaining strength, landed the aircraft safely. His citation concluded: 'By his skill, courage and fortitude this officer set an example of the highest order.'

In four months of routine bombing operations, up to Christmas, 39 targets were attacked, of which Duisberg and Essen were hit four times and Cologne three.

On 27 December the squadron began its move to 100 Group, a newly formed specialist Group which waged a war of its own, a war of the ether, jamming and confusing the enemy's radio and utterly confounding his fighter controllers. In addition to 'spoof raids' when Window was dropped in huge quantities to give the impression that a much larger force was attacking than was actually the case, aircraft of the squadron dropped bombs and incendiaries, flew protective patrols and sometimes bombed with the main forces.

Another operation which highlighted the airworthiness of the Halifax and the courage of one Australian wireless operator. In March 1945, just as the aircraft was leaving the target, Frankfurt, it was hit and severely damaged by anti-aircraft fire. One member of the crew was killed and Warrant Officer K. J. Dennis was badly wounded, being hit in both legs and having one foot almost severed. Despite his wounds and the loss of much blood the wireless operator persevered with his duties until the badly damaged aircraft had been landed.

In the four months of the Special Duties Operations, the squadron carried out 63 different operations, including operating on nineteen different nights in March. The squadron had carried out 1,069 sorties by the time VE day arrived, at which time it was operational from Foulsham.

No 460 RAAF Squadron formed in East Anglia during November 1941, operating with Wellington bombers. Nine months later the squadron began converting to Halifaxes. Squadron aircraft included B-Baker DT481 and F-Freddie W7781. Only a few Halifaxes were issued to the squadron and they were not used on raids. Before operations could commence the squadron converted again to become the first RAAF Lancaster squadron.

The Australian No 466 Squadron was formed at Driffield, Yorkshire, in No 4 Group on 10 October 1942, as a medium bomber squadron equipped with Wellington III aircraft. Although the ultimate intention was the creation of an all-Australian squadron, the majority of the aircrew and many of the ground staff at the outset were RAF. The only Australian aircrew in the original formation were the squadron commander and the gunnery leader. The policy of replacing non-Australian personnel by Australian was a gradual process and after two years of operations some half the flying personnel including all captains of aircraft were Australian. Of the original fourteen captains, Britain, New Zealand, Canada and Malaya were represented but not Australian.

To gain some operational experience for his captains, the commanding officer, Wing Commander R. E. Bailey, arranged flights with No 102 Squadron, based at Pocklington. Accordingly on 15 November eight flew as second pilots in Halifax aircraft to raid Genoa, and were the first of several captains to do their 'second dickie' trips with 102 Squadron.

Towards the end of December No 466 Squadron commenced its move to Leconfield in appalling weather conditions. In the middle of January it commenced its operational career on sea mining at which its aircrew became expert. On this occasion the mines were laid off the Frisian Islands. Its first bombing attack was on Lorient two nights later.

Eight months and 787 sorties later, No 466 Squadron became non-operational owing to its conversion to Halifax II aircraft at the beginning of September 1943. From this date it became a heavy bomber squadron. Now the aircrew strength had changed in balance to 83 RAAF and 121 RAF personnel. Wing Commander D. T. Forsyth became the new commanding officer.

The Halifax training for aircrew was carried out at first at the conversion units at Riccall and Marston Moor. The majority of ground crews were attached to No 158 Squadron at Lissett and Nos 1653 and 1663 conversion units at Marston Moor and Rufforth for experience on Halifax maintenance. Later in the month Halifax II's began to arrive at Leconfield and training continued from base. During October, Halifax III's arrived and began to replace the earlier models. Training continued throughout November, interspersed with 46 sorties on air sea rescue work.

The squadron became operational once more on 1 December, covering old ground, when twelve aircraft carried out a Gardening mission off Terschelling Island.

Englishman George Haggard was one of the RAF aircrew on this first Halifax operation. He joined his Australian crew at 1658 Conversion Unit at Riccall. He had joined up as a wireless operator/air gunner in 1941 but was failed on eyesight, remustered to a flight mechanic until the medical standard was lowered for flight engineers. He passed out from St Athan proudly wearing his tapes and brevet, and, like many others, without ever having flown.

He says: 'I made the mistake of taking my first flight as second engineer on a fighter affiliation exercise, violent evasive action avoiding a Hurricane, and I was as sick as a dog. Not a recommended introduction to flying!

'The bomb-aimer was the only other English member of the crew; the skipper, Johnny Cairns, was by no means a typical Australian either in appearance or temperament. He was originally a pilot on Lancasters but had badly damaged one and so was put back on to twin-engined Wellingtons. I never had any doubts about flying with him; as engineer if your pilot didn't co-operate it could throw your fuel log and consumption completely out, but we always worked very well together. My only criticism, and this may have been shared with some of the rest of the crew, was that if anything, he was too conscientious. It tended to be a joke with the crew that on a routine flight he was inclined to make a bumpy landing, but if there had been any trouble he'd make a perfect three-point landing.

'My first operation coincided with the squadron's first on Halifaxes on 1 December, mine-laying off Ameland Island. It was notable only for the fact that the pilot's escape hatch flew open on take-off. This had happened previously on a cross-country flight and there was trouble when they aborted so the pilot decided to carry on and drop the mines. It was quite impossible to close the hatch against the slipstream. The Halifax didn't rise above 3,000 feet but it was an uncomfortable trip.'

The aircraft was diverted to Lissett on return where the crew enjoyed a good supper after their near open cockpit flying. Another squadron aircraft crashed on landing at Catfoss in very poor visibility, but no casualties were sustained.

No 466 SQUADRON
AT DRIFFIELD
(*Top*) In the hangar
(*Centre*) Loading bombs
(*Bottom*) The crew approach

Three days later the next operation was also mine-laying off Terschelling and George Haggard was back at base before 2000. The Australian squadron was the first of Bomber Command's main force to have H2S and during a training exercise on the 16th, one Halifax crashed near Cranswick due to fire spreading from the starboard outer engine to the mainplane killing three of the crew. The pilot was placed on the seriously ill list. After a number of this type of operation, the squadron's first attack on Germany with Halifax III's was made on Frankfurt on the night of 20 December. George Haggard was on this raid. His Halifax arrived ahead of ETA to a heavy barrage of flak, fighter flares and no cloud cover over the target. Despite this, the pilot decided to do a circuit and come in again so as to arrive on time. The thoughts of the flight engineer were, 'Let's drop our load, and get to hell out of it.' They landed at Catfoss on return. The raid achieved little. Sixteen aircraft from No 466 Squadron formed part of a bomber force of 650 aircraft. Although the raid opened accurately many of the main force were deceived by dummy TI's, and the majority of the bombs fell outside Frankfurt. One aircraft was shot up by a night fighter when committed to its bombing run, and on return it was forced to land at Foulsham. Two of the squadron's Halifaxes failed to return to base.

George Haggard continues: 'Our Christmas Eve trip didn't count. About two inches of hydraulic oil swilled about the rest position on take-off, so we aborted. We jettisoned our mines in open country and landed. The bomb aimer had to map read his way to where he'd dropped them; he was accompanied by the armament officer who had to defuse them and some members of the RAF Regiment who had to guard them. The rest of us had gone to a dance; we weren't very popular with the searchers as it took until midnight to locate the mines.'

George Haggard's fourth legitimate trip was to Berlin on 29 December. It was the first attack on the German capital by the squadron. On the way to the target one of the aircraft was attacked by a FW190 but sustained no damage. Four minutes later a Ju88 loomed up on the port quarter and as the gunners opened up it disappeared, only to take up a position directly astern. Both gunners fired while the sergeant pilot carried out evasive manoeuvring. George Haggard saw no fighters, but experienced widespread flak and it was the highest he ever flew in a Halifax, 24,800 feet. Most of the squadron had returned to base by midnight.

The squadron did not open its account for 1944 until 6 January, when seven aircraft mined off Schiermonnikoog. Its first major attack was directed at Berlin on 20th, with eighteen aircraft, two of which returned early through technical failures and one that did not return at all. Cloud conditions made observation of results difficult, but some good results were seen in the target area.

The following night, 16 aircraft were briefed to attack Madgeburg. Take-off time was 2000. George Haggard was on this raid and evasive action caused him to be airsick. There were plenty of fighter flares and heavy flak. Everyone reported very large-scale fires in the target area and bombed on them. Later, the Intelligence Officer told the crews that they had bombed a dummy target set up by the Germans on the wrong side of the river! Leader Ted Eagleton had a collision on return and landed with one rudder unserviceable.

George Haggard was more fortunate. On the circuit waiting their turn to land he suddenly heard on the intercom: 'Dive, Johnny, dive, dive, dive,' and down they went, just missing a collision with another Halifax head-on, going the wrong way round the circuit. Fortunately the other Halifax pilot climbed. After seven hours in the air this was the final straw to shatter already jangled nerves. One Halifax failed to return from the raid.

The month of January concluded with two more raids on the Reich capital. On 28th sixteen formed part of a force of 673 heavy bombers. George Haggard described that night:

'Take-off was at midnight; we had a second dickie from the conversion unit with us. Just after leaving, as we climbed into cloud, still with our navigation lights on, the bomb aimer yelled, "Dive, Johnny, dive, dive, dive!" Johnny said, "There's nothing there," but the bomb aimer screamed, "Dive, dive, dive," and we dived. There wasn't anything there – he may have seen the reflection of our own navigation lights on the clouds. Needless to say, we started this trip on edge. We arrived over Berlin at 0330 to be greeted by a heavy concentration of flak and an attack by a Me210 which did not score any hits. The hydraulics were holed by flak and I spent twenty minutes pumping the bomb doors closed. I was soaked in sweat although it was about minus 40 degrees outside. When I got back to the astrodome the fires from Berlin could still be seen glowing through the cloud.'

George Haggard landed at 0815. Three aircraft failed to return and another crash-landed at Matlaske with minor injuries to two of the crew. The squadron scribe wrote:

> Large explosions and fires were reported and smoke was seen rising to 20,000 feet. There were several inconclusive scrimages with enemy aircraft.

For the final January raid twelve aircraft were briefed to attack Berlin: only six attacked the target successfully; the remainder returned early owing to technical failures. The aircraft captained by Flying Officer J. H. Stevens sustained three attacks on the homeward route from enemy aircraft. Though the Halifax was slightly damaged on the third one, the pilot successfully evaded the attacking aircraft.

Berlin was again the target for 466 Squadron on 15 February, when twenty aircraft were airborne. The force this time consisted of 891 aircraft, the largest force despatched against the capital on the second last of the great winter raids. Flight Lieutenant Johnny Cairns was piloting C-Charlie, with flight engineer George Haggard flying his seventh operation. George says:

'My recollection of the raid itself is rather hazy. There was 7/10 cloud over the target and very little opposition. It was not until we were returning, and approaching the Zuider Zee that we struck trouble; when I went back to change to our final fuel tanks, each of which should have contained approximately 200 gallons of fuel, as soon as I switched the fuel cocks the engines started cutting in quick succession, much to the annoyance of the skipper, who wanted to know, "What the Hell is happening?" I changed back to the previous tanks and the engines picked up again. The pilot flung the Halifax about in an effort to clear any possible airlocks in the fuel pipelines. I then tried No 2 tanks again, only to get the same results. The engines started to miss again so the skipper turned the aircraft inland so that we would not have to bale out over the sea.

'We began going out at 12,000 feet; the bomb aimer stayed with the skipper to help him hold the aircraft level to allow the rest of us to get out, until Johnny ordered him out at 7,000 feet, by which time all the engines were dead. He followed himself after making sure the bomb aimer had escaped. The whole crew landed safely I was later to discover.

'Personally, I remember nothing between sitting on the edge of the escape hatch with the slip-stream on my legs and waking up flat on my back in a very dark, damp field, with the sound of the main stream going home above. Very depressing. After pushing my parachute into a ditch, I tried to find my way out of the field, only to keep walking either into deep dykes or barbed wire fences. Deciding the effort was a bit pointless until daylight, I climbed a tree and went to sleep until dawn. On waking, I put my rollneck sweater over the top of my battledress blouse and tore the tops off my escape boots. I then started to walk in the direction from which I'd heard train whistles during the night, in the hope I might be able to jump a freight train. After a short time I came to a large farmhouse where I was met by a little man in a peaked cap and clogs. The first thing he asked me by signs was if I had a gun. I hadn't, but so much for my disguise! He took me into the farmhouse where there were a number of women and children, and gave me some coffee and bread. He put my boots in front of the fire to dry. By this time the village kids were beginning to go to school, stopping on the way to come in and look at me, and I was convinced that I was just waiting for the Underground to come along and pick me up.

'Later in the morning a shepherd who spoke English came in and there was a general discussion about the war. Then, at about midday, a small character in civilian clothes, but wearing a peaked cap and jackboots appeared; his first words to me were, "How many little children have you killed today?". Later in the day I noticed he had a Nazi badge in his lapel, and I found out later he was the local *Gauleiter*, and it at last sunk in that I was in Germany and not Holland! My immediate reaction was to answer his question with, "What about Warsaw, what about Rotterdam and London?" Deciding that discretion was the better part of valour I stopped arguing with him, and he calmed down and asked if I'd hurt myself baling out. Shortly after this a Luftwaffe truck arrived with my skipper and navigator in the back guarded by a *Feldwebel* and three privates. We were driven for some three hours through a snow storm to the guardroom of the airfield at Oldenburg.'

Halifax HX336 had crashed two kilometres south-west of Borgerwald, Papenburg. George Haggard was captured in the village of Borger which is situated approximately 20 to 30 kilometres east of the Dutch frontier, between Papenburg and Meppan. The officers finished up in Luft III and the NCO's in Luft VI.

One other Halifax also did not return to base and three had returned early. It was recorded that the bombing had been concentrated in the western part of Berlin.

This was followed on the 19th by a raid on Leipzig. Out of the seventeen briefed, three failed to take off, three returned early and one was reported missing. Cloud over the target made observation difficult, but fires seemed to be taking a good hold. By a lucky chance the night fighters caught the bomber stream over the Dutch coast when they were returning from attacking minelaying aircraft because Mosquito aircraft were attacking their Dutch airfields. Flight Sergeant Pope's aircraft was chased by three Ju88's from Hanover to the target. The enemy aircraft made no less than ten passes, but there was no damage or casualties and no claims made.

The following night the squadron was represented in the raid on Stuttgart. Most of the bombs fell outside the city to the north but there was scattered damage throughout the city, severe in places. The most valuable result was the damage to the Bosch Works, Germany's biggest manufacturers of sparking plugs and fuel ignition pumps.

On the 24th Schweinfurt was attacked. This was the follow up of a heavy daylight raid by US bombers. Reconnaissance revealed that the five ballbearing factories had been affected and that damage was spread throughout the town. The following night a similarly planned raid was carried out against Augsburg. A double bomber stream attacked the city in two waves within two and a half hours. Amongst other damage, the leading diesel engine works of the MAN factory complex was severely damaged.

In 466 Squadron's eighteen months with Halifaxes, there were 170 raids on 92 different targets, which included 6 on Berlin, 8 on Essen, 5 on Stuttgart and 4 each on Cologne, Duisberg and Calais. The final operation of the war for No 466 Squadron was an attack on the coastal batteries at Wangerooge in the Frisian Islands by 18 Halifaxes on 25 April. In May 1945 466 Squadron transferred to Coastal Command and disbanded five months later. The contribution of the Australian Squadrons had been considerable.

CHAPTER EIGHT

All Return from the Happy Valley

Essen was always high on the list of Bomber Command priorities but early attacks had not been too successful because of the difficulty of locating the necessary pinpoint target areas through the industrial haze that often covered the area. Apart from the leading role played by the huge Krupps works in the manufacture of finished weapons, such as tanks, armoured cars, artillery tractors, heavy guns, torpedo-tubes and bombs, they turned out a large range of special components and semi-finished products on which a great number of other manufacturers depended. Thus the output of Krupps was of vital importance to the enemy's war industry as a whole and, whenever possible, work was resumed in the buildings ruined in 1943, and again in March and April 1944. In the five months following the last of these attacks a very considerable amount of repair work had been undertaken and photographs showed that almost every building in the huge works had received attention.

Over a thousand Halifaxes and Lancasters were sent to attack Essen on the night of 23/24 October 1944, and 770 in the daylight operation which followed on 25 October. As expected strato-cumulus cloud below 10,000 feet completely obscured the target during the heavy night attack, but crews bombed on skymarkers which were well maintained throughout the bombing period. A strong red glow under the clouds increased as the attack progressed. Skymarking was again employed for the daylight attack, owing to the presence of cloud. However, some crews were able to identify ground detail through a break in the cloud, and confirmed that the marking of their aiming point was accurate. Large explosions were reported and a good fire area was established.

Photographs taken after these two attacks revealed widespread and severe destruction. Nearly 200 buildings in the Krupps works were damaged and two of the largest buildings, covering a total area of more than 140,000 square yards were virtually destroyed.

At least thirteen other factories in the city, two gas works, two power stations, a tramway depot, and four railway stations were also hit; and business and residential property was again widely devastated. An Essen newspaper lamented a week later:

> The fact remains, that life in the ruined Rhine and Ruhr towns is becoming increasingly difficult. Today it resembles the front . . . Things which are a matter of course elsewhere, constitute a problem here: water, electricity and gas supply. Food supply demands the utmost effort on the part of all concerned when communications are interrupted, stores destroyed, streets torn up by bomb craters. If we predict that the difficulties will further increase and may reach a stage when compensation is no longer possible, we do not deserve to be reproached with pessimism, for we are merely following the logic of events. We do not know when our leaders will be able to use a new means to give the war a different turn and therefore we must be prepared for the fact that for the time being we shall be compelled to endure the enemy air terror, and must draw the necessary conclusions.

This barely-concealed defeatism was soon justified. Two further attacks followed before the end of the year.

Let us zoom in on to the briefing for the first of these raids. We go to the pre-war station at Leconfield, Yorkshire, home of No 640 Squadron. The squadron had been formed ten months earlier to fly Halifax III's. The briefing is for the attack on 28/29 November 1944. All the crews listed on the battle order for the raid are sitting waiting for the station commander and other high-ranking officers to unveil the target. There is a thick cigarette smoke haze in the room as the commander enters. The banter stops and there is a scuffling of chairs as the crews stand to attention. The commander motions them to be seated. Wing Commander John Viney opens the briefing with:

'Sit down please', then after a short pause 'Right, fellows, well we have our old target again tonight and it's entirely a Group effort, we have some 340 aircraft going. The target as you can see is Essen.'

Squadron Leader Crawley, the Intelligence Officer, takes over:

'You have all been to Essen before and it doesn't need much introduction from me. I want to remind you that it has a famous Krupps works there in the northern part of the town and also the railway facilities are most important now, they are feeding the front line troops. Your point of aim in the morning is in the south eastern part of the built-up area of the city; it's adjoining the fully built-up residential part. The Germans will be asleep about that time in the morning so you will be able to wake them up with a good fire. It's a 4 Group effort in the morning, there are 340 aircraft on the target, including the Pathfinders. The attack will be carried out in four waves of two minutes each, the whole attack is scheduled to last eight minutes. No 640 Squadron are in the second, third and fourth wave. Here are the aircraft and captains on various waves; will you make a note of the times.

'Now, the H-Hour is at 0530 with the second wave time on target 0532 to 0534. Aircraft B, Flight Lieutenant Anderson; I, Warrant Officer Trelfer; Q, Flying Officer Jeeves and Y, Flying Officer Fielder.

'The third wave time on target 0534 to 0536. Aircraft A, Flight Lieutenant Easton; C, Flying Officer Jenkins; D, Flying Officer Harper; H, Flying Officer Boyes; J, Flying Officer Wakeman; K, Pilot Officer Cooke and L, Flight Sergeant Brown.

'The fourth wave time on target 0536 to 0538. Aircraft V, Flying Officer Mills; M, Flight Lieutenant Morris; S, Warrant Officer Smith; T, Squadron Leader Rogers; U, Flying Officer Povey; W, Flying Officer English; X, Flying Officer Buckland and Z, Flying Officer Goodrum.

'Decoys. There are too many decoys round Essen for me to give you a whole list of them but there is one very important one which will be just on your starboard side three miles before you get to your aiming point and it's quite possible they will shoot up down the Pathfinder markers there, look out for them. They are always weaker in colour and they don't go as long as the genuine ones. The Pathfinder method is Musical Sky marking and ground marking. The attack opens at H minus six minutes. The Musical Mosquitos will drop red ground markers, red and yellow sky markers and green and yellow sky markers. You are to aim your bombs at these in the following order of preference.

'One, at the red TI's if you can see them; they ignite at 4,000 feet. Two, at the red shooting yellow stars skymarkers. Three, at the green shooting yellow stars skymarkers. The skymarkers ignite at 17,000 feet. If you attack the skymarkers you must do so on an exact heading of 084 degrees True. Remember, the red ground markers are the ones to go for if you can see them. There will be no Master Bomber.

'Now, the same time that you are on Essen, No 3 Group are sending 150 Lancasters to Neuss, which is south of Düsseldorf. Their route joins yours here,' he says, pointing to the map, 'and they come this way and back north about. Now, with regards as to jettisoning any bombs: if you get over Germany you must drop your bombs live there, but if the question of an aircraft making an early return having to jettison some bombs, you must jettison them at least eighty miles in the North Sea, and avoid any shipping, of course.

'All aircraft are carrying propaganda leaflets tonight; you will find two packets stacked in the rest position in each aircraft. The mid upper gunners will put these into the bomb bays through the inspection hatches immediately after take-off.

'One final warning, remember you must empty your pockets before you leave the briefing room. Don't take any papers across with you that may be of assistance to the enemy and remember the Golden Rule should you bale out over the other side; the only thing you are allowed to tell the enemy is your name, your rank, and your number.

'Are there any questions?' He pauses. 'No? Thank you.'

The next speaker is the Scottish meteorological officer.

'Well, your front tonight is lying about six degrees east, that is some 50 or 60 miles west of the target area. It's a fairly stable affair and I'll give you details later on.

'For take-off it will be clear with only moderate amounts of cloud, and visibility about three miles. You'll have the same conditions all the way down England until about Reading, but from there on to the enemy coast, or rather the French coast, you'll have small amounts of cumulus, building up over the Channel to three to six times, well broken with tops at about 10,000 feet. There may be one or two tops at 12,000 feet but these are very scuddy and you shouldn't bump into these anywhere. From there, on until six degrees east, the same conditions. The tops will level off at 8,000 feet and there will be some large gaps in the cloud with 10/10 from the front into the target area. The strato-cumulus tops are 5,000 feet. There are one or two holes in the strato-cumulus over the sea, decreasing to low near Norfolk and cloudless all the way home, with smoke haze and visibility about two miles. Freezing level is about 3,000 feet, icing index moderate but you shouldn't be flying in cloud anywhere and the temperature tonight, about minus 24 degrees at 20,000 feet; this will be the minimum.'

The commanding officer, John Viney, is next to speak:

'I'll just run over the flight plan,' he begins. 'First, we are taking off on runway 32 and climbing up over base to 6,000 feet and setting course to Reading at a speed of 175. We hold 6,000 feet right the way down to Reading and there we open up and start climbing to cross the English coast at Beachy Head at 12,000 feet and we are climbing at 160. Now we level off here and fly at 12,000 feet to 03 degrees east. We do that leg along there at 170 and here we start climbing again to be at 19,000 feet by 0450 at 160, now we hold 19,000 at 160 right the way through and into the target area. Our bombing height is 19,000 feet and we are the lowest height tonight, the others are bombing at 19, 20 and 21,000 feet. After bombing, increase speed to 170 on the short leg out of the target area and maintain our height right through the Ruhr defences until we reach just north of Cologne; here we turn starboard and have a gentle dive losing 2,000 feet, increasing our air speed to 190 and crossing our own lines where we have a very rapid loss of height down to 8,000 feet. We are losing height at 220 on that leg. At 8,000 feet we shall be just above the cloud tops and we are holding 8,000 straight and level at 190 to 03.20 degrees east. Here we turn starboard again and head up towards the French coast. There is one point that you want to watch: Dunkirk. Avoid going within three or four miles of the town, and here we are having a gentle climb to cross the French coast again at 12,000 feet just in case we are too close to the town. At 12,000 feet and then, once we leave the French coast behind, we lose height again at 190 and cross back over the English coast at Orfordness at 8,000 feet. We are going to hold 8,000 feet right the way up to the Humber at 190. At the Humber we are breaking cloud and so down to base.

'Well, you will probably tonight have 10/10 over the target. You may be lucky and get a break so that you can see the TI's but, anyway, there is one thing about that – you won't be troubled by the searchlights.

'I have some times here. I'll see the pilots and engineers at 0030. The buses for your aircraft will leave at 0045; the first aircraft will take off at 0205. There is a set course from base at 0245, the raid opens at 0530 and you should be back for breakfast at 0800.

'You will see that your chief bother probably will be night fighters, as it is expected to be a full moon and it will be very, very bright over there. I think visibility will probably be somewhere like a mile. The signals officer will tell you all about the 100 Group's work tonight and their efforts to jam the enemy's RDF.

'After leaving a point here, out of Cologne, we do lay on this rapid loss of height of some 8,000 to 9,000 feet and that is primarily to try and fox the fighters. The rest of the way back, I should think, will be quite quiet. Just one or two points: we have radar silence to 05.30 east, and there are to be no navigation lights on after we leave the English coast. I think that's about all I have to say. Are there any points following the flight plan at all?' Before waiting for an answer he concludes, 'I think it's a very good flight plan.'

The bombing leader, Flight Lieutenant Smiddy, is next on his feet:

'We have got three different loads tonight. I'll just read out the aircraft letters followed by their respective loads. First of all, aircraft A, C, D, H, J, T and V, one 2,000 lb HC and eleven 500 lb clusters. Aircraft M, L, S, U, W, X, Z and K, one 2,000 lb HC and twelve SBC's, containing ninety 4 lb incendiaries. The remaining four aircraft, B, I, Q and Y, one 2,000 lb, five 1,000 lb American SAP's and six 500 lb GP's. All aircraft are carrying photo flares and all cameras, of course. Master bomber switch tonight will have to be on for take-off, and you'll switch it off once you set course and do not put it on again until you reach 06.30 degrees east; then it has to be entered in the navigator's log. Your camera heater switch: put that on before you take off and leave it on right through the target and switch it off after you have cleared the camera. Choose your bombs once you have left the English coast and switch on your bomb sight a good twenty minutes before you reach your target so you will be quite prepared for your run up.

'Remember, if you have to bomb on Wanganui flares, apart from the heading 084 True, you have to have zero wind set at true heights on the bomb sights. That is very important. The aircraft carrying the HE load will have a delay between release of the HE's and the 2,000 lb HC's. So, bomb aimers, count that delay very religiously. After bombing, put the jettison bars across and then return to normal. After you have passed through the target just press the bomb-tit once, clear the camera and then put the camera heater off. If possible, do your visual check on the bomb bays over Germany because then if you have any hang up you can release it live on Germany; otherwise do it over the Channel on your way back and remember once again it has to be entered in the engineer's log this time. I'll see the bomb aimers fifteen minutes before MT time and I will give you all the data gen then.'

The signals officer, John Tocher, takes over:

'As you've already been told, there's both W/T and radar silence up to 04.30 degrees. Keep your H2S switched on up to that point and then use it throughout the trip. It is a point that's worth knowing, I think. The mid-upper gunner should switch the modular off when you get into the aircraft and, navigators, switch your H2S on normally, and when you reach 04.30 degrees tell your mid upper to switch the modulator on for you to save you running back and forward.

'Enemy counter-measures are getting a bit of attention tonight as a special force of aircraft is covering you. There's a Mandrel screen which their navigation officer will give details of to the navigators. There's HF, AI and VHF and Würzburg plotting which are all being jammed, and there's a special Windowing force out covering you. We're carrying our own Window; start that off at 05.30 to the target, to 04.00 degrees. You're carrying two types, the broad type and the ordinary type. The rates are: broad type, two minutes throughout the area, and the ordinary, two minutes to within twenty miles radius of the target area. Your R/T call-sign everywhere is 'Beatem'. The Group frequency at H-15. Watch check with your navigator as you get into the aircraft. Check with the navigator what the H-hour is. The type Z should be used; switch it on taking off, and switch it off at the English coast coming in. The usual rules for IFF apply.'

There is a final encouragement from John Viney: 'Right, fellows, well it's a really good target tonight. It's the largest armament works in the world, so let's have a really steady bombing run and put an end to it.'

The station commander, Group Captain R. H. Waterhouse, has the last word: 'Well chaps, you know the job tonight is to complete the destruction of an already heavily devastated town. There isn't much of Essen left, so it needs all the more accurate bombing. Let's see if 640 Squadron can finish it off once and for all. Best of luck.'

Y-Yoke running up prior to take off

Now for the squadron effort. Unfortunately, L-Lucy did not take off as its rear turret was found to be unserviceable. S-Sugar took off at 0230 but had not reached enemy territory before the starboard inner engine became unserviceable. The pilot decided to carry on but had no option other than to turn back when the port inner engine began to surge. The mission was abandoned and the bombs were jettisoned before the aircraft landed at base at 0832.

The report of Pilot Officer R. S. English flying W-William, is typical of reports made on return.

> We attacked primary at 0537 from 19,000 feet heading 084. Bombed on green/yellow flares through 10/10 cloud. The glow of incendiary bombs showed they were fairly well concentrated.

So, from No 640 Squadron 17 Halifaxes attacked the primary target; there was one non-starter and one 'early' return. The weather turned out to be much as forecast, with cloud commencing inside the continental coast to mainly 10/10 at target, tops 8,000 to 10,000 feet. Visibility was good above cloud with some small breaks in the cloud over north eastern France.

The result of the raid compiled for the squadron record said:

> Skymarkers were not plentiful. The green/yellow appeared to be half-a-mile south of red/yellow. The glow of red target indicators, or fires, could be seen below cloud together with a white glow of incendiaries. The raid appeared to be fairly concentrated but it is impossible to state whether on the target or not. One Ju88 claimed damaged by V-Victor over the target, only two other fighters were seen. Very moderate heavy flak well below our height. No searchlights. The quietest trip to the Ruhr yet.

On the night of 28/29 November, 316 bombers were despatched; 308 attacked, dropping 1,199 tons of bombs on Essen comprising 1,024 tons of high explosive and 175 tons of incendiaries. All the aircraft returned. This was not quite unique but a very unusual and welcome occurrence. Much of the credit could be given to 100 Group aircraft which swamped the Ruhr defences, so much so that the fighters were not able to take instructions from the ground.

The report on the photo-reconnaissance said that the attack again spread destruction over the whole area of the city and works and it particularly noticed new points of damage throughout the Krupps armament works. Some of the points were clearly from new hits, others appeared to be the result of collapse or clearance of structures damaged in the very concentrated attacks of the previous month. The identified buildings to which new or further damage was seen included power houses, foundries, rolling mills, furnace shops, engineering shops and others concerned with armament and heavy steel production.

In view of the vast scale of damage in Essen alone it could be realised how almost every branch of German war production suffered directly, or indirectly, as the result of the administrative, social and industrial chaos produced by the intensive bombing of October and November. After the Essen raid the aircrew of No 640 Squadron had little sleep, for those on battle orders were out again the following night on another Ruhr target: Duisberg.

CHAPTER NINE

Gardening in April

Minelaying, planting mines, soon became known in RAF parlance as 'Gardening'. The value of sea mining was quickly realised by both sides. German aircraft began dropping mines round the English coast in October 1939 and Handley Page Hampdens opened the RAF campaign in April 1940. After the fall of Norway, Holland, Belgium and France the areas specifically selected for Bomber Command minelaying were: Norwegian waters, those of the Kattegat and the Belts, the Baltic, Kiel Canal, the mouth of the Elbe and the Bay of Biscay. Later on an area round the Frisian Islands was included.

The mines, cylindrical in shape and upwards of ten feet long, were very sensitive and attached to a parachute to check their speed of descent. In the early days mines could only be released from a low altitude to make sure they would drop in their pre-designed position; otherwise the parachute attachment could have caused a drift through the air.

Mines were usually dropped close to land and precise navigation was essential. On making landfall near the selected dropping point the navigator checked his position by landmarks on the coast and told the pilot. The pilot then descended very low and flew for a given number of seconds at a predetermined speed on a straight course. The navigator had to be sure of his exact position or the mines would not be dropped in the right area. Occasionally it was necessary for a pilot to fly round the area for a considerable time while the navigator checked for accuracy. When the precise spot was reached the bomb aimer released the mines, the aircraft rose as it was relieved of its load and the airmen would fly back to base with the satisfaction of a job well done though they would see no tangible results of their work.

At the end of 1943, making use of the Schnorkel device, new U-boats, speedier under water than their predecessors, posed a new threat to the Allied merchant fleets. The new Type XXI U-boats were prefabricated, built by a number of firms throughout Germany and assembled in the three main northern shipyards at Bremen, Danzig and Hamburg. All three of the yards received regular attention from Bomber Command. Nevertheless, as the U-boats were being produced on a massive scale, other means had to be found to stop these boats becoming operational. Mining of the Baltic was an obvious solution. Hampdens had been replaced by their stable companion, the Halifax and these aircraft, which carried either mines or bombs, opened the minelaying season of 1944 by dropping mines in Danzig Bay which had long been the main area for the acceptance trials of new U-boats.

When the nights were long enough Halifaxes were out on their missions which called for great skill and resolution.

Minelaying was a thankless task, a great deal of effort for possibly little reward. The mine, really a type of delayed action bomb, flopped from the aircraft, floated down on its parachute, sank into the water, no splash, no flame and no flash. One pilot said, 'It's one of the most monotonous jobs in the world. You take your orders, fly for hours in the dark, reach the target area, drop the mine, then go back home. No thrills. No bangs. Just monotony.'

That this was not always the case will be shown as we follow two operations that took place in April 1944. The squadron is again No 77 whom we met earlier at Elvington.

On 12 April there was a call for 15 crews to drop mines in the Heligoland Bight. Thirteen aircraft dropped their mines successfully, the other two returned early. The pilot of W-William was unable to reach sufficient height due to a coolant leak developing in the starboard outer engine; the pilot of the other aircraft was Ian Robertson piloting P-Peter. Ian took off at 2105, carrying four mines, in his usual Halifax LK728. Jack La Planche, the navigator, describes what happened:

'As an experienced crew we were allocated extra large mines. These would not go into the bomb bay and we had to take off with the bomb doors partly down with mines hanging out. Ian said it did not affect take-off, but he had to use full power. At 7,000 to 8,000 feet the port outer engine showed excessive flame and eventually caught fire. We made a turn towards the coast, we were supposed to go to Flamborough Head to jettison. Ian switched on Graviner and by the grace of God the fire went out, but we were losing height with a full load of mines and fuel still on board.

Denmark and Northern Germany

I decided we could not make Flamborough Head and told the pilot to fly 090, which was about thirty miles to the coast, and prepare to bale out. I shouted to the crew not to bale out yet as we were over a high tree-growing area and we were less than safety height above ground to bale out. We almost scraped the top of the trees as we lost height. The ground fell away towards the coast. The flight engineer had the controls full power through the gate; the engines could not last long like this.

'We were firing off colours of the day and distress signals as we flew out to sea over Hornsea at 200 feet; it must have scared the life out of the residents. At the most half a mile out to sea we let the mines go at 2136; the aircraft seemed to rise in the air, we gained another 100 feet and breathed again. The pilot was able to make a flat turn and once more the gods were with us. Catfoss had seen our signals and lit up the runway. We went straight in and landed at 2150.'

Pilot Ian Robertson received a second green endorsement for his action. He thought he had flown a mile out to sea before dropping the mines and says: 'All the crew reckoned it was the most nervy trip of the tour – all for 45 minutes airborne time!' The rest of the aircraft found good conditions over the whole route. Known enemy defences were active and six sightings were made of enemy aircraft, but no attacks developed. Mines were laid in the correct position.

On 18 April there was a further minelaying operation. The crews encountered difficulties and despite spending a long time searching they could not be certain that their mines had been laid in the correct position. Subsequent information convinced the Intelligence Officer that the mission had not been successful. This was probably the reason why another operation was mounted on 23 April. This was one of the last minelaying operations to be carried out before the Second Front opened six weeks later, for in the meantime all of Bomber Command's resources would be required in strategic bombing in support of the Invasion.

On this Sunday, 23 April 1944, the weather in south Yorkshire was cloudy as the parishioners made their way home from Evening Service. At Elvington six crews had been detailed for a minelaying operation and they, plus the reserve crews, had been briefed to drop their mines off the port of Rostock in the Baltic Sea. At the last moment W-William LL126, a Halifax V which it will be remembered had given trouble nine days earlier, captained by Pilot Officer Wickham-Jones, did not take off. A reserve aircraft, back from a major overhaul, not air-tested, the perspex covered with dust, was wheeled out of the hangar. This aircraft had been designated P-Peter, to replace the one Ian Robertson had left at Catfoss. Derek Sykes and his crew were not at all happy to be called in as the replacement crew. Originally they had been second reserve for the mission as they were due for five days leave.

The six crews, who took off five minutes either side of 2100 were:

C – LW260 – Halifax II
PO Brown E .A. DFC
Sgt Davison P. DFM
F/Sgt Duff B. DFM
F/Sgt Tarpey M. DFM
FO Butterworth R. L.
F/Sgt Bird G. R.
F/Sgt Green R. A.

V – LK744 – Halifax V
Fl Lt Wodehouse S. E.
Sgt Roberts D. D.
Sgt Bulmer J. H.
FO Nutt J. S.
Sgt Needham J. S.
Sgt Cottar R.
Sgt Brown J. H.

A – LK737 – Halifax V
F/Sgt Blair R. A. W.
Sgt Moore L. H.
F/Sgt Pratt P. G.
F/Sgt Armstrong G. A.
F/Sgt O'Meara J. P.
Sgt Tustin D. C.
FO Date J. M.

R – LL131 – Halifax V
PO Robertson I.
Sgt Symes C. J.
F/Sgt La Planche J. S.
F/Sgt Spears W. A.
F/Sgt Paine G. H.
F/Sgt Walters F. W.
F/Sgt Presbury A.

L – LL235 – Halifax V
Fl Lt Thompson E. N. DFC
Sgt Armstrong J.
PO McClelland G. DFM
FO Robbins A. E.
F/Sgt Harvey F. W.
Sgt Redall R.
Sgt Harris D.

P – LW270 – Halifax II
F/Sgt Sykes P. D.
Sgt Jones G.
FO Murray J. H.
Sgt Haynes F.
F/Sgt Power W. A.
Sgt Loverock W. H.
Sgt Harrison J. J.

All six aircraft carried a load of four different types of sea mines as they took off from Elvington with a moderate south-westerly wind behind them. The visibility was good enough for the navigators to visually identify Flamborough Head as they turned out across the North Sea.

We will follow the progress of each aircraft in the order they are listed above.

Pilot Officer E. A. Brown, a veteran squadron pilot, was well on course when at 2300 the port outer engine overheated. With oil pressure low the engine was feathered. The Halifax was still over the sea so the four mines were jettisoned, unprimed, off the south west coast of Denmark, from 14,000 feet. The return flight was made on three engines and C-Charlie landed safely at base at 0150.

Flight Lieutenant Wodehouse in V-Victor located the dropping position and after a timed run of 189 seconds from the position indicator released the mines, in good visibility, from 13,000 feet on three red markers which, he reported, appeared to be well concentrated. The Halifax returned to base without mishap at 0315.

Flight Sergeant Blair in A-Able had a similar experience. He reported a slight haze at release point and dropped his mines from 13,000 feet in the correct position after a run of 189 seconds from the position indicator. This Halifax landed at 0330.

The other three Halifax flyers were not to be as fortunate as their companions. Ian Robertson says: 'We did not fly P-Peter, our usual aircraft, that night. It would only take two mines with bomb doors slightly open; we were given R-Rodger which carried a full load.'

Jack La Planche, navigator of the same crew, says: 'As an experienced crew we were once again chosen for the special pinpoint mission,' This is how their flight was reported in the press:

MINE LAYING HALIFAX CLAIMS TWO FIGHTERS

Excellent team-work enabled members of the crew of a Halifax which was engaged in a recent minelaying operation, to claim the destruction of an enemy night fighter, and the probable destruction of another. At 2331 when the bomber, R-Rodger, was some distance from its target, the rear gunner, Flight Sergeant Alf Prestbury, of Derby, saw a Me110 preparing to attack from starboard. He immediately warned his pilot, Pilot Officer Ian Robertson, of the attack, and as the Halifax turned in evasive action, the rear gunner and Flight Sergeant Mike Walters, mid-upper gunner, of Pocklington, were both able to open fire.

The fighter did the same, at about 450 yards range, but evasive action had saved R-Rodger, and the fighter's bullets passed above it. In contrast to this, the fire of the Halifax's gunners was accurate and damaging, for when the Me110 broke away, at close range, smoke was pouring from both its engines. It disappeared into cloud, and the crew claimed it as probably destroyed.

The second combat a few minutes later was more conclusive. Another Me110 was sighted, also to starboard, and prompt warning given of its approach. Again the pilot manoeuvred so that his two gunners could engage the enemy, and fire was exchanged until the distance separating the two aircraft had been reduced to less than 100 yards. Then, the Me110 burst into flames, and spiralled to the ground, where it exploded.

Both the pilot and the flight engineer were able to watch its descent, and to confirm the accuracy of their gunners' marksmanship.

R-Rodger, which was undamaged, completed its task, and twenty minutes later when returning home, the crew had the satisfaction of seeing the second fighter still burning on the ground.

The mines were dropped from 12,000 feet. Ian Robertson and his crew, who were all uninjured, landed safely at Elvington at 0325. It was later found that the Halifax had not been damaged at all.

Halifax L-Lucy crashed in the sea off Traner Odde on Als, an island to the south-east of the mainland of Denmark. The reason for the crash is not known for certain. The Halifaxes had experienced light and heavy flak from Esberg and Fano when crossing the west Danish coast, but as the aircraft had flown over Denmark before crashing it is most likely that it was attacked and shot down by Me110's from the same squadron that tangled with Ian Robertson.

The body of the pilot, Flight Lieutenant Edward Thompson from Grays in Essex, was buried on 1 May. Sergeant Roy Redall was buried on 6 June. Navigator, Flying Officer Gerald McClelland, was buried on 18 June and wireless operator Flight Sergeant Fred Harvey a day later. Of the other crew members, one survived to become a prisoner-of-war and the other two were never found.

On the last aircraft, P-Peter, brought in as a reserve when W-William developed a fault, Sergeant John Harrison, the six-foot tall rear gunner, who incidentally had attended the same school as his pilot, remembers: 'Our regular aircraft, G-George, had a bomb hang up on an earlier operation so on this night we flew in a reserve aircraft. Originally we were loaded with two mines but the Armament Officer came on the tarmac and insisted we took a full load.'

Navigator James Murray of the same crew says: 'We were detailed to lay anti-shipping mines in the waters off the port of

Rostock. The aircraft we were flying were too old to be used against well-defended main targets in Germany and were therefore used on operations like minelaying. When we had four mines on board the bomb doors could not be closed completely, so our speed and manoeuvrability was diminished.

'We were a fairly inexperienced crew; this was our eighth operational mission. The mid upper gunner William Loverock was a new member of the crew. We flew out over the North Sea and crossed in over Denmark north of Sylt, which was heavily defended. Our course took us over South Jutland and Lolland Island towards our target. Over Jutland we were tracked by a Me110 obviously carrying air radar. We were warned by Monica and began taking evasive action. The night fighter attacked and we exchanged shots with him.'

John Harrison, in the rear turret, continues the story: 'The German did not use tracer so we could not see where he was firing from; he attacked from behind and below, sighting on the bomber's exhausts. I did not see the fighter until its first, unsuccessful attack. The pilot was reluctant to jettison the mines when we were so near to our objective.'

James Murray continues: 'The second attack was successful and the port mainplane started burning. Some bullets appeared inside our fuselage and I think our mid upper gunner was killed at this time for we heard nothing from him.'

Witnesses on the ground said the Halifax looked like a flaming torch.

James Murray: 'Our situation seemed hopeless. During the fighting we had lost height and were down to 12,000 feet. Before the attack we had been flying at 15,000 feet. The pilot asked me where we were and I told him we were over the coast of Lolland, but our course had been changed during the evasive action and that we were flying out over the sea. The pilot immediately changed direction and set course for Lolland, ordering us to bale out when we came over land.

'Assisted by the bomb aimer I opened the hatch in the floor of the navigator's compartment and looked down. When I saw we had passed the coast I baled out. Due to my inexperience I opened my parachute at once and then looked around. I was frightened to see that the wind was carrying me out to sea. I tried to steer my chute, but in vain and I landed well over a mile off shore. I kicked off my boots, inflated my Mae West and began swimming.'

Frank Haynes, the bomb aimer, was next to leave the doomed aircraft. He delayed his jump and landed on the island of Falster. John Harrison was the third survivor. He landed by parachute, a bit shaken, on Lolland in a field near the sea. He says: 'We were still over the sea when the pilot gave the order to bale out. I landed on my feet and buried my parachute and Mae West. I didn't know where I was.'

Paddy Power, the wireless operator, landed close to where John Harrison came down. Glyn Jones, the flight engineer, was most unfortunate. His parachute did not open and his body was discovered in a gravel pit near Nykobing.

An explosion was heard at 0015 as the Halifax exploded and crashed on farmer Markersen's field at Skibeholt, on the tiny island of Hjaelm, situated between Lolland and Falster.

The Halifax grazed a cliff and its completely pulverised wreck was spread over 600 yards, with parts still on fire. No bodies were found but four mines, three yards long, amazingly survived. Pieces of wreckage were found on the beach below the cliff.

The final moments of pilot Derek Sykes must remain a mystery. At 1800 fishermen found his body floating between Lolland and Falske. It was picked up, brought into harbour and thence to the mortuary. There were no injuries or no identification papers on the body which had no shoes, and no parachute was attached. The following night a patrol boat picked up a parachute near Christian IX bridge at Nykobing. This parachute almost certainly belonged to Sykes. The conclusion is supposition, but it would appear that once the five live crew members had baled out, Sykes himself managed to follow them. He landed in the sea, disposed of his parachute and possibly his footwear, and then drowned or died of exposure before he could reach land. He was buried with Glyn Jones on 30 April. The heavily decomposed body of 19-year-old Sergeant William Loverock, the new gunner, probably mortally wounded in the mid-upper turret, was found at sea by fishermen and brought ashore at the north coast of Lolland on 19 May. His remains were buried a week later.

For the survivors, the nightmare over, their adventures were just beginning, although Frank Haynes, who had landed on Falster, was fortunate. He was ferried across to the Swedish port of Malmo the same day.

This leaves James Murray, John Harrison and Paddy Power. We left nineteen-year-old John Harrison rather shaken, burying his parachute and Mae West in a field. He continues: 'I didn't know where I was. My first impression was that I was in Germany so I started scouting for ways of escape. I walked by night and hid during the day. After I had been walking for three nights I realised I had landed on an island because no matter in which direction I ventured I came to the sea. It was a lonely feeling being on the run. I dared not ask the way and I could not read the road signs. On the north coast I caught sight of Bandholm harbour, decided to steal a fishing boat and sail to Sweden. As I sneaked closer to the harbour I found myself face to face with a man. We were equally surprised, and scared. Should I attack him or run away? I decided to try and explain the situation. I wrote RAF in the sand on the beach and sketched a parachute. The man was one of the locals who worked at a pumping station, draining water from low lying fields. He hid me in the pumphouse. Later he returned with food and beer for me, accompanied by three other men who took me to a small fishing shed where we discussed the situation. Then we went to one of their houses, where I was hidden. I was really well cared for, with delicious food, the like of which I had not tasted before.

'My rescuers, Skipper Christensen and the brothers Marius, were not members of the Resistance but they had contacts. One day they told me that a doctor would come and see me, to test my story. This was necessary because the Germans smuggled in fake airmen to try and infiltrate the Underground.

'The doctor, Ib Hansen, from Maribo, spoke excellent English, and knew a great deal about England and interrogated me in a very clever way. For my part I was pleased to speak English again, without having to gesticulate. I passed the scrutiny and later I was supplied with civilian clothes. Late one night I was taken by bicycle to Maribo where I received a welcome from the Resistance people. I gave them the escape money I always carried. I spent the night in the doctor's house and was reunited with James Murray and Paddy Power. The Canadian, Murray, had swum a mile to the shore, and Irishman Power had landed not far away from me, on Lolland.'

Early next morning Resistance workers took the three airmen to the station and joined the train for Copenhagen. The airmen

Ian Robertson (extreme left with cap) his crew and that of Laurie Ellis and Pete Cadman

P-Peter (LK728) Halifax V with air and ground crew (l to r) GC, GC, J. La Planche, A. Presbury, W. Spears, C. Symes, GC, GC, G. Paine, GC, I. Robertson.

were placed in different compartments as were the two escorting agents. Naturally, the airmen were nervous, not only because of possible identity checks and the fact they were wearing civilian clothes, but because there were more than one hundred German soldiers on the train. John Harrison shared a compartment with three of them, one of whom was very keen to lend him magazines to read.

However, the airmen were fortunate and reached Copenhagen without incident. Here they were met by Allan C. Christiansen, a Resistance worker, who hid them at his parents' apartment. He promised to return later to take them to another safe house, but unhappily he was arrested by the Gestapo a few hours later. His brother-in-law arrived with the news and the airmen were quickly moved into a flat belonging to a Communist Underground worker. Here they remained while arrangements were made for transporting them to Sweden.

On Saturday evening they were led on board a small ship in Tuborg docks. Here they joined thirty-six others who were going to Sweden illicitly. They heard a German patrol on the dockside, the ship's papers were checked and the soldiers drank a beer with the skipper before the ship sailed. The way to Sweden was open.

In Swedish territorial waters they met a Mr Handil of the Danish/Swedish Refugee Service and were landed in Malmo. It was just a week since they had taken off from their Yorkshire base. The return flight was quicker; they returned from Sweden in a Mosquito.

Meanwhile, back at Elvington, the destruction of two Me110's by the guns of R-Rodger, was confirmed; one straightaway and the second within 24 hours. There were immediate awards of the Distinguished Flying Cross to pilot Ian Robertson and immediate DFM's to gunners Mike Walters and Alfie Presbury for 'courage and devotion to duty when their aircraft was attacked by enemy fighters'.

We now leave Bomber Command, and their maritime operations, to follow the Coastal Command Halifaxes who spent many a long hour scouring the seas and oceans in search of targets.

CHAPTER TEN

Coastal Halifaxes

At the beginning of the war Coastal Command began with one advantage, it had been fully mobilised a fortnight before the outbreak of hostilities. Due to an appeasing and parsimonious Government it was ill-equipped with aircraft of sufficient range to do more than provide close escort to coastal convoys.

From the very first, Germany adopted unrestricted submarine warfare. By the end of 1940 U-boats were operating rather further away from our coasts and scoring considerable successes against convoys in areas where their routes converged a hundred miles out into the Atlantic. All this time Britain persisted in the purely defensive policy of escorting every convoy for which aircraft could be made available. As a result the U-boats were free to sail to their appointed patrol areas without hindrance. The air had made little or no contribution to the defeat of the U-boat and the capture of the Biscay ports had greatly eased the problems of the rapidly expanding U-boat fleet.

By May 1941 Coastal Command had made two notable advances, first in respect of types and ranges of aircraft and, secondly, in weapons: the first airborne depth charge had made its appearance. The technique of offensive air action against the U-boat had been carefully studied. There were two principal areas through which U-boats had to pass, the Bay of Biscay and the northern waters between Iceland and the Shetlands. The problem was to find and attack them during their passage through these areas and thus to prevent them from reaching their patrol areas, or at worst to harass and delay them.

The two chief factors which influenced the planning of such operations were, first, that the average rate of progress of a submerged U-boat was two to three knots, and, secondly, that at this time it was compelled to come to the surface for several hours in every twenty-four in order to recharge its batteries and ventilate. If, therefore, the area through which a U-boat could pass at submerged speed in twenty-four hours could be kept under constant observation by aircraft, sightings of surfaced U-boats at some time during that period were, in theory at least, a certainty.

Unfortunately, however, there were several practical factors which entered into the problem. In the first place there were limits to the ranges at which a U-boat could be detected visually from an aircraft, even in the clearest weather, and in bad weather these ranges were considerably reduced. The tracks of individual patrolling aircraft had, therefore, to be close enough to each other to ensure that there was no gap between the visual ranges of adjacent aircraft. Secondly, no spot in the whole patrol area could be left unobserved for a period longer than the minimum required by the U-boat for surfacing and recharging its batteries in order to catch it. Thirdly, at night except in bright moonlight, the chances of sighting a U-boat were negligible, since at that time there was no reliable means of illumination in service.

Coastal Command at this time felt justified in embarking on an offensive policy and accordingly, the number of aircraft employed on convoy escort was reduced to the minimum consistent with safety; all remaining aircraft were turned on to patrols in the two main transit areas and to offensive sweeps along the convoy lanes and in other areas where U-boats were believed to be operating.

In spite of the limitations in numbers of aircraft, the new policy immediately produced results. There were many sightings and attacks by aircraft, and, although kills were still very rare, U-boat captains found themselves compelled to submerge in areas where they had formerly moved freely on the surface. This slowed up their rate of progress, shortened their time on patrol, and materially reduced the potential threat to shipping.

It was not long before the U-boats were driven 300 miles and more from our coasts, where they could operate beyond the range of our aircraft. This distance gradually increased till, eventually, only very few of our ships were sunk within 450–600 miles of our bases.

By 1943 the U-boat building programme had reached enormous proportions and it was clear that the Germans were once again prepared to stake everything on success in the Battle of the Atlantic. It was obvious that so long as they even held their own in this battle, there could be no question of an invasion of the continent. However the strength of Coastal Command was steadily

Flight Lieutenant A. I. Sladen DFC.

being built up and more and more squadrons were trained in anti-U-boat detection and attack.

Flying over the sea called for a particularly high standard of navigation. There were few landmarks, and Coastal Command aircraft spent most of their time flying out of sight of land. Pilots took perils for granted, but the one most feared was not flak nor fighters but weather.

Among the squadrons with the Command was No 502 (Ulster) Auxiliary, which had started the war with Ansons at Aldergrove under the command of No 5 Group at Plymouth; they were later equipped with Whitley twin-engined bombers. Ex-Bomber Command Squadron No 58 also flew Whitleys with Coastal. Both these squadrons converted to Halifaxes. An official order was issued in January 1943 that all Halifaxes diverted for Coastal Command would be finished in extra dark sea grey on upper surfaces with white sides and under surfaces. A month later a further order stipulated white for all front and side views, including engine cowlings and spinners, with upper surfaces in extra dark sea grey. Serial numbers were to be light grey, with codes in red.

The Coastal Halifax II was fitted with three 330 gallon overload tanks in the bomb bays, each with submerged electrical fuel pumps to feed petrol to the main wing tanks. As a result of this, and the transferring from twin-engined aircraft to Halifaxes, extra crew members were needed, flight engineers and WO/AG's.

Trained ground wireless mechanics, twenty-four of them, were sent from the Gunnery School direct to the squadron at St Eval, in Cornwall, but the Coastal 58 and 502 Squadrons were at Holmsley South near Bournemouth. In Cornwall the new WO/AG's had one or two trips, thirty-minute stooges, before being sent to join their new squadrons. The squadron commanders were not pleased to see these inexperienced newcomers, with not even OTU training. Among these twenty-four pioneers were Jack Spackman, who joined Dick Collishaw's crew, and 'Blondie' Wilson who was to team up with Algernon Sladen, both in 58 Squadron.

Before the war Sladen was studying agriculture at Cambridge University, but from 1937 until the outbreak he was one of the 'week-end pilots', a sergeant in the university squadron. He did considerable flying in his own aircraft, one of which he won in a raffle. Before completing his first operational tour in Iceland and joining 58 Squadron, he served for a year with a unit which was carrying out some of the early experiments with the Leigh Light.

During the hard winter of 1941–42 he was one of the pilots who dropped mail bags laden with food for passengers of snow-bound trains travelling from Inverness to Wick. On 26 January, piloting Whitley K-King of 612 Squadron he dropped 500 lb of food to two trains. Nearly eight months later, while flying another Whitley of the same squadron, he attacked a U-boat and estimated a direct hit and much oil was seen on the surface. This, however, was not credited as a kill.

By the time he joined 58 Squadron at Holmsley South, at the end of February 1943, Toby Sladen, as he was sometimes called, had completed nearly 1,200 hours of flying. At the beginning of the next month he was flying as second pilot on Halifaxes and practised attacks on a submarine off Eddystone rocks. On 6 March he flew with Flying Officer Eric Hartley on an anti-U-boat sweep in the Bay of Biscay. The Halifax had to land at St Eval before returning to Holmsley South. On 13 March Toby Sladen flew solo on Halifaxes and was out flying the four-engined aircraft all through March and April.

Algernon Sladen acquired the nickname 'Moonpath' as he was one of the originators of the radar-less moonpath attack on surfaced U-boats, who, unwarned by radar response, were often caught napping. He was often seen sitting in the mess with hands swooping in a light beam planning his next attack.

In May 1943 Coastal Command were at last in a position to 'flood' an area with aircraft. The month saw the turning point in the Battle of the Atlantic when a total of 41 U-boats were sunk, many of them from the air in the Bay of Biscay. Wing Commander Wilfred Oulton, commanding officer of 58 Squadron at this time, was responsible for the destruction of three of them. Squadron Halifaxes had been unsuccessfully searching the Bay for six weeks before Wilf Oulton sank *U-663* on 7 May. Halifax D-Dog of 58 Squadron sank *U-528* on 11 May and L-Lucy of 502 Squadron accounted for *U-753* on 14 May. On 15 May Wilf Oulton sank *U-463*. On 31 May he was flying R-Rodger, when on patrol over the Bay with J-Jig, flown by Flying Officer Eric Hartley, they, with the help of a Sunderland, disposed of *U-563*. This U-boat was a doughty opponent and it took the combined total of 24 depth charges from the three aircraft to finish it off.

May was a record month, with 18 U-boats destroyed by Coastal

(***Top left***) George Martlew and (***top right***) F/Sgt Greig, Sgt Laffy and F/Sgt Frape with the Halifax which was shot down. (***below***) F/O Griffiths crew. F/Sgt Greig, Sgt Laffy, W/O Young, W/O Moody – (front) F/Sgt Martlew, F/O Griffiths, F/Sgt Frape, F/O Quinn

Command alone; the great majority were killed on the surface while fighting back. Dönitz recalled his boats to harbour so there was a lull in sightings for the first half of June, before the U-boats were found trying to get out by hugging the Spanish coast. No 58 Squadron were soon aware of this and Flight Lieutenant Sladen flew on Spanish coastal patrols during June.

In May Prime Minister Winston Churchill and Foreign Minister Anthony Eden visited the United States. Before returning to Britain they flew via Gibraltar to North Africa for the Casablanca conference, and this was widely reported later. It was thought at the time that their presence in these parts was the reason that Ju88 night-fighters attacked a civil aircraft on its way to Britain from Lisbon, on the grounds that a man resembling the Prime Minister in build, and smoking a cigar, boarded the KLM plane just before take-off. Among the 13 passenger victims was Leslie Howard, the well-known film actor. This act took place on 1st June.

The first operational flight for George Martlew, flight engineer with Flying Officer Griffiths' crew, was a few days later on 5 June. They took off at 1435 from St Eval flying 58 Squadron's G-George HR764 on an anti-submarine patrol in the Bay of Biscay. The tragedy of Leslie Howard's death was still fresh in their mind when George suddenly spotted a Ju88. The time was 1630, and the Halifax was at 2,000 feet some sixty miles off the French coast. George continues: 'After I spotted the Ju88 at 4,000 feet on our port quarter I turned and saw another and another; in fact seven in all. The person in the mid upper turret was a spare bod, a pilot who came along for the ride, and it was he who opened fire as the first Ju88 made its attack from the port quarter and above. The second attack came from almost dead ahead and the closing speed was frightening to say the least. However, the attack was dealt with and we dived to starboard hotly pursued by two Ju88's. Attack after attack was made and each time beaten off. This was the first time that any of the crew had seen the enemy; we were very inexperienced, but held out.

'Eventually we saw some cloud about six miles away to eastward at 3,000 feet and made for it. At the skipper's command I opened up the taps of all four engines as we made for the cloud cover with the seven Junkers following. We managed to reach the cloud, and comparative safety. From time to time the skipper would break cloud momentarily for me in the astrodome to give the position. Each time I had to report they were still there, circling the bank of cloud. On our fifth look they had gone and we assumed they must have been getting short of fuel and returned to their base.

'During our dash for the clouds we had dropped our depth charges to give us more speed to gain height more quickly. One other point was that on the very first attack I fired a Very light and the attack was broken off; no doubt the German pilot thought this was some sort of signal, but they were not fooled for long.'

Halifax O-Orange HR744 of the same squadron had a similar experience while flying at 1,500 feet on an anti-submarine patrol in the Bay of Biscay. The pilot sighted seven Ju88's which crossed the bows of the aircraft from starboard to port. One enemy attacked from the starboard bow as it passed, opening fire at 600 yards. The Halifax went into a diving turn to starboard, opening fire with front guns on the enemy aircraft, which immediately broke away and passed astern. The Halifax then made for cloud cover, about fifteen miles distant, increasing speed to about 230 mph. It was followed by the Ju88's at 3,000 yards, except one, which kept strict station on the starboard quarter at 1,000 yards. The enemy then carried out a port beam attack which the Halifax countered by a sharp turn to port. The mid upper gunner opened fire on the enemy aircraft which immediately broke off the attack. The Ju88's then manoeuvred astern and above the Halifax but did not make any further attacks.

The period between 1 July and 2 August marked the climax of the air operations by the Bay of Biscay patrols and was the period of their greatest success. We now know that 86 U-boats crossed the Bay during those weeks. Of these 55 were sighted; 16 were sunk by aircraft and one by a surface ship, while six others were forced to turn back. In addition, the air patrols off Cape Finisterre and the coast of Portugal sank three more U-boats and damaged a fourth. Losses to the anti-submarine aircraft were, however, heavy. Fourteen did not return.

While Algernon Sladen was flying long, fruitless patrols over the Bay to Cape Finisterre and Corunna, other flyers from his squadron were enjoying some successes. Early in the morning of 13 July Halifax O-Orange was flying over the Bay at 500 feet; there was a moderate sea with a visibility of twenty miles. Two white streaks were observed 6–7 miles away, and then two U-boats were sighted on the surface travelling at about eight knots. The Halifax turned slightly to starboard in order to get up sun, when a third U-boat was seen; the three boats were in tight V formation, proceeding at speed. No radar contact was made until after the visual sighting.

A Sunderland appeared from the north and turned to port to circle the U-boats clockwise. The Halifax followed in the circuit keeping five to eight hundred yards from the enemy. All three U-boats immediately opened fire at both aircraft. The fire seemed to come from abaft the conning tower. The U-boats took evasive action by making tight turns at high speed, the outside boat nearest the aircraft continually drawing away and turning stern on so that the stern fire of the whole formation could always be brought to bear. The flak was accurate for elevation and bearing but short for range; it gave the impression that the enemy gunners were attempting a box barrage between themselves and the aircraft. No tracer was seen. The aircraft took evasive action by gentle switchback flying but did not open fire.

Eventually the Halifax succeeded in getting in touch with the flying-boat by flying alongside, and the pilot told the other aircraft that he was going to fly on a reciprocal course. The Halifax then turned and began to circle the U-boat anti-clockwise. This manoeuvre was successful in splitting the fire of the U-boat's gunners, who slackened off and finally ceased fire after the aircraft had made two more circuits. The Halifax intercepted words on the R/T in German, and immediately afterwards the starboard U-boat, a Type VIIC, broke formation and started to submerge. This Hamburg-built boat, *U-607*, was attacked by the Sunderland. The remaining two U-boats then turned to port; the outside one submerged, the inner one remained on the surface and re-opened fire as if to cover his colleague's dive. The Halifax was then on a course of 360 degrees when the last U-boat was seen to be diving. The aircraft turned to starboard and flew straight in. The attack was made from the U-boat's starboard beam from a height of 50 feet. Eight Mark XI Torpex depth charges were released set to shallow depth, spaced 60 feet, five seconds after the U-boat had disappeared. The periscope feather was visible about 50 feet ahead of the swirl at the time of release. The depth-charges straddled the U-boat's track 100 feet ahead of the swirl; three under-shot, two exploded on or near the U-boat itself producing a considerably larger plume, and the remaining two overshot and exploded with smaller plumes.

The aircraft made a tight turn to starboard and on tracking over the bombing mark again saw the brown explosion scum with black bubbles beginning to form in the centre. On the next circuit eight men were seen swimming in the centre of a spreading patch of black oil 200 feet across. On circling a third time a number of other men were seen swimming through the oil patch towards the rim of bubbles that ringed the area. O-Orange was asked by the Sunderland to photograph the explosion mark of the Sunderland's attack, but no photographs were taken as only a patch of lightish green water was visible. *U-607* was sunk.

Attacking U-boats from the air had been rather inconclusive with loose ends and unanswered questions left in the minds of the crews. In many cases it was certain that the U-boat had been sunk, but aircrews rarely found out how or why. The U-boat sinkings yielded many prisoners and some of them supplied the answers to these questions.

On 20 July 1943 *U-558* was sunk by a USAAF Liberator while on its tenth patrol. The vital factor in the sinking apparently was chlorine gas. The aircraft achieved a large measure of surprise and dropped an accurate stick. Although, according to the prisoners, the nearest depth charge fell fifty feet away, the explosion was near enough to cause a serious entry of water. This water got into the batteries and quantities of chlorine were generated. The U-boat was unable to dive. Then Halifax E-Easy of 58 Squadron appeared and relieved the damaged Liberator. This was particularly unfortunate for the Germans as the Halifax engaged in a gun duel so effectively that the Germans used up all their ready-use ammunition and were prevented by the gas from going below to fetch more. Most of the casualties were caused by this chlorine.

When the boat finally sank, the few survivors spent five days in a dinghy. They were very depressed by the sight of innumerable Allied aircraft and only one German, a FW200. One of the officers said that the U-boat commanding officers did not greatly fear depth charge attacks by surface craft, but dreaded attacks from the air, particularly from searchlight aircraft. Another interesting fact about *U-558* was that its engines had been sabotaged at a French base.

Although these survivors only saw a FW200, the Germans had

long-range fighter units operating over the Bay. The activities of the group, V/KG.40, operating with Ju88's were stepped up during the spring and summer of 1943, as V-Victor of 502 Squadron was to find out. The Halifax was flying at 2,500 feet on anti-submarine patrol in the Bay when it sighted a Ju88 diving out of the sun on the starboard beam. The Halifax immediately took evasive action with a steep diving turn to starboard. During this manoeuvre it was seen that there were three more enemy aircraft following in line astern. The enemy aircraft now positioned themselves two on the port quarter and two on the starboard quarter. The Halifax jettisoned its bombs and set course for the nearest cloud cover, which was 2/10 strato cumulus. This did not provide much cover, and one enemy aircraft positioned itself immediately above the Halifax apparently shadowing and directing the attack of the others. The captain of the Halifax decided that the cloud cover was insufficient and started to climb at maximum boost and revs. One enemy aircraft was now on each bow, and one on each quarter at approximately 600 to 800 yards range. While one enemy aircraft made a feint attack, the other carried out the real attack. These were counteracted by violent corkscrew evasive action. One Ju88 closed to 100 yards and the rear gunner of the Halifax got in a long burst from 500 yards. When the enemy aircraft broke away black smoke was seen. Two of the Ju88's turned away and circled the damaged aircraft.

The remaining Ju88 now carried out an attack on the starboard bow. The Halifax countered with a steep diving turn to starboard and the enemy aircraft passed ahead at point-blank range. The front and rear gunners of the Halifax opened fire and succeeded in obtaining many hits. As the Ju88 passed astern smoke was seen pouring from it. A few moments later the navigator and rear gunner saw white objects in the sky which appeared to be parachutes, and the Ju88 was seen to dive through the clouds. The three remaining attackers then set course eastwards. The only damage to the Halifax was one bullet hole in the port aileron.

At twilight on 24 July another Ju88 flew across the bows of HMS *Woodpecker*, with the Second Escort Group. On board the ship was an RAF officer who kept a diary of the Escort Force's activity, to which we will return later.

On 30 July two Type XIV boats, 'Milch-cows' and another U-boat were located sailing in a group. All three were accounted for:

the supply U-boats, *U-462* by Halifax S-Sugar of 502 Squadron, *U-461* by Sunderland U-Uncle of 461 Squadron, and the other, *U-504*, by the Escort Group. With their meagre armaments the U-boats had given the aircraft a certain amount of punishment.

The sheer quantity of air and sea offensive which the British threw into the attack illustrates the determination to confirm their superiority in the U-boat war. *Woodpecker* picked up survivors including the captain and first officer of *U-504*. Other ships in the Group picked up a further fifty or so survivors. The RAF officer aboard had seen the whole action.

On 1 August Sunderlands accounted for another two U-boats in the Bay. The morning of the next day found many Allied aircraft and two Escort Groups searching the western part of the patrol area for enemies; several U-boats were seeking their damaged colleagues, and the Germans had sent out three destroyers to help them. It was probably these that fired on 'Moonpath' Sladen. He saw five sloops picking up U-boat survivors and later met three 'Narvik' Class destroyers which fired on him. Second pilot Sergeant Upshall was wounded by the attack.

There were many indecisive attacks and gun duels between aircraft and U-boats; but late in the evening on 2 August *U-106*, which had been very persistently hunted, was finished off by two Sunderlands. The enemy destroyers, which had been reported as large destroyers, caused the commander-in-chief at Plymouth to send out reinforcements to the Escort Groups; but inaccurate sighting reports prevented a junction being made, and the German ships thus rescued *U-106*'s survivors and reached harbour safely. Four U-boats had, however, been sunk in two days. This, coming so soon after the heavy losses of the previous month, caused Dönitz to recall the last six boats to leave, and to cancel all group sailings. His inward-bound boats were ordered to make Cape Finisterre, and then use Spanish territorial waters to reach home.

Dönitz told Hitler on 31 July: 'The enemy is directing his main efforts against the exit lanes of our submarines . . . consequently our losses are still very high.'

U-boat sinkings provided proof that aircrews who never even saw a U-boat materially contributed to the success of the crew that did. One petty officer told his captors:

'We were six days out, past 10 degrees west, and thought we were out of immediate trouble, when an aircraft attacked unexpectedly. There had been no warning on the search receiver. The skipper was on the bridge when one of the ratings saw the aircraft and yelled, "Aircraft alarm". The engineer promptly uncoupled the surface diesels to switch over to electric propulsion; in the meantime the skipper cancelled the order, yelling: "Too late, too late, man the guns."

'You can imagine the confusion, we were losing way and had practically stopped when the depth charges dropped, fortunately out of harm's way, on the port side. The commander was white and trembling; he had never got over his first aircraft attack, when he was first officer in another U-boat. The boat returned, but several of the crew were killed by machine-gun fire.'

Another prisoner said: 'We had aircraft alarms fifteen times in the space of ten hours; you've no idea of the unnerving effect repeated alarms have on one's nerves. The loud-speaker begins to sound like the voice of doom.'

The weeks following the beginning of August were an anticlimax; U-boats were only surfacing at night and then for the minimum period necessary to charge batteries. This lull worked out nicely for Jack 'Tinker' Bell who joined 58 Squadron after already completing a tour with 502 Squadron, flying Whitleys. He had amassed 1,164 hours flying when he started with the squadron on 14 August. He says:

'When I formed my crew at Holmsley South, we all went into Christchurch for a celebration drink or two. At about 2130 we arrived at a high-class pub frequented by select army officers. One officer, in particular, was saying how he disliked the RAF shooting so-called lines. Naturally this annoyed us, who by this time were full of the joys of spring, and strange to say this officer somehow mislaid his cane. To go with the cane we somehow or other also acquired a small pewter tankard, and on all our flights these souvenirs went with us.'

Halifax Y-Yoke of 502 Squadron was flying on anti-U-boat patrol on 2 September in the Bay of Biscay, when the navigator and second pilot sighted two unidentified aircraft some three to four miles ahead. The Halifax immediately climbed for cloud 3,000 feet above. As the range closed the aircraft were identified as FW190's. They positioned themselves, one on each quarter.

The first attack came from the port quarter; the enemy aircraft opened fire at 600 yards, closing to 400 yards. The Halifax evaded by corkscrew action and the rear gunner returned the fire with a long burst at 600 yards. A few moments later, the Halifax gained cloud cover, and altered course ninety degrees to port. Twenty seconds later, it emerged from the cloud to find the fighters, one on the starboard beam and one on the starboard quarter, a thousand feet above. The enemy aircraft on the beam made a beam attack, followed by the other enemy aircraft. The Halifax evaded by a diving turn to starboard. Cloud cover was again reached, but the enemy aircraft were resighted when the Halifax passed into clear patches. They were able to make another attack, before contact was finally lost. Neither the crew nor the Halifax suffered any hurt. The Halifax reached base safely.

Not all the Halifaxes returned safely. In the days of radar and the extent to which blind homing measures could be relied upon there was a temptation to dispense with legitimate navigation. Some time earlier one Halifax didn't quite get home. The navigator had kept quite a reasonable log, up to the arrival of the Cornish coast, when he dropped everything except a map, and changes places with the second pilot who tried inexpertly and unsuccessfully to get Gee fixes. It was dark and the aircraft flew over 10/10 cloud and set course for Holmesley South from a rather vague radar fix. No concern was felt when a pundit and an occult could be seen although these were not on the schedule, being in fact twenty miles north of the intended track – the rear gunner must have been mistaken, they thought. A little later some pyrotechnics, fired off in the Salisbury Plain, were imagined to be flak from Southampton although, needless to say, dead reckoning would have dispelled this belief had it been kept up to date. The Halifax partially executed a turn over a valley in the Salisbury Plain, which was taken to be Southampton water. It was the last flight of the crew as a whole.

It was also the last flight for two of the crew of HR982 on 27 September, and very nearly for the other six. Eric Hartley, already mentioned, took Group Captain Roger Mead, station commander at Holmsley South, on his first operation with 58 Squadron. The Halifax sank *U-221* but was so damaged in the attack it ditched three miles from the scene. Six of the eight crew escaped in the dinghy. They were rescued eleven days later. Eric Hartley received the Distinguished Flying Cross.

Wing Commander Wilfred Oulton, the U-boat killer, moved on and was replaced by Wing Commander J. M. D. Ker as commander of 58 Squadron. Bob Farrow also joined the squadron as a WO/AG in September. Two months earlier he had been crewed up with Flying Officer Dick Collishaw, who, before joining the RAF, had been a policeman. Dick told his crew, 'Well, boys, I don't necessarily want to be the boldest pilot on the Squadron, just the oldest!'

The activities that took place in 58 Squadron's Officers' Mess were many and varied. One was the game High Cockolorom: this consisted of teams racing against each other down the length of the mess and then leaping on the back of a fellow member who was bent facing the wall. 'Mouse' Grant, the commanding officer, led a team on one occasion and was the first to run. He went down the length of the mess like a bat out of hell and leapt on the proffered back. Unfortunately he was going too fast and his head came into violent contact with the wall, and he fell as though pole-axed. However, with a shake of his head, he got up, grinned, and climbed on the back.

Another activity was 'footprints', which entailed removal of shoes and socks and the use of a fire bucket filled with soil, beer and water. Chairs were piled on top of each other, and the selected people had their feet dipped in the bucket and were required to place the footprints up the wall. These were then continued across the mess ceiling and down the opposite wall. At times this became somewhat hair-raising when the chairs wobbled and the foot-printer made a heavy landing. There were also beer drinking upside down games but the commanding officer kept a very careful watch on those taking part and all standby crews were barred from parties.

On 12 October Algernon Sladen attacked a U-boat by moonlight, straddled it while on the surface but no results were seen. Four nights later he was again on moonlight patrol and on both occasions the crew were in the air for almost ten hours.

The Coastal Halifaxes carried four WO/AG's, most of them trained in America and Canada. These four alternated between the rear turret, radar, mid-upper turret and the W/T set, at intervals.

George Trott flew on 92 trips with 502 Squadron. On 29 November he was a 'spare bod' flight engineer with Flight Lieutenant Grant in D-Dog HR681. It was one of his early operations to the north coast of Spain. Here French, Spanish and Portuguese fishing boats had a defined limit outside which they were liable to be attacked without warning.

The flight engineer continues: 'The radar operator told the skipper he had picked up a contact ahead. The navigator checked and said it was a lot of fishermen outside the limit. Then a voice came over the intercom, "Our engineer has not seen anything, so let's bomb them." The order was given: "Bomb doors open." One of the crew took me back to the starboard rear, opened the floor panel and we both looked out. Flares and two 600 lb depth charges were dropped. As they entered the sea, one just missing a boat, the water rushed up to a great height, with fishing boats smashed all over the sea. What a sight!

"Bomb doors closed." The flares burned out, all was black again and we were on our way home.'

In December 58 and 502 Squadrons moved from Holmsley South to St David's, a new airfield near Solva, fourteen miles from Haverfordwest. This was a big undertaking but the Halifaxes continued operational flying throughout. Commanding 502 Squadron was Wing Commander Charles A. Maton, a South African from Capetown, the first air gunner ever to do so. He had resigned his position as Private Secretary to Sir Abe Bailey in 1938 to join the RAF. This popular man, whose squadron boasted the only Irish bagpipe band in the RAF, had earlier been given the Orangeman sash under armed escort, with the pipers playing as they never had before.

George Trott recalls: 'I did one trip with the Wing Commander. He flew with us as WO/AG and took his turn in the top and rear turrets and on the radar. He even relieved me, the flight engineer, and sat in for the second pilot. When we approached St David's on return I had to fire a special cartridge in the Very pistol so that the camera pointing downwards, in the front compartment, could take a picture of St David's Head. I did not like the look of this cartridge, because it did not seem to fit right in the gun. I told the Wing Commander, he had a look and cancelled the action. Next day it was checked and said to be satisfactory. That night a crew took off in the dark and flew around. One of the locals later told me he heard the Halifax flying low round the Head. Suddenly there was a "brilliant white light" which lit up everything around. The next thing he saw was the aircraft on fire, diving into the sea, and then darkness. Nothing was found and I often wonder if that cartridge had backfired into the Halifax.'

Earlier in December it was noticed that ships which had previously been engaged in blockade running to and from the Far East had dispersed to ports and anchorages between Brest and Bordeaux. It was believed that all these ships had loaded and it seemed reasonable to assume that a breakout had been planned. Also, as there had previously been arrivals in the Bay of Biscay simultaneously with departures, it was reasonable to suppose that some homeward ships were expected. In fact, due to German signals being read at Bletchley Park, it was known that blockade runners were shortly to arrive at Biscay ports. The presence at these ports of a strong escort force of five large and six small destroyers, showed that there would be escorts for any evaders.

There was no further activity until 23 December, when a westbound force of destroyers was sighted by 'Moonpath' Sladen in the Bay of Biscay. He saw destroyers going out and dropped flares over the force. Almost simultaneously a suspicious merchant ship of around 6,000 tons was sighted sailing independently on an easterly course, still far out in the Atlantic. It was clear that the destroyer force was on the way to meet the inward bound ship.

In the meantime Sladen's R-Rodger had landed at Predunnock after nearly twelve hours in the air; it returned to St David's the next day.

Heavy attacks developed in the Atlantic against the inward bound blockade runner, now identified as *Osorno*. A Wellington was the first to attack, with depth charges, just after midnight. Nearly seven hours later a Liberator also attacked; in both cases no results were observed. Further sightings were made during daylight by Liberators, Sunderlands and Beaufighters.

Following these sightings a striking force of eight Halifaxes of 502 Squadron, armed with 500 lb MC bombs, was detailed to attack. The convoy was located and attacks were made between 1700 and 1900 at heights varying from 5,000 to 12,000 feet. Violent evasive action made it difficult to observe results but several crews reported seeing dense clouds of smoke coming from *Osorno*.

In the early hours of the following morning, Christmas Day, nine further attacks were made but no confirmation of damage could be made and a force of 14 Mosquitos, 15 Torbeaus and 29 Beaufighters failed to make contact with the convoy in the afternoon. The ship was ultimately beached in shallow water off

Le Verdon, with lighters alongside, which showed that cargo was being unloaded.

The next incident was on 27 December when another inward bound ship was sighted far out at about 20 degrees west. She was *Alsterufer*, 2,700 tons, the smallest but fastest and most heavily armed of the blockade runners. She, too, had been expected by the British as the German codes had been broken and the Admiralty had put ships and aircraft on the alert.

The *Alsterufer*'s captain, realising he had been observed, held his easterly course, although he had been ordered to turn south if he was identified, as though he were a British ship independently routed to Gibraltar.

The *Alsterufer* signalled the Operations Directorate giving her position and asking for support. The Germans replied that support was being sent. The first three attacks were made by Sunderlands but the fourth attack by a Czech Liberator was lethal. The Czechs from 311 Squadron dived through intense flak and parachutes on cables and fired eight rocket projectiles in pairs, the first at 800 feet and the last at 600 feet. They also dropped one 500 lb MC bomb and one 250 lb GP bomb from 600 feet. Five of the rocket projectiles struck the stern above the waterline and one bomb hit the stern and set it on fire.

The German was again sighted at 1758 by four Halifaxes and seen to be blazing from end to end, listing to port and down by the stern. From time to time explosions were seen. Four lifeboats containing survivors stood off about a mile from the blazing ship. The 74 survivors drifted about the scene of the sinking until well into the next day. They still hoped that the German destroyers would reach the position and pick them up. However, the destroyer force had been intercepted by the cruisers *Glasgow* and *Enterprise* and against heavy odds sank three of them.

On 30 December 'Moonpath' Sladen was again over the Bay and sighted a German lifeboat with survivors from the three destroyers. The survivors from *Alsterufer* had been picked up the previous day by warships of a British Escort Group.

So ended the year 1943 which has many claims on history; high among them was that it saw the defeat of the U-boat menace in the Atlantic which, at the beginning of the year, bade fair to strangle the Allies' strategy in Europe and held out to the Axis their last remaining hope of avoiding decisive defeat.

The main object of the operations against the U-boat was to prevent the Allies losing the war. Coastal Command shared with the Navy in this successful task.

The year 1944 opened encouragingly for the Coastal Halifax squadrons.

George Martlew of 58 Squadron was flying with his regular skipper, Flying Officer Griffiths, on New Year's Day. They took off in G-George HR792 for an anti-submarine patrol in the Bay of Biscay. 'We obtained a blip on our radar screen' he remembers 'and investigated, using carbon flares, and saw a U-boat making eight to ten knots on the surface. The U-boat fired, initially shooting at the flares. We dropped down from 600 feet during the mile and a quarter run in. The flak passed under our port wing as we released the charges. We saw several plumes and the nearest was close to the port beam level with the conning tower. As we tracked over the U-boat the navigator fired some 100 rounds from the .5 nose gun, in two long bursts. The first was over the target but the second burst round the conning tower. The enemy replied with cannon fire but ceased after the second burst. Our rear gunner fired some 200 rounds as we passed over but did not see any results. We remained in the vicinity for seventeen minutes but saw nothing further of the U-boat.'

On 2 January L-Lucy of 58 Squadron, piloted by 'Moonpath' Sladen, was on patrol in the eastern part of the Bay of Biscay when shortly after 1930 a radar contact was obtained eight miles on the port beam from a height of 1,000 feet. The Halifax immediately began to home but contact was lost at six miles. The loss of radar when the nose was depressed was a common failing on Halifaxes. After searching for several minutes another contact was obtained, this time at a range of fifteen miles. The aircraft again began to home and altered course so as to make use of the moon path. During the run in contact was lost several times, but Sladen twice regained it by lifting the nose of the aircraft. When the range was closed to one mile the captain sighted a U-boat on the surface, fine on his port bow.

'We sighted the U-boat surfaced a mile ahead and travelling at about eight knots,' Flight Lieutenant Sladen said. 'We had to alter course 80 degrees to get it into the moonpath so that while remaining unseen ourselves we had a good view of our target. Then we lost height and went in as low and as fast as we could. We seemed to take the U-boat completely by surprise. Dropping from 300 feet to 50 feet, we released our depth-charges.'

Six 250 lb depth charges, spaced at 60 feet, were dropped and the mid upper gunner saw the plumes straddle the submarine between the conning tower and the bows.

'The enemy replied with a short burst as we passed over him,' continued the skipper. 'Machine-gun fire from four guns came straight up at us but missed their mark. During the forty minutes it remained on the surface we saw a regular flashing light from the U-boat: presumably the light of an electric lamp. We flew in the vicinity for an hour and returned for another hour-and-a-half without seeing anything more.'

After the attack a marine marker had been dropped and the aircraft circled this and kept in touch by radar. It was probably that damage was inflicted on the U-boat which stopped it diving for the forty minutes the flashing light was seen.

Two nights later the same crew, flying Y-Yoke, were on anti-U-boat patrol in the Bay when a radar contact was obtained at ten miles range from 2,500 feet. The blip was very weak at first but afterwards became clearer. The aircraft began to home until a wake was sighted at 1½ miles range and then the U-boat, at one mile. There was no moonlight to aid the aircrew in their second attack, it was made at almost the same time of night, but the moon was diffused by cloud.

'This time the wake, and not the U-boat itself, was the first thing we saw,' said the pilot. 'We sighted it a mile-and-a-half ahead. Then a mile ahead, the U-boat came into view, its decks awash but the conning tower clearly visible.'

The aircraft immediately went into the attack from the starboard quarter of the U-boat, which was on a north-easterly course indicating it was returning from a mission, and the stick of six depth-charges spaced at 60 feet was released.

'We saw the plumes from our depth-charges straddle the stern from a 50 foot attack', said the pilot. A vivid violet flash was seen and the U-boat was lifted out of the water by the explosions. The conning tower was seen apparently lower in the water and the contact then faded.

'After that we lost contact and saw nothing during the four-and-a-half hours we remained in the area before being relieved by

Sgt R. B. Lawrence, Lt. R. A. Tunnell (USAAF) F/Sgt J. Scott. (front) Sgt R. W. Wilson, W/O J. E. Abbey, F/Lt A. I. Sladen, F/O A. J. Starr.

VETERAN 58 SQUADRON CREWS

Sgt J. Spackman, F/O R. Collishaw, Sgt E. Arnold, P/O McKelvie, P/O G. Vandry (front) Sgt Hughes, Sgt R. Farrow, Sgt T. Gavin

another aircraft', said the skipper. The explosion of a depth charge was sometimes visible at night and this may account for the vivid flash that was seen. It is disappointing to record that neither U-boat was sunk.

Three nights later the same crew were on another anti-U-boat patrol off Spain. Four unidentified aircraft closed but the pilot soon lost them in cloud. These were probably Ju88's from the Kunkel Kommando, named after its Commanding Officer, Hauptmann Kunkel. This detachment of nine Ju88's had been set up at Nantes at the end of the previous year. Many Allied crews operating over the Bay at night reported being shadowed by supposed enemy aircraft, during the hours of darkness, but the number of actual attacks reported was very few. Kunkel achieved no success whatever although he personally made over forty night patrols.

Four nights later, on 11 January 1944, Wing Commander Ker joined the crew as second pilot on a search for a damaged U-boat. However, owing to engine trouble, the aircraft had to return early without completing the search.

On 15 January a communication was received from No 19 Group headquarters. Addressed to Flight Lieutenant A. I. Sladen of 58 Squadron St Davids, it said:

> The AOC and all at No 19 Group most heartily congratulate you on your immediate award of DSO.
> Your very fine achievement is a feather not only in your cap but also in that of No 58 Squadron.

At the same time other members of the crew, navigator Flying Officer A. J. Starr and Warrant Officer J. E. Abbey, the wireless-operator, were awarded the DFC.

At the end of the month the crew were given leave and together they first of all spent a weekend at a Swansea hotel. Here they took over the lounge from the elderly residents. Having consumed an enormous amount of drink they decided to form their own Halifax with chairs. On the first chair sat the navigator. On the two chairs behind him sat the two pilots. Then singly sat the engineer, W/OP, radar operator, mid upper and rear gunners. As they were on a 'secret mission' they moved round the lounge checking everybody's identity card. By this time the aircrew had drunk the bar dry but the tolerant residents had enjoyed the break in routine and much enjoyed the young airmen's little cameo.

The 'rest' trip continued by boat to Belfast, a few days at their own homes, then back to base.

Meanwhile on 5 January Halifax R-Rodger HR983 of 58 Squadron flying at 2,200 feet on a night patrol in the Bay of Biscay had been investigating some fishing vessels when a radar contact was made at 22 miles. The aircraft homed and sighted first a wake and then a U-boat on an easterly course four miles away. The U-boat was not clearly identified until three anti-U-boat flares were released from 800 feet. She was then between one and two miles away. At first the German gunners fired at the flares but then elevated their guns to fire at the Halifax. Six Torpex depth charges were released from 150 feet in a starboard beam attack and the stick was seen to overshoot, probably caused by flying at too fast a speed while losing height. The depth charge seen nearest to the U-boat burst to port of the bandstand. The Halifax then circled and released another flare. The fire from the U-boat again increased and again was seen to be clearly directed against the flare. The Halifax gunners were given an opportunity to reply before contact was lost five minutes later.

Although no major damage was inflicted the U-boat's crew must have been severely shaken at being attacked so close to base.

In the latter part of January a spell of fine weather, improved radar tactics, and lack of caution on the part of the U-boats produced a number of promising attacks, particularly in the Bay of Biscay and off the west of Ireland where U-boat concentrations were located. Most of these attacks took place by night.

Despite some successes, it soon became apparent that the radar homing technique was far from perfect, and that it was necessary to put a greatly increased effort into training in this field. Bob Farrow found that the relay in the radar modulater unit occasionally stuck. He discovered that a kick sometimes cleared the fault, a case of 'brute force and bloody ignorance' solving highly technical problems in the air.

It was also about this time that the enemy began to achieve satisfactory results with his 10 cm search receivers using improved amplifiers and aerials; for this reason the difficulties of locating and killing U-boats at night increased. Nevertheless, our night performances improved and one of the reasons for this was the introduction of the new 1.7 in flare. There were always new techniques being tried out, as John Bell found:

'Instead of using high level flares the scientists had worked out in theory that low level flares could be used in a similar way to Leigh Lights, and I was selected to do the trials with the boffins in St Bride's Bay. It was a pitch black night and we took off loaded with dozens of these flares which were to be pushed down the flare chute when required. The target was a buoy in the Bay. We made about three or four runs at 150 feet but didn't see the buoy until we passed over it. The boffin on board decided that this would improve if we reduced height to 100 feet. This we did, but after a further three runs he decided that the distance of sighting was still not good enough. He reckoned that if we reduced to 50 feet the distance would double, and an attack would be possible. By this time I was getting somewhat alarmed, but decided to try one run, even though I realised that I would have to be careful how I pulled up after the run. We made the run, with little improvement, and it was only the words from the rear gunner, "Christ, if we go any lower I shall need a diving suit," that brought the boffin back to earth.

'On the night prior to his wedding the squadron navigator was included in my crew to check the navigation. This, of course, happened to all crews. We were on an anti-U-boat patrol down to Spain, and all went well until about two hours from base when the radar picked up a contact on the port bow. We homed on the contact and carried out a flare attack, but didn't release depth charges as it turned out to be a motor vessel. According to our intelligence, no ship should be there, so we again released flares, but still couldn't identify it. We circled this ship for about 45 minutes until finally the ship identified itself. Imagine the language when the word EIRE was illuminated! We then proceeded back to base, but when 45 minutes flying time away from St David's we received a diversion signal instructing us to land at St Eval, in Cornwall. There was a hurried discussion with the bridegroom-to-be, the outcome of which was that we would not acknowledge the signal until we were nearer St David's. This we did and said that as we were very near to base we would try to land there, and if impossible would then divert to St Eval. Eventually, we landed safely, and the grateful bridegroom bought the beer to repay the telling off I received from the Commander.

'The one and only time I saw a U-boat', Bell continues, 'in two tours of operations, occurred on the night of 7 February when on an anti-submarine patrol in the Western Approaches. We were on our way back when the radar picked up a contact thirteen miles distant. I homed on this so that the moon was behind the contact, a technique used by "Moonpath" Sladen, and had a visual at about three miles. The attack signal was sent to Group and a depth charge attack carried out, followed by both turrets opening fire. No anti-aircraft fire was encountered until the charges had been dropped, then it arrived and removed the fixed aerial. We did a circuit and picked up the contact on the downwind leg and turned in to assess results. However, when we levelled into the approach, the contact had disappeared and no trace could be seen in the moonlight. Pete Webb, one of the WO/AG's, fixed up the aerial and transmitted an attack report while I circled the flame float which I had dropped. He was then instructed to home another aircraft on to the position, which he proceeded to do. For this he was given an immediate award of the DFM. Later I received the DFC.'

Flight Engineer George Trott, mentioned earlier, was still freelancing as a spare bod and his life was not without excitement. When he was flying with Flight Lieutenant Evans in 502's K-King JB895 on 29 February, the starboard outer propeller came loose well out to sea. Fortunately they were just passing some zig-zagging naval ships. The Halifax fired off red flares and sent out a Mayday signal. The aircraft was losing height so everything portable was thrown overboard and ditching station positions were taken up. Luckily the pilot regained control, cancelled the distress signal and finally returned to St David's. After landing, the propeller fell off.

Ten days later the maverick was flying in R-Rodger JP166 with Flight Sergeant Younster. They attacked two German destroyers in the Bay of Biscay. A near miss blew the rudder and screws off the rear destroyer which had to be towed back to port by his colleague.

When landing, Flight Sergeant Younster was in the No 2 pilot's position. Running along the tarmac something happened, and the Halifax went to port, the port engines were ticking over. The whole aircraft crashed down. What a mess! An Irish ground crew member came up, and, in an accent that could be cut with a knife, said, 'Any bombs on board?' Someone said 'Yes' and he was off as fast as his legs would take him. Everyone was out by the time the fire tender arrived. The flight engineer received a back injury that still plagues him but only spent three days in the sick bay at the time.

The following month, on 25 April, he was flying F-Freddie with Flight Lieutenant Holdeness, with Flight Lieutenant Clarke as second pilot. George Trott continues:

'While on a special patrol we had a radar contact in the Bay of Biscay, which looked like a U-boat. We were at close range and the bomb doors opened quickly. We dropped delayed action flares and circled while we waited for them to ignite. "Stand by for attack, port, starboard, starboard, bombs gone." The Halifax rose as the six depth charges fell away. I was looking out of the starboard hatch – what a sight! The bombs dropped in the sea, but the target, all lit up by our flares, didn't look like a U-boat. Wreckage hurtled up as the ship went down. Cheers on board from us all, but the skipper calmed us down, saying we had been hit by flak in the port mainplane and tailplane. I hadn't seen any firing, but the navigator had. When we returned to base Wing Commander Maton phoned Group Headquarters with news of our success. Later we were told we had sunk a 5,000 ton *Sperrbrecher*, with a crew of 184 men. It was out on a trial following an overhaul.

Jack Hochkins, an Australian WO/AG of 58 Squadron, who flew with Flight Lieutenant Faneco, had practised the new radar homing technique, mentioned earlier. Their Halifax G-George HR744, was a 'colossal aircraft with no bugs and was shot up but always came home' says Jack. This was illustrated at the end of April when it was shot up on an anti-submarine patrol in the Bay of Biscay after attacking a U-boat and a flak ship. A heavy calibre cannon shell hit the mainplane and went through the Elsan and bullet holes punctured the fuselage. The Halifax made it back to Chivenor, where it was left as unserviceable.

The radar on the aircraft was fitted with an attenuator, a device to reduce signal as it homed on to a U-boat so that the strength of the signal received by the enemy remained constant and it was hoped they would believe the aircraft was still some way off, not closing on them rapidly.

Jack Hochkins continues: 'We used Sonar, coloured homing buoys which were dropped in a pattern in the sea near a suspected

U-boat. We could tell which buoy the enemy was nearest to, its course and speed.

'As a special crew we were sent to Leuchars in May on loan to scientists who were carrying out what were called Z tests. Highly secret homing torpedoes were wheeled out to our aircraft, under cover and security. The problem was how to get them into the water without damaging their complex equipment, by parachute. It was claimed that if they were successfully dropped within half-a-mile of a submarine, they would home on to it. This became known as a "Creeping Jesus" attack. They were only used well away from the enemy coast because it was thought that if one had been captured it could have been developed and used against our proposed invasion fleet.

'Apparently it was an honour to our crew, and myself as a radar specialist, that we were selected for these tests.'

'The only time I was in formation with an enemy aircraft was on 17 May,' says John Bell. 'During an anti-E-boat patrol between Southampton and Cherbourg we had located an E-boat force that was returning to port, when on my starboard side was the familiar orange light of a Ju88. Both turrets were fixed on it, but in order to shadow the E-boats no attack was made. When we reduced height he did likewise, when we turned he did and this lasted for about five minutes. Then, without warning, he flew off to investigate some Royal Navy ships about ten miles away where he received a very warm welcome. I shall never know why we were told not to attack the E-boats.

'While stationed at St David's,' Bell continues, 'my crew were adopted by the two ladies who managed the Cambrian Arms. We were able to buy our beer when it was shut, and as a bonus the two good ladies supplied us with lobster suppers almost every week. To repay them we started the fishing run. Local coastguards supplied a boat and by using a dinghy sail we were able to go out in the bay with our fishing lines. We used red pieces of wire and caught numerous pollock which were donated to the pub and other local people.'

Bob Farrow, at much the same time, was enjoying a spot of leave, also fishing, but from the RAF launch at Fishguard. This was a rest period before D-Day.

The main anti-U-boat operations in the English Channel and its western approaches opened on D-Day. Previous to that date single

U-boats had penetrated into coastal waters with the aid of Schnorkel, but both equipment and experience were lacking, and when the invasion came the U-boats put to sea from the Biscay ports and made their way to the Channel on the surface. This resulted in a record rate of sightings and attacks. During those first vital four days from D-Day, Coastal Command sighted 37 U-boats, of which 24 were attacked. In every case the U-boats fought back desperately with flak, but despite this, and the limitations imposed by the difficulties of night attack which applied in the case of no less than 18 attacks, 6 U-boats were destroyed and 5 damaged.

These successes were decisive. A blow was inflicted on the enemy from which he never really recovered in so far as the invasion operations were concerned. From now on, the enemy again adopted extremely cautious tactics and the opportunities for killing became less and less, as his skill with the Schnorkel became greater.

Flight Lieutenant Sladen was over the Bay on D-Day for some nine hours during which time he encountered flak while investigating eight armed trawlers off Lorient. Three days later he was airborne for 11 hours 40 minutes on a strike. He sighted launches off St Malo and some enemy survivors being picked up by destroyers in the Channel.

Edward Beesley joined 502 Squadron for a second tour in June. On the 20th he was flying in E-Easy which took off at 0055 for a night radar exercise. The starboard aileron control rod broke on take off and for five hours, waiting for first light, the pilot used up petrol doing flat turns and lining up with the runway. The instructions on R/T were to point the aircraft out to sea and all jump. The pilot, Flying Officer Frank Muir and the second dicky, to stay and the rest jump, or all try to come in. The pilot brought the Halifax in all right; the blood wagons and the fire engines were lining the runway with the promise of an operational breakfast on success.

The following day George Trott, now finally crewed up with Canadian pilot Flight Lieutenant James, was aboard 502 Squadron's T-Tommy JP169. Their Halifax came upon a Sunderland that had just attacked a U-boat and a Halifax of 58 Squadron diving down for a low level attack. The U-boat dived leaving an oil slick. Base told all aircraft to return to patrol, except T-Tommy which, just having started its patrol, had plenty of fuel. Flight

Lieutenant James was instructed to track the oil slick and turn on the radio contact so that the Navy could home on to the position. The Halifax flew up and down the track in low cloudy weather and, over the Atlantic, flew through a dead zone for radio. It was five hours before the Navy showed up. T-Tommy returned to St David's after 11¼ hours in the air, many of which were flown in cloud, and the last 75 minutes in darkness.

No U-boat was sunk on this day.

In July Nos 58 and 502 Squadrons at St David's, found themselves carrying out three different types of operation. They carried out anti-submarine patrols night and day, anti-shipping patrols round the French coast and armed reconnaissance in the Channel Islands area in support of the Normandy invasion.

Despite all the hard work there were still light moments. Bob Farrow remembers Flight Lieutenant A. R. Clutterbuck, captain of a wild crew who had tangled with a BV222 the previous October, shooting at crews with a revolver! There were complaints from the Vicar at Solva when a Halifax 'buzzed' his church just as wedding photographs were being taken. Flight Lieutenant Ben Bentley was taking off crosswind with a full bomb and petrol load when his Halifax hit Flying Control and split in half. Fortunately, the aircraft did not explode. After that a new expression was coined, 'Swing and sway the Bentley way'.

In mid-July, on a Scillies–Ushant patrol, Sergeant R. W. 'Blondie' Wilson, in 'Moonpath' Sladen's crew picked up a contact which appeared and disappeared. This was probably a Schnorkel which was being lapped by waves. It was difficult, even in a moderate sea, to pick up a Schnorkel on radar. Six days later the same crew were in action, looking for reinforcements by sea from St Malo to Granville. The radar failed, so the bombs were dropped on Granville jetty.

On 20 July, while twenty-two miles west of Ushant, Sladen saw enemy aircraft bombing an Escort Group from 7,000 to 8,000 feet. He immediately called for fighters, which arrived too late. One frigate was hit. Six days later, while on a patrol between the submarine bases of Brest and Bordeaux, Sladen sighted two E-boats and two minesweepers and attacked the latter; unfortunately two bombs hung-up.

This was the last operational flight for Flight Lieutenant Algernon

Sladen with No 58 Squadron, his seventieth. He completed 390 hours day and 301 hours night operational flying with the squadron and a further 133 hours non-operational. His total RAF flying time then was 2,016 hours – his assessment by Wing Commander J. B. Grant was 'above the average'.

The development of the Allied land operations during August not unnaturally affected the work of the anti-shipping squadrons. The rapid over-running of Western France increased the importance of operations in the Bay of Biscay.

The capture of Cherbourg and the fall of St Malo finally separated the German surface forces in the Channel from those in the Bay of Biscay. The sea forces in the Biscay area at the beginning of August consisted of three destroyers, a torpedo boat, four escort vessels, some 20 *Sperrbrechers* and 30 M Class minesweepers and smaller auxiliaries. Their chief task was to maintain supplies for the isolated garrisons of Brest, Lorient and St Nazaire, and many of the smaller anchorages and harbours, so that the Germans could continue to operate the U-boat bases, even though they were entirely cut off from the landward side. On 7 August 502's T-Tommy flew over HMS *Warspite* which was shelling Brest. The naval signalman flashed 'Clear Off'.

The next day pilot John Bell of 58 Squadron was busy: 'While on strike standby, I was briefed with two crews from 502 Squadron to carry out a shipping strike against three transports, two smaller vessels and two escorts which lay between the Ile de Groix and the French mainland. We were assured by the Intelligence Officer that there would be no enemy aircraft and no flak, so we could treat this almost as a practice bombing exercise. It was decided that we should attack together from different directions at differing heights: 4,000, 6,000 and 8,000 feet. I drew the lowest level. On arriving off the Ile de Groix all three navigators saw the targets and duly set their bomb sights. R/T was used throughout as it was thought, wrongly, that no one would be listening. We set off to our points of approach at our respective heights, and on the signal from the Australian squadron leader we mounted the attack.

Within two minutes both aircraft of 502 had called off the attack for different reasons, and I was left blissfully ignorant of what was to come. The ships were sighted and the bombing

F/Lt John A. Bell flying No 58 Squadron Halifaxes. (*Above*) Returning from shipping strike on 8 August 1944

commenced. About a mile from bomb release the flak started, and my rear gunner gave a running commentary on how close it was. He was politely told to wrap up, and I lowered my seat and flew the rest of the run-in on instruments. My navigator, Ben Collins, released the bombs and on hearing this, I pushed the nose down and dropped to almost sea level and relative safety. In the meantime the other two Halifaxes, who had watched me, did their bombing runs. One stick of bombs demolished an ack-ack battery on the island; the other aircraft decided to make another attack but no hits were obtained. So we returned to base – to tell the Intelligence Officer what we thought of him.'

It was thought that one of the *Sperrbrechers* was seriously damaged. Later John Bell was awarded the Croix de Guerre for this and other missions.

On 21 August, Wing Commander Grant, who had taken over as commander of 58 Squadron took off in O-Orange JP296, a modified Mark II Halifax on an anti-submarine patrol. As second pilot there was an American, C. D. Hendrickson, and the flight engineer, Flight Sergeant George Martlew, now tells of that fatal Bay of Biscay patrol.

'It was about 0130 and we had just been to look at the U-boat pens at Bordeaux. As we flew westwards from the mouth of the River Garonne, the radar operator reported three blips on the screen. The skipper decided to illuminate and identify the blips. At this time I changed the fuel system to feed the engines from tanks 1 and 3 in each wing, these being the tanks to use for take-off, combat and landing. I then went to the starboard gun opening and mounted the beam gun. The skipper then dropped flares and we spotted a U-boat slightly to port and almost at once saw a second and third U-boat to starboard. They immediately put up light flak and then opened up with heavier stuff. The mid upper gunner, Flight Sergeant Greig, and I, on the beam gun, replied as we were only about 800 feet high at the time.

'As we had some difficulty getting the U-boat in our sights we did not bomb on the first run. Attempts later to illuminate the submarines failed. We judged the course and speed of the U-boats, however, and at about 0200 were flying towards Royal Navy ships to guide them to the area. Suddenly there was a violent explosion from what appeared to be a shell amidships and within seconds the Halifax struck the sea.

'Our dinghy release could not be pulled as the port wing, which contained the dinghy, had been torn off when we hit the sea. Water began to fill the aircraft quickly and I climbed out through the mid-upper escape hatch and then on to the starboard wing, from which I was soon swept off by the waves. I lost the other crew members immediately I came out of the aircraft. After some ten to fifteen minutes oil and petrol from the Halifax began to burn on the surface, so I swam away. After a further ten to fifteen minutes I saw the torchlights of other members of the crew and swam over to join them. It appeared that only five of us had escaped, both pilots, the navigator, Flying Officer Young, one of the WOP/AG's, Sergeant D. Laffy, and myself. We estimated we were twenty miles from the coast and decided to swim in that direction. We made use of our compasses and began to make plans for our escape when we reached land. However, the navigator had been badly injured and his scalp was flapping about with the waves; he died after a short time and we took off his Mae West and let him go under. The sea then became very rough and it rained heavily. Sergeant Laffy decided he had had enough and broke away from the rest of us and drowned himself by taking off his Mae West and going under. This left just three of us.

'As dawn broke we saw some pieces of wreckage from our aircraft, but they gave us no support. However, the skipper tore off a strip of metal about five feet long by five inches wide; it was too dull to act as sort of reflector but nevertheless it was as well he kept it. During the morning we saw a Liberator and Sunderland, the flying boat came straight towards us only to turn off when about three miles away. Three tiny specs in the Bay of Biscay are hard to locate and you can imagine our feelings. Just as we were beginning to wonder if ever we were going to be seen we suddenly saw a warship on the horizon, heading straight for us. The captain of the ship had seen one of our aircraft wheels floating on the sea and decided to investigate. He then saw the metal strip which Wing Commander Grant was waving. As the ship came alongside us it did not stop engines but threw a boarding netting over the starboard side. The ship's crew said that we looked like three torpedoes coming for the netting. All that I can remember was holding on to the netting and two huge arms grabbing hold of my wrists. The next thing I knew it was 36 hours later, when I found myself in one of the ship's officers' bunks, with my left leg heavily bandaged. Apparently I had suffered a cannon shell injury of which I had no knowledge, no doubt due to the excitement and apprehension of the occasion. We had spent 10½ hours in the sea before being rescued by the Canadian frigate, HMCS *St John*. We spent two weeks on board, during which time we were repeatedly shelled from the shore batteries off La Rochelle.

'This adventure qualified me for membership of the Goldfish Club, qualifications for which are escaping death by the use of an emergency dinghy.'

While the Wing Commander was recovering from his nasty experience off the French coast the squadron moved up from St David's to Stornaway in the Isle of Lewis.

Flight Lieutenant James, piloting G-George JP171, carried out one of the last operations by a 502 Squadron Halifax from West Wales, when flying from Brawdy. The port inner engine failed so the pilot flew out to sea and jettisoned the depth charges 'safe'. One hung up but nevertheless the pilot managed to land without mishap. Later he learned that two Welsh fishing boats were nearly wrecked by blast waves, as the depth charges had exploded on hitting the sea. The fishermen were not at all pleased.

Naturally there was a large party before the departure and four crews felt brave enough the next morning to 'shoot up' the WAAF's quarters. As an encore they decided to do the same to the officers' mess. For some reason it was decided not to be such a good idea at the last moment. Unfortunately for him, Dick Collishaw's R/T set was not working and he carried out the 'attack' alone. Needless to say he appeared on the mat for the escapade.

The move to the Outer Hebrides was not at all popular. Even the huts had to be anchored to the ground. The NCO crews found themselves on a site that had been condemned. There were pools of water everywhere, even under the mice infested huts. There was so much water that ducks swam beneath the huts. The food in the mess was bad, so much so that the crews turned to cooking their own food on the hut fires. There was not much relief when the airmen went to town, for although the beer was good, the natives were found to be hostile. This was a naval town! There was also some slight animosity between the air and ground NCO's that might have had its origins in that aircrews were allowed sheets and pillowcases and the others were not.

Wing Commander Grant rejoined the squadron on 29 August

and four days later, it, together with 502, was declared operational with 18 Group.

By September, the anti-shipping campaign had shifted eastwards in the wake of the Allied armies and it was on 8 October that 58 and 502 Squadrons learned that their future would be carrying out strikes off the Norwegian coast and in the Skagerrak and Kattegat.

The interruption of troop transportation in ship convoys making night passage from Norway to the Western Front, via Danish ports, was considered very important. The Halifaxes with the Mark XIV bombsight, using the flare technique and dropping 500 lb MC bombs carried out the strikes, despite bad weather. The introduction of these bombs, fused with the No 44 air burst pistol was a success. It was expected that the fragmentation effect from near misses would cause both material damage and casualties. This expectation was realized.

Bob Farrow flew in a Halifax with Dick Collishaw for the last time on 10 October for air test and training. It should not be thought that this was not dangerous. A very experienced crew flying Y-Yoke who had survived a landing on the sea off the Scillies and flown home 350 miles from Norway with a large hole in the fuselage, were killed on one of these flights when it crashed ten miles south-east of Shaint Isles in the Minches.

Jack Hochkin's Halifax was shot up on one of the early Skagerrak raids and Wing Commander Maton and his crew were later shot down in the same area.

Firefly aircraft from HMS *Implacable* attacked *U-1060*, a rare Type VIIF U-boat. The U-boat, launched at Kiel in April in 1943, one of only four of its type, and under the command of Herbert Brammer, had a 32-foot section added abaft the conning tower which was used to stow twenty-five torpedoes as cargo to replenish operational boats at sea. On 29 October two Czech Liberators further attacked the U-boat which was beached off the northern tip of Fleina Island, Norway. Despite depth-charges and rocket attacks it was still considered that the U-boat could be salvaged, so consequently on 4 November it was marked down for further attacks.

'Tinker' Bell says: 'We were briefed that the boat lay between the island and the mainland and it was covered by enemy aircraft. I was timed to arrive at the position at dawn. We duly set off and encountered rain and low cloud. When we arrived, west of the position we reduced height to about 300 feet, just below the cloud, and searched for an opening between the islands, the tops of which were in cloud, found one and went in. For the next twenty minutes it was a case of "I spy"; there were islands to port bow, and ahead on starboard bow. It wasn't the enemy aircraft we worried about, just survival in the mist and rain and hills. Needless to say we never did see the U-boat and I was thankful when we turned to the west through a gap and headed for the open sea. I think that was the most hair-raising twenty minutes I have ever spent in an aircraft.'

Nevertheless, two other Halifaxes, D-Dog and T-Tommy of 502 Squadron, had also been briefed to carry out an attack. In order to avoid radar detection both aircraft flew below 1,000 feet when within a hundred miles of the Norwegian coast. The sea was calm, the weather had cleared with 5/10 cumulus cloud. When the U-boat was sighted at 0830 the bows down to the conning tower were projecting sharply out of the water, with one of the hydroplanes visible. There was no opposition, it was obvious the submarine had been abandoned.

The pilots decided to attack in their own time; it was like a practice with the added spice that enemy fighters could appear at any moment. D-Dog attacked from the south-east at 2,500 feet, releasing seven 500 lb MC bombs, spaced at 50 feet. The stick ran the whole length of the U-boat but fell 30 feet to port between the U-boat and the island.

T-Tommy made two attacks from different directions dropping four, and then two more 600 lb A/S bombs from 1,300 feet. An almost exact straddle was made on the first run and an overshoot of about one length of the visible part on the second. Afterwards the conning tower was no longer visible and the bows were projecting less out of the water than before. The U-boat was assessed 'known sunk' by Y and H/311 and D and T/502, in conjunction with aircraft from HMS *Implacable*.

John Bell continues: 'On Bonfire Night we took the insides out of various coloured Very cartridges. At midnight we celebrated Guy Fawkes' feat by climbing certain huts and dropping the cartridges down the stove pipes. There was a sudden rush of the occupants to get out and they were quickly followed by green, red or yellow smoke!'

In the Skagerrak and Kattegat the war against the enemy's shipping was waged mainly at night. The enemy was employing some 50,000 tons of medium and large ships solely to withdraw troops from Norway. With this tonnage, it was estimated that he could move a division every fortnight. Attacks were aimed primarily at the traffic sailing between the Oslofiord area and the Danish ports. In the Kattegat traffic was found that had safely rounded the dangerous waters of south-western Norway on the last lap of the route to German ports, and thence to the Western Front.

Altogether there was no shortage of targets; distance was the main limiting factor.

During the early hours of darkness on 22 November Halifax E-Easy of 502 Squadron, while on patrol in the Skagerrak, bombed on a radar contact, and, dropping flares, illuminated *Sund*, a merchant vessel of over 3,000 tons. The aircraft attacked with 500 lb bombs and scored a direct hit. A dull red glow was seen on the ship: this developed into smoke and flames which rose to a height of about 500 feet.

Some two hours after this attack Y-Yoke of the same squadron, also on anti-shipping patrol in the Skagerrak, sighted the same vessel still on fire. An attack was made with 500 lb bombs, one of which fell on the forward part of the ship, and started a fresh large fire.

Smoke billowed up to 1,000 feet, and the flames could still be seen from a distance of over 40 miles. Swedish fishing boats later picked up some 30 survivors.

Two days later, during the early evening, Halifax C-Charlie of 502 Squadron sighted three merchant vessels after homing on to a radar contact in the Skagerrak. The ships opened fire, but the aircraft took evasive action and then attacked the largest ship, a vessel of 3,000 tons. Two direct hits were scored with 500 lb MC bombs and, in the light of flares, smoke was seen issuing from several parts of the ship.

During the month a total of 28 attacks were made against enemy shipping despite most unfavourable weather.

Flying from Stornaway in the dark John Bell picked up a radar contact. Using a high level flare he saw a vague outline with no lights. He attacked with depth charges and on the run out lights suddenly appeared on the vessel; it was a Scottish fishing boat!

After circling for 15 minutes to make sure all was well the Halifax continued on patrol.

Due to the large number of attacks off Scandinavia the squadrons at Stornaway were short of bombs for anti-shipping patrols and so John Bell was detailed to fly to Leuchars to collect twelve 500 lb bombs. He continues:

'I took off just before dark and arrived in the Fife area and requested permission to land. This was granted so I approached the flare path and touched down on the end of the runway and came to a screaming halt at the other end, with me sweating and the brakes full on. I taxied up to the control tower, to be met by a naval rating who gazed at me in amazement. I was told that I had landed at a naval airstrip which was only 800 yards long. The RAF base at Leuchars was about 5 miles away. I then had the job of getting the Halifax off the runway. Fortunately, we were carrying very little petrol, and we scraped off the end of the runway at ten feet and landed safely, and wiser, at our true destination.'

Jack Hochkins was out again in December; on the 7th he recorded: 'Strike on Kristiansund, heavy defences surprised by low approach. Bombed a 6,000 ton motor vessel anchored along the fiord. We undershot, however a violent red flash was seen. We kept straight on 20 miles into Norway and turned out and came back further up the coast to avoid known flak areas. Over Aalsunde we saw the other strike wing getting a terrific flak welcome, it was coming up from all sides and dropping into the centre like a gigantic but deadly candelabra. On 13th a strike on Kristiansund and anchorages, Norway pretty by moonlight. On 20th strike on Aalsunde, weather hopeless. On 28th shipping patrol, two vessels attacked but unable to see results due to the bad weather. Enemy aircraft were also out.'

During the early hours of 29th Halifax C-Charlie of 502 Squadron sighted a 5,000 ton tanker accompanied by two escort vessels north-east of the Skaw. A bombing attack was made on the tanker and one pair of bombs fell on the forward hatch. An explosion followed and bright yellow flames came from the ship and were followed by dense black smoke, billowing up to a height of 3,000 feet. Two hours later the same tanker was seen by Y-Yoke, also of 502 Squadron, and again attacked. Two direct hits left the tanker burning furiously.

The Air Correspondent of a national newspaper was taken on patrol at the end of the year – he reported from 'A Coastal Command Station Northern Scotland':

It was cold and clear last night as the giant Halifax bomber's engines were run up. Even the ground seemed to vibrate with the sound. I jammed myself into the engineer's cockpit and we bumped across the landing ground. The bumps stopped, and we climbed steadily, making out to sea. The engineer's cockpit in a Halifax was my best vantage point, but there was not much to see then – just a wide expanse of sea ahead and flimsy clouds on all sides.

The Halifax in which I was flying, V-Victor, had taken off shortly before nightfall to find and bomb German shipping believed to be in the area of Northern Norway.

'It's a very long trip,' the Intelligence Officer said at the briefing of the crew, 'but it's an important one. Any ships you may see will be loaded with either troops or vital war supplies.'

It was very soon dark, but everyone in the bomber was busy. The intercom was as restless as a London telephone exchange. Guns were tested, the route to be followed was mapped by the navigator, recognition flares were checked over. Nothing could be left to chance when we were over the target area.

'Turn 30 degrees to starboard,' the navigator's voice crackled over the intercom. 'We are now flying at 25 miles from the Norwegian coast,' he said a few minutes later after the aircraft had swerved slightly on its course. 'We shall reach the target area in two hours' time.'

The only excitement during these next two hours was seeing an immense fire. I could see huge flames and dense clouds of smoke. 'Pity we can't go in and stoke it up a bit,' said the captain of the aircraft, Flight Lieutenant A. Swain. 'We might look in on the way back if we have time.'

Two hours passed very quickly. There was nothing much to be done until the target was reached, so we ate sandwiches and drank sweet, milkless tea. The bomber tore on through the night.

'Pilot to navigator . . . turn 45 degrees to starboard.' There was a silence for several minutes, but I could still hear that the navigator had his intercom switched on. Then – 'We have crossed the Norwegian coast.'

Down below everything was in darkness, though in the Arctic night I could dimly see snow on the tops of hills. We were flying low and after crossing the coast dropped to about 1,000 feet.

V-Victor's job was to find ships. We dived and began methodically searching the fiords, rather like a terrier beside a rabbit warren pushing its nose into each hole. Over each fiord we dropped flares, turning night into day. Then we circled round. An anti-aircraft gun started popping at us, but most of the time, I was relieved to notice, it was shooting very wide. It was joined later by other guns, and even rifles were used, but the Halifax and its crew continued going in and out of the fiords, dropping flares, then diving down to see if ships were lurking there.

For nearly two hours we searched, but there was not a ship to be found. 'Seems to be no joy at all,' said the captain of the aircraft, using RAF slang which means, in common parlance, that there was nothing to bomb. 'How soon will we have to start back for home?' The engineer checked over the petrol levels. 'We'll have to start back now,' he said, 'and we haven't time to have a look in at the fire.'

So the long, long flight back to Scotland began, with the Northern Lights flashing in the sky. It was morning when we got back to base. The flight had lasted nearly 12 hours. We had flown 1,700 miles.

A typical Coastal Command operation this – long, monotonous hours in the air, keeping a constant and unrelenting vigil over the seas and oceans from the Arctic to the Equator, from Biscay to the American shores, an area of over 10,000,000 square miles; ready at all times to strike at enemy shipping, to lay a heavier strain on his land communications and to keep the seas open.

The skipper of V-Victor said there had been 'no joy' on the trip, but I was grateful to have seen something just like that – arduous, patient and often unrewarding work which the men of Coastal Command perform. Naturally I shared their disappointment that we had found no shipping to bomb; but it is by such flights that the enemy's sea transport is kept under tribute and in constant peril.'

So ended 1944, a most successful year for the Allies. The new role Coastal Command was playing, in attacking reinforcements from Norway reaching the front line, had not gone unnoticed. General Eisenhower, the land commander, signalled to Air Chief Marshal Sholto Douglas, the AOC-in-C Coastal Command: 'I should like all those serving under you to know that the Allied Expeditionary Force feels a debt of real gratitude for Coastal Command's great contribution to the success of our operations in France.'

January 1945 was a month of extremely bad weather but aircraft kept flying, although 'Blondie' Wilson, now crewed up with another pilot says many trips were aborted due to the weather. He says there was often trouble in Stornaway as the natives did not like Englishmen. Flight Engineer Trott says they walked or went by bus to the town to the dance halls or picture houses. The pubs closed at 2100 and the McEwans beer was popular. Some airmen visited the American Club just outside the camp. He continues:

'The Irish ground staff were very close and clanny, as they were all volunteers. When they were recommended for promotion they accepted the "honour" but would not sign the form as it meant they would be posted away from 502 Squadron, so they stayed where they were so as not to be posted to the "big island" as they called the mainland. Each time this happened they would have a

NCO Coastal Command crew, including Australians, checking photographs at Stornaway.

No 58 and 502 crew members, including W/Cdr Holderness, F/Lt Bell, F/Lt Spurgeon and F/Lt Derry in good voice in the Mess at Stornaway.

good party. I attended one of these, it was some do, which included Irish moonshine!

'The aircrew were not so clanny. We had some airmen from Bomber Command. One joined our squadron on return from three months' rest from operations after 40 consecutive trips. On his first trip with us he came up to me after five hours' flying and said, "When are we going home?" I told him, "In about another five hours". He was none too happy.'

Most of the 58 and 502 Squadron aircrew were now in the veteran stage and this last four months of the war was to claim many of them.

Edward Beesley, mentioned earlier, says: 'We had identical twins as pilots on 502 Squadron, Peter and John Davenport. Wing Commander Sos Cohen was public relations officer between the RAF and Royal Navy; he wore an observer's beret. He flew on a night operation from Stornaway. He had 62 operations to his credit, one for each year of his age! He was awarded a DFC, but what made him unique was that he had served in four wars, Matabele, Boer and both World Wars!

'Lord Londonderry, the Honorary Air Commander of the squadron, was threatened with a right hander if he didn't shut up bragging of his friendship with Herman Goering, in the mess at Stornaway.'

Flight Lieutenant James, flying C-Charlie JP338 of 502 Squadron had some bad luck on 13 January when his bombs hung up when attacking vessels in the Skagerrak. The same pilot, flying T-Tommy JP330, was more fortunate thirteen days later when he successfully attacked five vessels, one of which was believed to have blown up.

Jack Hochkins was busy again in early February: 'We located two small motor vessels on the 8th in bad visibility. It was a hard job homing as the radar was playing up, probably frozen. After several runs suddenly our rear gunner screamed out "Flak" and then, "Fighters – Fighters on port quarter!" We took really violent evasive action, toppling gyros; the whole crew was jumpy as we had been told Bomber Command had lost 17 out of 50 aircraft in mining Oslo Fiord, in the same area. However, we recovered ourselves, and we were really scared for the first time in a long while.

'I did a fair radar homing, we bombed, returned to base and

reported we had probably damaged the enemy vessels. Flares from other aircraft kept lighting us up and we were glad to get out of there in one piece.

'Three days later there was a strike on Egersund Fiord, large motor vessels and other ships in harbour. How we got through it we will never really know, although we tried all the right things. It was just one of those times you think, "Well, this is it boys, we're finished at last!" '

On the night of 20/21 February 58 Squadron's C-Charlie obtained a radar contact while on patrol in the Skagerrak. On homing, the pilot sighted six merchant vessels on an easterly course. He attacked one, a 3,000 ton ship, and scored a direct hit on the bows with a 500 lb bomb. This was followed by flames and smoke and the vessel was left blazing. Less than an hour later G-George, of 502 Squadron, sighted a 6,000 ton merchantman and four other vessels, about 40 miles east of Kristiansund. The pilot attacked and obtained four hits on the large ship, which became enveloped in flames, and ammunition appeared to be exploding. The ship was still burning fiercely an hour later, when the Halifax left the scene, and subsequently sank. H-How JP173 of 58 Squadron failed to return this night.

Shortly before midnight the next day 58 Squadron's Y-Yoke homed on to a radar contact in the Skagerrak, and sighted a 4,000 and 3,500 ton ship steaming at 10 knots on an easterly course.

The Halifax attacked and hit the larger ship with a 500 lb bomb on the stern. The vessel slowed down and then stopped, emitting great clouds of dense black smoke.

On the night of 25/26 February George Trott was flying in L-Lucy JP172 with Flight Lieutenant James on a Skagerrak raid: 'Nine vessels – we hit one, she blew up just as a Liberator was going to see what was on fire. The aircraft survived but what that crew said to us when we had to land at their airfield near Elgin cannot be repeated here!'

On the same night one of 58 Squadron's veteran Halifaxes P-Peter HX224, which John Bell had flown operationally thirteen times from as far back as the middle of December 1943, went missing.

The aircraft, with its crew of three Australians, three Britons and three Canadians, crashed into the Skagerrak twenty miles north of

Hirtshals in northern Denmark.*

Newcomers joining the squadron were inexperienced, sensed the war was nearly over and wanted to get in on the action. Perhaps the squadron commanders should have made them serve an apprenticeship with the more senior members but Jack Hochkins says: 'When our mates were lost we didn't make friends with the replacement crews coming in, because they were green and too cocky, and they got shot down.'

George Trott was one of the flyers that had been with 502 Squadron for an extremely long time; he had flown with 22 different pilots. He mentions landing at the Liberator base near Elgin: 'The Halifax III Bristol engines used up too much oil so quite a few aircraft had to cut their patrols short and land at Wick or Elgin.' Coastal Command reported:

> Merlin XX and XXII engines of the Halifax II and V aircraft have not given satisfactory service under operating conditions, and action has been taken to improve the engines by the incorporation of a number of essential modifications, but as these Marks are now out of production, some modifications cannot be incorporated. It has therefore become necessary to ask higher authority for a later Mark of engine for these aircraft; it appears that this will be approved.

Nevertheless the Halifaxes kept on flying.

During the night of 2 March, Halifax K-King of 502 Squadron, on patrol in the Skagerrak with an Irish pilot and navigator aboard, homed on to a radar contact and sighted a merchant vessel escorted by a trawler type auxiliary and a destroyer. An attack was made on the merchantman, *Isar* of 9,026 tons, and two direct hits were scored. The ship caught fire and flames from it were visible at a distance of 15 miles. There were 1,500 Service personnel on board. Nearly 100 dead and many wounded were put ashore at the Norwegian town of Moss, and a number of dead horses were washed ashore. The Irish, known horsemen, were upset, so drowned their sorrows when they heard about it.

Some aircrew members also took to drink as a release for the

* The wreckage of HX224 was found by a lobster trawler 39 fathoms down in position 57.56N, 10.04E on 14 November 1979. In the haul were aluminium sheets, metal wreckage, machine gun ammunition, a harness buckle, lighter, gold watch and parts of a skeleton. The gold watch was inscribed as being presented to Hugh MacLean, an Australian, on his 21st birthday in 1936. Despite an exhaustive search none of his relatives could be traced and his remains were buried with full Military honours at Copenhagen in June 1980.

tension and strain they were suffering and one of 502 Squadron ended up at the special hospital in Scotland.

George Trott, who flew as a spare engineer on 92 trips remembers another drink story:

'Just as we were due to take off, the second pilot was taken ill. The only replacement pilot had consumed too much alcohol; nevertheless, we poured him into the Halifax, put him in the centre seat and the navigator took over as second pilot for take-off. Our drunken pilot came to after three hours and was astonished at what had happened. He shook himseif out of it and did his job perfectly, as if nothing had happened!'

George Trott recalls some other hobbies carried out by different crews he flew with:

'I joined one crew that carried a spare wireless operator. The flight was a long range one and after we cleared the Cornish coast the pilot switched over to "George", told the second pilot to take over, and told me, the flight engineer, to double up as second pilot. He then went back to the centre of the Halifax and played chess with the spare wireless operator for two hours.

'On another trip, I saw one WO/AG, on his rest period, stripped off doing physical training at the rear of the aircraft near the Elsan. Another Halifax WO/AG was seen reading his bible in the top turret, fingering his rosary, and once I went down to the front turret to give the navigator a fix I had taken in the astrodome and found him doing card tricks! A gunner in another crew I flew with played his banjo in the rear turret.'

Early on 6 March, E-Easy JP301 of 58 Squadron sighted and attacked a thousand ton merchant ship south-east of Homborsund Light. One 500 lb bomb was seen to hit amidships, causing a bright glow and a huge pall of smoke. The vessel was seriously damaged. In the late evening of the same day the Irish crew of K-King, 502 Squadron, homed on to a contact in much the same area. With the aid of flares the pilot sighted two merchant vessels of about 3,000 tons each. He attacked one of them with bombs and obtained a direct hit on the stern. A great column of smoke rose from the stricken ship, and when more flares were dropped she was seen to be stationary with the other vessel circling her.

On 16 March Flight Lieutenant James piloting Halifax B-Bertie PG365, a Mark III of 502 Squadron just managed to get back to Wick when the compass was found unserviceable and the starboard inner engine packed up and the other three showed signs of failing. Lifeboats and the Navy had been alerted and were standing by in case of a ditching in the sea.

On the night of 20 March U-Uncle of the same squadron homed on to a radar contact in the Skagerrak and sighted five merchant vessels on an easterly course. The pilot attacked a 2,500 ton vessel and obtained a direct hit. As the aircraft turned away the ship was completely obscured by explosions and smoke.

On the night of 4/5 April J-Jig JP299 of 58 Squadron homing on to a radar contact in the Kattegat, illuminated a 4,000 ton merchant ship and three escort vessels on a northerly course. The pilot attacked with six 500 lb bombs and scored at least one direct hit. There was a great explosion on the ship, followed by a large mushroom of flame, and debris was seen flying in all directions. When the aircraft left the area of the attack a pall of smoke had risen to a height of 3,000 feet.

Early on 10 April N-Nan of the same squadron, in the same area, homed on to a radar contact and sighted an 8,000-ton ship accompanied by another merchantman, a destroyer and two escort vessels. An attack was made with 500 lb bombs and a straddle amidships was scored on the 8,000 tonner and the jubilant aircrew left the ship enveloped in flames and smoke.

During the night following the above attack Halifax M-Mike of 502 Squadron attacked shipping, two direct hits were obtained on a 4,000 ton merchant vessel in the Kattegat. The hits were followed by a great orange explosion on the target.

Although the war was nearing its close relentless pressure was still being applied by the Coastal Halifaxes and to celebrate Hitler's birthday on 20 April H-How of 502 Squadron scored a direct hit amidships on a 4,000 ton merchant vessel, starting a fire which was still visible when the Halifax was fifteen miles away from the Kattegat. The following night M-Mike of 502 Squadron set fire to another merchant vessel of 4,000 tons.

These excellent results were not obtained without casualties, four aircraft were lost during the month, including J-Jig of 58 Squadron which had been successful earlier in the month.

The Halifax squadrons were credited with nearly 6,000 tons of shipping sunk and 58,000 tons damaged in April from the record number of 101 attacks.

The good work was continued in the last week of the war with six attacks in the Skagerrak and Kattegat.

In the last seven months of the war Nos 58 and 502 Squadrons were credited with 26,104 tons of shipping sunk, 35,523 tons seriously damaged, and 66,629 tons damaged. Included in these figures are those of several transports. *Isar* has already been mentioned, *Rolandseck* of 1,845 tons, was sunk about a week later when southbound with troops on board, while in April *Feodosia* of 3,075 tons, which had just started service as a transport, and the *Hansa I*, 1,923 tons, another transport, were sunk. A rapidly increasing number of other ships carrying general and specialised cargoes were also sunk or damaged.

The two Halifax Squadrons had a total combined strength of 27 aircraft when the war in Europe ended.

At the end many men had seen too much action. Jack Hochkins said: 'I was good at my job and indeed often requested to fly extra trips with the commanding officer and others. I received a commission on active service, but no medals. I ruined my health but am left with a host of memories, including those many uneventful, boring and futile trips over the trackless sea, risking all and seeing nothing.'

Air Chief Marshal Sholto Douglas, the Air Officer Commanding-in-Chief of Coastal Command signalled:

> During my visits around the Command over the past eighteen months, and these have included nearly all stations, I have been forcibly impressed by the keen spirit which has been so evident in aircrew and ground crew personnel alike.
>
> Our victory in the war at sea, which has been a 5½ years' battle with many ups and downs, would not have come about but for the united efforts and the will to win of the RAF and WAAF, and our Dominion and Allied colleagues.
>
> Many of you, like myself, will be leaving Coastal Command in the near future, but we shall all, I am sure, recall with affection and respect a Command with a war record that should long be remembered.

When the war ended George Trott was on leave. His pilot Flight Lieutenant James thought that he had looked a bit off colour. He did not return to Stornaway, but from his 92 trips he certainly knew what it was like flying in a Halifax on a *Night Flight*.

Glossary

AI	Airborne interception, night fighter radar equipment
AOC	Air Officer Commanding
Caterpillar Club	Eligibility – Life saved by (silk) parachute
CGM	Conspicuous Gallantry Medal. Until 1942 this had been a naval decoration. After this date it was awarded to the other two services for action against the enemy.
Flak	FLiegerAbwehrKanonen; Anti-aircraft gun
G	Gravity
GEE	Radar aid to navigation and target identification
Goldfish Club	Qualification – To escape death by use of emergency dinghy (or Mae West)
GP	General Purpose (bombs)
HC	High Capacity
HE	High Explosive
HCU	Heavy Conversion Unit
H2S	Radar aid to navigation and target identification
IFF	Identify friend from foe
LMF	Lacking moral fibre
Mandrel	Radio swamping of German early warning system
MC	Medium charge
Monica	Radar fitted in rear of Bomber Command aircraft to provide 'early warning' of night fighters
MT	Motor Transport
Musical Sky	Marking by coloured markers dropped blindly
NAAFI	Navy Army and Air Force Institute
RDF	Raider Direction Finder
SBC	Small bomb container
Serrate	Radar device enabling fighters to home on
TI	Target indicators
u/s	Unserviceable
Wanguani	Pathfinder Force skymarking

Additional Reading

Every Dane over the age of 45 has an RAF story to tell – there is even a branch of the RAF Association in Copenhagen. Consequently many books on the subject have been published in Denmark and I would recommend two by Anders Bjoernvad, *They found a way* and *Fallen Allied Airmen 1939–45*

Although I had some stories of No 158 and No 76 Squadrons I did not include them because of the excellent books *In Brave Company* – the history of 158 Squadron and *To see dawn breaking* – the history of 76 Squadron. Bill Chorley wrote and produced the latter 272 page book which was printed by Midland Counties publications and like the earlier book, written with Roy Benwell, is of a very high quality and magnificent value. The book can be obtained from the author for £6.50 UK (Inc p & p) or £7.25 Abroad in International money orders at 13, Washbrook View, Ottery St Mary, Devon EX11 1EP.

Finally, if any of you have not read my *Raider – the Halifax and its flyers*, which includes all the roles performed by the wartime Halifax, I am told that some copies of the reprint are still available.

Index

Aachen, 99
Aalsunde, 206
Abbey, J.E. W/O, 190
Achères, 93
Ahrweiler, 28
Aircraft:
Anson: 172
Beaufighter: 185
Do217: 131
Flying Fortress: 99
FW190: 99, 110, 143, 181
FW200: 178
Hampden: 58, 157, 158
Hurricane: 141
Ju88: 74, 122, 126, 147, 153, 174, 176, 179, 190, 195
Lancaster: 29, 35, 52, 77, 102, 139, 141, 148, 151
Liberator: 178, 185, 186, 201, 203, 212
Lysander: 58
Magister: 44
Me109: 78
Me110: 50, 128, 162–164, 168
Me210: 144
Mosquito: 147, 168, 185
Mustang: 55
Spitfire: 55
Stirling: 15, 29, 44, 60, 77
Sunderland: 177, 178, 180, 185, 201
Swordfish: 98
Tiger Moth: 44
Wellington: 84, 98, 116, 117, 140, 141, 185
Whitley 58: 172, 173, 182
Alderson, A. Rev, 13
Alexandria, 113
Allen, E. F/Sgt, 112
Allen, F. (Mrs. Booth), 58
Alsterufer, 186
Anderson, R. H. F/Lt, 150
Anderson, W. B. S/Ldr, 93
Armstrong, G. A. F/Sgt, 161
Armstrong, J. Sgt, 161
Badcoe, S/Ldr, 22, 24
Bailey, A. Sir, 184
Bailey, R. E. W/Cdr, 140
Baldersby, 108
Bandholm, 116
Banks, F/Sgt, 128, 132
Barham, HMS, 113
Barker, N. Sgt, 14
Batty, W. Sgt, 22
Bayreuth, 55
Beaulieu, 83
Becker, M. Hptmn., 28
Beesley, E., 196, 200
Belfast, 191
Bell, John, 181, 192, 195, 198, 200, 204–206, 211
Bennett, D. C. T. W/Cdr, 112, 113
Benson, 97
Bentley, F/Lt, 197
Berlin, 18, 28, 69–71, 77, 78, 80, 82, 93, 118, 143–145, 147
Bird, G. R. F/Sgt, 161
Birkenhead, 111
Blackpool, 25
Blair, R. A. W. F/Sgt, 161, 162
Bochum, 20, 33, 36, 106
Bonn, 35
Bordeaux, 185, 197, 200
Bournemouth, 98, 172
Boyes, W. F/O, 150
Brammer, H., 203

Brannigan, A. Sgt, 14
Brawdy, 202
Breighton, 45, 54
Bremen, 158
Brest, 105, 185, 197, 198
Brookes, F. E. AVM, 84
Brown, D. B. F/Sgt, 150
Brown, E. A., 16, 25–27, 161, 162
Brown, J. H. Sgt, 161
Buckland, P. J. C. F/O, 150
Bulmer, J. H. Sgt, 161
Burn, 59
Burn, R. Sgt, 86
Burton, G. Sgt, 108, 110
Butterworth, R. L. F/O, 161

Cadman, P. S/Ldr, 16, 17, 19, 22, 24, 71, 80, 82
Caen, 32
Cairns, J. F/Lt, 141, 145
Calais, 147
Capetown, 184
Carnaby, 33, 38
Carter, W/Cdr, 118
Catfoss, 141, 160, 161
Chambres, H., 13
Charleroi, 36
Chemin, A., 13
Cherbourg, 195, 198
Chevalier, R., 13, 43
Chichester, 28
Chivenor, 194
Christchurch, 181
Christiansen, A. C. 168
Churchill, Winston, 86, 174
Clayton, H. F/Sgt, 22
Clarke, F/Lt, 194
Clarkson, Doreen, 58
Clutterbuck, A. R. D. F/Lt, 197
Coblenz, 35
Cockerill, A. J. P/O, 138
Cohen, S. W/Cdr, 210
Collins, Ben, 200
Collishaw, R. F/O, 172, 183, 202, 203
Cologne, 18, 34–36, 38, 40, 139, 147, 152, 153
Cooke, G. P/O, 150
Copenhagen, 166, 168
Cottar, R. Sgt, 161
Cranswick, 143
Crawley, S/Ldr, 149
Crawford, Joan, 84

Daffey, R. J., 16, 17, 71
Danzig, 158
Dalton, 98, 99, 107
Darlington, 107
Date, J. M. F/O, 161
Davenport, John, 210
Davenport, Peter, 210
Davison, P. Sgt, 161
Davy, E. G/Capt, 15
Declerk, A. Sgt, 117
Dennis, K. J. W/O, 139
Derby, 162
Deremore, Lord, 59, 60
Derna, 117
Dieppe, 93, 94
Dimmock, N., 56
Dinsdale, 107
Dishforth, 59
Dönitz, Karl Adml, 174, 180
Dortmund, 106, 107
Douglas, S. Sir ACM, 208, 215
Dresden, 40
Driffield, 136, 140
Duff, B. F/Sgt, 161
Duisberg, 106, 138, 139, 147, 156
Dunkirk, 152
Düsseldorf, 22, 23, 38, 151

Eaglescliffe, 107
Eagleton, T. S/Ldr, 144
East Grinstead, 59, 111
East Moor, 93
Easton, F. F/Lt, 150
Eden, Anthony, 174
Edmunds, D. W. W/Cdr, 118, 127, 133
Egan-Wyer, S/Ldr, 31
Eisenhower, D. D. General, 208
El Alamein, 117
Elgin, 212
Elizabeth, Princess, 93
Elizabeth, Queen, 93

Elvington, 13–16, 19, 24, 25, 28, 31, 33, 34, 38, 40–43, 59, 60, 63, 72, 158, 160, 161, 163, 168
English, R. S. F/O, 150, 154
Enterprise, HMS, 186
Esberg, 163
Essen, 18, 32, 33, 37, 38, 55, 118, 139, 147–149, 151, 154, 155
Evans, F/Lt, 193

Fairwood Common, 64
Faneco, F/Lt, 194
Fano, 163
Farrow, R. R. Sgt, 183, 191, 195, 197, 203
Fauquier, J. W/Cdr, 83, 84
Feodosia, 215
Fielder, R. R. F/O, 150
Finch, Pam, 56, 58
Fishguard, 195
Flemming, M. M. W/Cdr, 108
Ford, 52, 53
Forsyth, D. T. W/Cdr, 140
Foulsham, 139, 143
Frankfurt, 18, 25–27, 32
Fuller, L. F/Sgt, 118, 127
Full Sutton, 31

Garson, Greer, 84
Gelsenkirchen, 37
Genoa, 140
George VI H.M. King, 93
Gibbons, B. Sgt, 117
Gibraltar, 174, 186
Glasgow HMS, 186
Gneisenau, 112
Goering, H., 210
Goodrum, R. W. F/O, 150
Gransden Lodge, 83
Grant, J. B. W/Cdr, 183, 198, 200-202
Grant, F/Lt, 183
Granville, 197
Graveley, 84
Grays, 163
Green, R. A. F/Sgt, 163
Greig, F/Sgt, 200
Griffiths, F/O, 174, 187
Grimble, H. P/O, 51
Gross, Gordon, 98, 99, 104, 105, 107

Hagen, 42
Haggard, G. F/Sgt, 141, 143–146
Halifax, Yorks, 108, 111
Hamburg, 18, 101, 118, 120, 126, 127, 158
Hansa I, 215
Hansen I, 166
Hanover, 128, 129, 134, 147
Harper, W. N. F/O, 150
Harris, A. T. ACM, 126
Harris, D. Sgt, 161
Harrison, J. J. Sgt, 161, 163–166, 168
Hartley, E. F/O, 173, 183
Harvey, F. W. F/Sgt, 161, 163
Haynes, F. Sgt, 161, 165
Haverfordwest, 184
Hendrickson, C. D., 200
Heslington, 60, 61
Hirtshals, 211
Hitler, Adolf, 180
Hochkins, J. F/O, 194, 203, 206, 210, 215
Holdness, F/Lt, 194
Holliday, Matthew, 22, 28, 30, 112, 113, 117
Holme-on-Spalding Moor, 45, 54
Holmsley South, 172, 173, 181, 183, 184
Homburg, 41
Hornsea, 160
Howard, L. F/Sgt, 27
Howard, Leslie, 174
Hull, 108, 130
Hurst, R. F/Sgt, 126, 132

Implacable, HMS, 203
Inverness, 173
Isar, 212

James, F/Lt, 196, 197, 202, 210, 211, 213, 215
Jeeves, A. J. F/O, 150
Jenkins, J. G. F/O, 118, 124, 126, 127, 134

Jenkins, S. S. F/O, 150
Johnstone, A. V. R. AVM, 64
Jones, G. Sgt, 161, 165
Juvisy, 50

Kalgoorlie, 135
Kalle, R. A. P/O, 108, 110
Kamen, 40
Karlsruhe, 93
Kassel, 25
Keens, P. F/Lt, 133
Ker, J. M. D. W/Cdr, 183, 190
Kiel, 203
Knaresborough, 84
Krefeld, 108
Kristiansund, 206, 211
Kunkel Hptmn, 190

Ladbergen, 40
Ladybird, HMS, 116
Laffy, D. Sgt, 201
Lamarr, Hedy. 84
La Planche, J. S., 31, 158, 161, 162
La Rochelle, 202
Leconfield, 140, 149
Leeds, 54
Leeming, 84, 93
Leipzig, 18, 40, 93, 147
Le Mans, 50
Leuchars, 195, 206
Le Verdon, 186
Leverkusen, 28
Lille, 50
Lisbon, 174
Lissett, 141
Liverpool, 98
London, 48, 69, 79, 86, 146, 207
Londonderry, Lord, 210
Lorient, 196, 198
Lossiemouth, 20
Loverock, W. H. Sgt, 161, 164, 165
Lowe, A. E. W/Cdr, 15, 16, 39, 80
Ludwigshafen, 38, 55

Magson, L. Sgt, 110
Maidenhead, 111
Mainz, 55
Malmo, 165
Mamby, 51
Manchester, 59, 60
Mangione, J. Sgt, 94, 97
Mannheim, 18, 24
Mansan, F/Lt, 17
Manston, 40, 48
Margaret, Princess, 93
Maribo, 166
Markland, A. W/Cdr, 47, 50
Marston Moor, 19, 59, 140
Martlew, G. Sgt, 174, 187, 200
Matlaske, 145
Maton, C. A. W/Cdr, 184, 194, 203
Mauretania, 98
McClelland, G. P/O, 161, 163
McClorry, E. G. F/O, 22
McCrindle, E. P/O 136
McEwan, C. M. AVM, 98
McIndoe, A. Sir, 59, 111
Mead, Harry, 13
Mead, R. G/Capt, 183
Melbourne, 136
Melbourne, Yorks, 38, 57, 117, 118, 130, 133
Metcalfe, L. Sgt, 110
Middleton St George, 58, 107
Miller, Glenn, 61
Mills, F. W. F/O, 150
Montorgueil, 52
Moore, L. H. Sgt, 161
Morris, J. T. W. F/Lt, 150
Muir, F. F/O, 196
Münster, 33
Murray, J. H. F/O, 161, 163, 164, 166

Neale, G. V. Sgt, 108
Needham, J. S. Sgt, 161
Neuss, 151
Newcastle, NSW, 117
Northern Echo, 13
Nuremberg, 14, 18, 127
Nutt, J. S. F/O, 161
Nykobing, 165

O'Meara, J. P. F/Sgt, 161

Orfordness, 152
Osnabruck, 55
Osorno, 185
Ostend, 47
Ostre, G., 13, 42, 43
Ottawa, 98
Oulton, W. W/Cdr, 173, 183

Paddington, 111
Paine, G. F/Sgt, 31, 161
Palmer, R. A. F/Lt, 20
Papenburg, 164, 147
Paris, 32, 47, 99, 116
Peck, Gregory, 59
Peenemunde, 47, 127
Pershore, 98
Peter, King of Yugoslavia, 83
Plymouth, 56
Pocklington, 59, 62, 162
Pope, F/Sgt, 147
Povey, C. C. F/O, 150
Powell, A. F/Sgt, 22
Power, W. A. F/Sgt, 161, 166
Pratt, P. G. F/Sgt, 161
Predunnock, 185
Presbury, A. Sgt, 31, 161, 162, 168
Pritchard, Eric, 44, 45, 47, 50, 53, 54

Queen Elizabeth, HMS, 113
Quine, P. F/Sgt, 22, 27, 28

RAAF Squadrons:
460: 139
461: 180
462: 135, 136
466: 66, 136, 140, 147
RAF Squadrons:
10: 22, 112, 117, 126
35: 84, 112
58: 172–174, 178, 181, 183, 184, 187, 190, 196–198, 205, 210, 211, 214, 215
76: 45, 55, 112, 135, 136
77: 14, 19, 22, 72, 117, 158
78: 45, 48, 53, 55, 56
83: 83
RAF Squadrons *continued*
97: 83
102: 140
158: 140
311: 186, 204
346: 14, 31, 32
347: 13, 14, 31, 40, 42
502: 172, 173, 179–181, 184, 193, 196–198, 204–206, 208, 210–215
612: 173
614: 136
640: 149, 154, 156
Raymond, Rene, 13
RCAF Squadrons:
405: 83
408: 84
419: 84, 107, 108
420: 84, 108
424: 84
425: 84
426: 84
427: 84
428: 84, 107
429: 84, 93
432: 84
433: 84, 98, 104, 107
434: 84
Reading, 35, 151, 152
Redall, R. Sgt, 161, 163
Reisholz, 40
Rheims, 35
Riccall, 66, 130, 140, 141
Ripon, 107, 108
Ritchie, G. Sgt, 93
Robbins, A. E. F/O, 161
Roberts, D. O. Sgt, 161
Robertson, Ian, 19, 20, 31, 158, 160–163, 168
Rodney, W. F/Lt, 45, 50–52, 54
Rogers, E. B. S/Ldr, 150
Rolandseck, 215
Roncoroni, J. A. W/Cdr, 30, 31
Rostock, 116, 160, 164
Roy, Jules Capt, 32, 34, 36, 39–43
Rufforth, 140

San Giorgio, 116

St Athan, 45, 141
St Davids, 184, 185, 190, 192, 193, 195, 197, 201, 203
St Eval, 172, 174, 192
St John' HMCS, 202
St Malo, 196, 197
St Nazaire, 198
Scarborough, 107
Scawton, 13, 43
Scharnhorst, 112
Schweinfurt, 147
Shannon, D. S/Ldr, 136
Short, Neville, 27
Skipton-on-Swale, 98, 104, 105, 108
Sladen, A. I. F/Lt, 172–174, 176, 180, 183, 185–187, 190, 193, 196–198
Smiddy, S/Ldr, 153
Smith, B. W/O, 150
Snaith, 59
Solva, 184
South, G. J. G/Capt, 83
Southampton, 183, 195
Spackman, J. F/Sgt, 172
Starr, A. J. F/O, 190
Spears, W. A. F/Sgt, 31, 161
Steer, Sgt, 117
Steere, G. F/Sgt, 94, 97
Sterkrade, 55, 136
Stevens, J. H. F/O, 145
Stockton, 107
Stone Sister, 67
Stornaway, 202, 205, 206, 208, 210, 215
Stuttgart, 28, 32, 118, 147
Summers Jack, 83, 84, 89, 97, 98, 107
Sund, 205
Sutton, J. S/Ldr, 127
Swansea, 64
Sydney, 117
Sykes, P. D. F/Sgt, 161, 165
Symes, C. J. Sgt, 31, 161

Tangmere, 15, 38
Taranto, 113
Tarpey, M. F/Sgt, 161
Tedder, Sir A. ACM, 113
Tholthorpe, 108, 110
Thompson, E. N. F/Lt, 161, 163
Tirpitz, 112, 116
Tiverton, 56
Tobruk, 115, 116
Tocher, J. S/Ldr, 154
Topcliffe, 107, 108
Trappes, 50
Trelfer, K. J. W/O, 150
Trenchard, Lord MRAF, 115
Tripoli, 136
Trivett, W. F/Sgt, 15, 16, 18, 22, 25, 30, 71
Trondheim, 113
Trott, G. D. F/Sgt, 183, 184, 193, 194, 196, 208, 211–213, 215
Turner, Lana, 84
Tustin, D. C. Sgt, 161

U-boats
U-106: 180
U-221: 183
U-461: 180
U-462: 180
U-463: 173
U-504: 180
U-528: 173
U-558: 178
U-563: 173
U-607: 177, 178
U-663: 173
U-753: 173
U-1060: 203
Upshall, Sgt, 180

Valiant, HMS, 113
Vancouver, 110
Venot G. E. Lt/Col, 31
Verdun, 38
Vertican, N. W/O, 135
Villeneuve St George, 99
Viney, J. W/Cdr, 149, 152, 154

Wakeman, R. F/O, 150
Walker, G. A. A/Cmdr, 15, 36, 118, 126

Walters, F. W. F/Sgt, 31, 161, 162, 168
Wangerooge, 147
Warner, P. S/Ldr, 116
Warsaw, 146
Warspite, HMS, 198
Waterhouse, R. H. G/Capt, 154
Watten, 136
Webb, P. F/Sgt, 193
White Waltham, 110
Wick, 173, 213
Wickham-Jones, P/O, 161
Wilson, R. W. Sgt, 172, 197, 208
Wodehouse, S. E. F/Lt, 161, 162
Wolverhampton, 111
Wombleton, 45
Wood, Mrs Alice, 13
Woodbridge, 48, 88, 89
Woodley, 15
Woodpecker, HMS, 179, 180
Wuppertal, 108

York, 14, 28, 41, 54, 57, 60, 61
Young, F/O, 201
Young, W/Cdr, 55
Younster, F/Sgt, 193